CASE STUDIES IN
CULTURAL ANTHROPOLOGY

GENERAL EDITORS
George and Louise Spindler
STANFORD UNIVERSITY

THE SWAZI

A South African Kingdom

Second Edition

THE SWAZI

A South African Kingdom

Second Edition

By

HILDA KUPER

University of California

HOLT, RINEHART AND WINSTON, INC.

FORT WORTH CHICAGO SAN FRANCISCO PHILADELPHIA
MONTREAL TORONTO LONDON SYDNEY TOKYO

Library of Congress Cataloging in Publication Data

Kuper, Hilda.
  The Swazi, a South African kingdom.

  (Case studies in cultural anthropology)
  Bibliography: p.
  Includes index.
  1. Swazi (African people).   2. Swaziland—History.
I. Title.   II. Series.
DT971.42.K87   1986   306'.0968'3   84-25130

ISBN: 0-03-070239-9

Printed in the United States of America

ISBN 0-03-070239-9
4 5 6 7 016 8 7 6 5

Holt, Rinehart and Winston, Inc.
The Dryden Press
Saunders College Publishing

Dedication

To the memory of King Sobhuza II,
a good king, a wise statesman, a gracious man.

Acknowledgments

I cannot adequately express my gratitude to the many people in Swaziland who befriended me and assisted me in my work. I find it impossible to mention only a few by name since in this 'revised case study' I relied on information given to me over some fifty years.

At another level, I gratefully acknowledge funding granted at different times by the International African Institute, the University of California Research Council, the (American) National Science Foundation, the Ford Foundation, the Guggenheim Foundation, the National Endowment for the Humanities, and the Wenner Gren Foundation. I am also appreciative of the help of a series of UCLA graduates in anthropology who were my research assistants, more particularly Beth Rosen Prinz, Sondra Hale, Victoria Lockwood and Donald Joralemon, Michael Paolisso and Daniel Hilton-Chalfen. Thoko Theresa Ginindza played a special role in both Swaziland and America as student, researcher, and friend. Finally, as always, my deepest debt is to Leo Kuper without whose continued encouragement this work would not have been completed. But for the interpretation and presentation of data, I alone am responsible.

FOREWORD

ABOUT THE SERIES

These case studies in cultural anthropology are designed to bring to students in beginning and intermediate courses in the social sciences insights into the richness and complexity of human life as it is lived in different ways and in different places. They are written by men and women who have lived in the societies they write about and who are professionally trained as observers and interpreters of human behavior. The authors are also teachers, and in writing their books they have kept the students who will read them foremost in their minds. It is our belief that when an understanding of ways of life very different from one's own is gained, abstractions and generalizations about social structure, cultural values, subsistence techniques, and other universal categories of human social behavior become meaningful.

ABOUT THE AUTHOR

Hilda Kuper began her association with the Swazi in 1934 and has continued it to the present, spending a total of five years in Swaziland accumulated through intermittent visits to continue her research or, since 1972 in her capacity as official biographer of King Sobhuza II. In 1982 she received the Medal of the Royal Order of Sobhuza II. Her play, *A Witch in My Heart* has been translated into siSwati as well as Zulu and is used in the government schools of Swaziland. Her tribute to Sobhuza, given by her at his funeral in 1983, is presented in the Appendix to this book. It is this long and intensive association with the Swazi that has made it possible for her to write this case study and provide a knowledgeable and moving account of the years in Swaziland since independence.

Hilda Kuper is now retired from her professorship in anthropology at the University of California at Los Angeles, which she occupied from 1963 to 1978. Before that she taught anthropology at Witerwatersrand University, Johannesburg; the University of Natal, Durban; the University of North Carolina; and headed the department of anthropology at University College, London, replacing Michael Smith for one year.

She has received numerous fellowships and awards, including the Rivers Memorial Medal from the Royal Anthropological Institute of Great Britain and Ireland for her fieldwork in Swaziland and South Africa. She has published numerous books, including the well-known *An African Aristocracy* and *The Uniform of Colour,* a novel of Africa, *Bite of Hunger,* and as editor, with her husband, Leo Kuper, *Adaptation and Development of African Law.* She has also published many articles on the Swazi and from her fieldwork in 1953–58 on a Durban Hindu Community. Hilda Kuper was born in Rhodesia (Zimbabwe) and finished her Ph.D. in Anthropology at the London School of Economics in 1942.

ABOUT THIS CASE STUDY

This new edition of *The Swazi* is in two parts. The first part is an analysis of Swazi society and culture as it existed when the first edition was published in 1963. The second part is the story of the past twenty years, beginning with the struggle for independence; to its achievement in 1968, and subsequent developments. The two parts are contrasting in coverage and style.

The first part, "From Kingdom to Colony," describes the monarchy, the centralized Swazi state, the clans and lineages, the functions and meaning of the homestead, the royal lineage and household, and the inter-relationships among these elements of the complex Swazi sociopolitical system. The analysis follows the functional paradigms of British social anthropology, though history is not left out. We see how the clans were welded into a centralized state by the conquering Nguni aristocracy and how this state was lost to the Boers and the British. We also see how the impact of western industrialization threatened the formulations of traditional Swazi society.

The second part, "From Colony to Kingdom," is historical and biographical in style. It presents a close-up view of the events of the past years as Sobhuza II, the Swazi King, steered the Swazi government and society through the last years of colonial rule and fourteen years of post-independence. The immediacy of the events, in all their detail, as presented in this study, is only possible because Dr. Kuper, a Swazi citizen and appointed biographer of Sobhuza, was a persistent observer for the entire period and enjoyed the confidence of the ruling house.

Sobhuza's informed and statesmanlike influence is apparent throughout the study. He gave his people, and the world, good advice, such as "language differentiates people from animals . . . Talk with your enemies." The alternative, he warned, was "confrontation, arms manufacturing, and stockpiling of military weapons," (Jubilee speech, September 4, 1981). He had a sophisticated understanding of culture and of its processes of change, identity, and alienation. He self-consciously and purposefully guided the development of his kingdom so as to keep tradition and change from opposing and destroying one another. His own wisdom and humanitarian world view made it possible for him to apply this understanding to the guidance and development of his own people.

Sobhuza died just fifteen days before the fourteenth anniversary of post-colonial independence, on August 21, 1982. In the brief period since his death power confrontations have occurred that threaten the stability and unity that marked his long reign. Dr. Kuper's combination of history and biography gives us an understanding of both the reasons for stability and unity under Sobhuza, and the reasons why they are threatened today.

There has never been a publication in anthropology resembling Part II of this case study, and it is doubtful if there will ever be another one. History and its recorder Hilda Kuper, came together in time and space. The combination of Parts I and II of this case study gives us a perspective on a third world society and culture and its adaptations to the vicissitudes of our times that is unparalleled.

George and Louise Spindler
Series Editors
Calistoga, California

An Essential Preface

This new case study, based on information collected at different periods between 1934 and 1983, reflects changes that have taken place in both the culture of the Swazi and in my own approaches towards anthropological data.

When I agreed to bring *The Swazi* up to date I considered two alternatives. The first was to integrate recent material into the old framework; the second, was to add an entirely new section focussing on events since 1962, the arbitrary cut-off point of the original publication. The more I thought about integrating the new material the clearer it became that I would have to write not a revised edition but a totally different book. The second alternative provided a more satisfactory solution.

I finally decided to retain the entire text of the original study, except for a few changes in the introduction and a few factual corrections. The time frame and the statistics have not been revised or updated, and much of the writing is in the present tense. Though it would have been easy enough to update numbers or to change the present into the past tense, this would have obscured the contrast in style and perspective between the original and the new presentation of material. But even more important, Chapters 2 to 7 deal with the core of a traditional culture to which conservative Swazi continue to refer and frequently use to validate actions. Knowledge of that cultural heritage is an essential background for understanding the more recent events.

This book is divided into two parts titled respectively, for effect rather than accuracy, "From Kingdom to Colony" and "From Colony to Kingdom." Together they constitute a case study designed as an introduction to the history and culture of a small group of people in a country classified, in the language of international politics, as "an undeveloped British colony" in Part One, and as "a developing Third World nation" in Part Two.

Part One deals primarily with the Swazi in the years from 1934 to 1945 when I did my most intensive initial fieldwork, but the final chapter showed that the structure of Swazi society was less rigid than it had initially appeared. Part Two reflects my identification with the Swazi from the '60s until 1983, during which years I visited Swaziland eleven times for periods varying from two weeks to nine months. In 1970, Sobhuza granted me Swazi citizenship by *khonta* (allegiance) and in 1972 I was appointed to write his authorized biography. My last visit to Swaziland was in September 1982 for his state funeral. Information on subsequent events is derived from newspaper cuttings, correspondence with people in the country, and conversations with others outside.

Biography is not recognized as a conventional genre for presenting the material of anthropological research. It differs from the more impersonal monograph which treats the individual as "a type" or "a case." It is also different from the more narrowly focused "life history" based on information derived primarily from a single central character. A biography entails more documentary research and a deeper and broader historical perspective on individual actors.

The presentation in Part Two differs significantly from the more conventional ethnographic chapters of Part One. It is more historical and more personal. Though I began the original case study with a historical introduction, I was primarily interested in history as the "living past" shaping an "ethnographic present." Writing the biography of Sobhuza made me intensely aware of the chronological sequence of events and of the interaction between culture, history, and personality.

Part Two is not written in the present tense but in the past and explicitly challenges the concept of an "ethnographic present" in which time appears to begin with the arrival of the anthropologist in the field and end with her or his departure. Nor is it a diachronic study, in the sense of comparing the same society at two different periods of time (e.g. in 1945 and in 1962). Most studies based on return visits are presented in the context of "then" and "now." My close association with Sobhuza and his people enabled me to participate in, as well as observe, the unevenness, contradictions, and complexity of historical reality blandly labeled "the process of change" or, even more simply, "development." The approach in Part Two can be crudely labeled "processual" in contrast to the synchronic presentation of much of Part One. Process is rooted in the concept of time but is itself more than a sequence of events. It involves repetition and adaptation as part of continuity, and conflict and rejection as part of change.

Recent writings by historians and political scientists focus on Swaziland as part of a regional and world situation with emphasis on economic power expressed in dependency theory and class analysis. The emphasis in Part Two is on political power; other institutions and aspects of culture (economic, ritual, legal, et al.) are related to the central theme. The two approaches are different but not incompatible. The material in Part Two was selected to illustrate ambiguities in decision making, manipulation of cultural symbols, contradictions between ideology and practice, shifts in alliances, power struggles within and between political factions, and the extent to which individuals, through their personalities as well as their positions, influenced the complex and dramatic process of history in the making.

H.K.

Contents

PART ONE | From Kingdom To Colony

Introduction

The Swazi are part of the millions of Bantu-speaking peoples of Africa who migrated at different times from places farther north and eventually arrived in the southeastern region between the Drakensberg Mountains and the Indian Ocean.* From their homelands they brought cattle and seed for cultivation, and handmade products of iron, wood, skin, and clay. They did not use their cattle for transport, and, being their own beasts of burden, they probably traveled light. But they carried with them the heritage of all immigrants—the knowledge, memories, and experiences of the past from societies they had left behind. With this, they were able to shape their lives anew, adapting as they forgot.

The country they traversed was inhabited by peoples—hunters and pastoral nomads—whose ways of life were different from their own, and there was also infiltration from non-African outsiders along the eastern seaboard, where they settled. Long before the arrival of white settlers in the southeast, there was contact, to the point of intermarriage, between different groups. The modern Swazi, a handsome people, are predominantly Negroid in appearance, but with skin color ranging from dark brown to honey gold; occasional individuals have profiles reminiscent of friezes from ancient Egypt and others show Bushmanoid features. Distinct from physical mingling there occurred cultural diffusion and borrowing, and social adjustments, which may account for some of the striking similarities in both culture (material goods and the less tangible aspects of social beliefs and behavior) and social structure (ordered systems of relationship), found in areas far apart on the vast African continent.

Traditional Africa presents several models of political systems, ranging from large-scale states and highly centralized chiefdoms to small local communities, knit primarily by kinship and without defined political leadership. In the process of historical growth, the Swazi developed their particular system, a dual monarchy that was unique in some respects but which fits into the general category of centralized chiefdoms. At the head was a hereditary king, titled by his people *Ngwenyama* (Lion), and a queen mother, *Ndlovukazi* (Lady Elephant).

Beginning in the nineteenth century, boundaries drawn by white colonial powers

---

* *Bantu*, literally "People," is a linguistic label derived from the root *ntu*, "person," and the plural prefix *ba*. There are over 400 Bantu languages and many dialects, but their structure is sufficiently characteristic and distinctive to postulate a common origin.

3

cut through existing African political units. Swazi tribesmen found themselves dispersed in territories controlled by British, Boer (Afrikaner), and Portuguese. The claim to Swazi identity remains based on allegiance to the two traditional rulers, but Swazi living in the Republic (formerly the Union) of South Africa and in the Portuguese province of Mozambique fall outside their effective control. This book is limited to the way of life of those Swazi whose homes are in the small British High Commission Territory (now Kingdom) of Swaziland.

Swaziland, a lovely country of 6704 square miles—roughly the size of Hawaii—offers the challenge of considerable regional variation. In the west are rugged highlands where grass is short and sour, trees grow mainly in deep ravines, and the weather is cold and exhilarating. The mountains slope into the undulating plains of the more fertile and warmer midlands, which, in turn, gradually give place to bush country where cattle thrive throughout the year on green foliage. Between the lowlands and the eastern seaboard, the high windswept Lubombo Plateau forms the fourth topographical region.

Of great cultural importance to the Swazi is the abundant supply of water. Rain comes with the beginning of spring, in August or September, and falls in heavy showers, saturating the land and filling four large rivers and many tributaries, until the end of summer, in January or February. Throughout southern Africa, the Swazi queen mother is famed for her rain medicine. Her people do not consider floods and droughts acts of God or nature, but signs of royal displeasure or punishment from royal ancestral spirits. In more arid areas it is safer for the rulers to employ others as rainmakers. In Swaziland rain supports the traditional monarchy.

Its temperate climate, fertile soil, and potential wealth have made Swaziland an area of white settlement. In 1946 the population was approximately 184,750, of whom 181,000 were Africans, 3000 Europeans ("Whites"*), and 750 Eur-Africans ("coloreds," people of "mixed" descent). The Whites own roughly half the territory, and the majority of Swazi are concentrated in scattered reservations, called "Native Areas" or "Swazi Areas." Swaziland illustrates graphically the point that geographical conditions and natural resources are subservient to social controls. The territory presents an economic patchwork, reflecting largely a pattern of land distribution between Whites and non-Whites, irrespective of the four major topographical belts into which the country falls. All major advances in mining, agriculture, industry, and commerce are concentrated in "European areas." Like most of modern Africa in which Europeans have settled, there are striking contrasts between the traditional African and the Western way of life.

Superficially, the most conspicuous symbols of difference are buildings and clothing. In Swazi areas, most of the people live in huts that are clustered together into homesteads and linked by winding footpaths. The huts are of three types, representing three main Bantu-speaking groups that have been absorbed into the Swazi Kingdom: Nguni, Sotho, and Tonga. The predominant style is set by the Nguni, the group of the royal Dlamini clan. Nguni huts are shaped like beehives

---

* The capitalization style used here reflects the usage in southern Africa of "White" as a proper noun to refer to caucasian residents, whose ethnic background may be English, Afrikaner, or European.

Carrying the framework of a hut to a new site, 1938.

with plaited ropes radiating from neat ornamental pinnacles and binding down the thatching grass. There are no special air vents, and the doorways are so low that even children have to crawl to enter. Sotho huts, which are increasing in number, have pointed, detachable roofs placed on walls of mud and wattle, or sometimes of stone; wooden window frames can be built in and there are higher doorways. Tonga buildings, which are restricted to the eastern region, have overhanging eaves as their main characteristic. In some homesteads more than one style is found, but this represents no difficulty in adjustment, no conflict in level of development. In all, the central structure is the cattle pen. The relative uniformity is maintained by the absence of special functional buildings for trade, administration, education, health, or worship. The Whites introduced a variety of domestic architectural styles ranging from simple brick bungalows to Hollywood-inspired mansions, and also built clearly distinguishable shops, offices, schools, hospitals, and churches. The contrast in the exterior of the buildings corresponds to a considerable extent to differences in interior equipment and furnishings. In conservative Swazi homesteads, there are no chairs or beds. The people sit and sleep on grass mats and use Egyptian-style wooden headrests as pillows. There are no stoves, tables, or cupboards. Cooking is done on an open fire in the hut, or in the yard. Utensils are limited, and wooden meat platters and clay drinking bowls, designed for group, not individual, portions are kept on the floor, which is of stamped earth smeared with moistened cow dung, to make it smooth, clean, and sweet-smelling.

Clothing, a more personal demonstration of cultural identification than buildings, always reflects major distinctions of sex and age. Small Swazi children are decked only in narrow waistbands of beads or plaited grass, with tiny charms to protect them against various evils. Older boys flaunt their manliness behind triangular flaps of animal skins, and later wear these over materials tied like a skirt and reaching to the knees. Young unmarried girls wear gay prints tied around the hips with a separate piece of cloth knotted over one shoulder. Married women are conspicuously set apart by heavy skirts of cowhide and aprons of goatskins, so tied that it is easy, with practice, to swing a baby from the back and suckle it at the breast. Whites, particularly missionaries, condemned traditional clothing as immodestly revealing, and Western clothing became for some Swazi synonymous with "Western civilization" and a first essential of Christianity.

Striking differences tend to mask the extent of borrowing and adaptation resulting from over a hundred years of white settlement. The effects are most visible on the outskirts of urban centers developed by Whites, where Swazi live in simple Western-styled-and-furnished houses, but even in the isolated backwoods of the bush county, woolen blankets, beads, tin trunks, and bottles are conspicuous clues of contact. Perhaps most significant, although also less conspicuous, are the pieces of paper symbolizing the penetration of the written word. We find in modern Swaziland a small group eager to imitate the ways of the Whites and, at the other extreme, a group that rejects all things Western and longs for an idealized golden age; between the extremes are the masses, whose choices are not consciously or deliberately made in terms of whether they are "traditional" or "Western." The need for cash drives many Swazi to work for long periods in the world of the Whites, but they do not live there as white men, and when their period of service is over, they return to their homes, unaware of the extent to which they may have been changed by their experiences.

Very few Swazi attempt deliberately to live in both worlds at the same time. The exception to this general rule is the *Ngwenyama* Sobhuza II, an educated conservative, with a deep pride as well as a vested interest in the traditional culture of his people. Applying the crude cultural indices of building and clothing, we find that he is the head of the most conservative homestead in Swaziland, but that he has also bought one of the most modern houses in the country which he named Masundvwini (Place of Palms). He retains the heavy drapes and solid furniture of the original white owners in the front rooms, where he serves hard liquor, and tea from bone-china cups. The rooms at the back have acquired a more traditional atmosphere; here one sits on mats on the floor with Sobhuza's wives and drinks beer from the common bowl. Sobhuza's clothing, like his housing, mirrors a duality of cultures. When he interviews white officials in their own offices, he wears a tailored suit and polished shoes, and when he goes visiting, he usually carries a cane and a hat. But in his own homes he dresses in cloth and loinskin and walks barefoot and bareheaded with conscious majesty. Sobhuza typifies the dilemma of many a hereditary African ruler. He is a king at the crossroads—and for him there is no green light. The contrast of cultures is part of a more basic conflict between two social systems: one, a small-scale monarchy with a rather feudal economy, the other a colonial structure based on expanding capitalism.

I met Sobhuza for the first time in 1934 in Johannesburg, where we were both attending an education conference. He agreed to help in a study of his people which was being sponsored by the International African Institute. When I arrived in

Swaziland a few weeks later, he arranged for me to live at the ritual capital, Lobamba, in the care of his mother, the *Ndlovukazi*, Lomawa. He also introduced me to his closest kin and to the national council, publicly gave me permission to attend meetings and ceremonies, and delegated one of his own trusted men to act as interpreter, cook, and liaison officer. When I visited other areas, I usually stayed in the homes of local chiefs who were informed by runners of my intended arrival. I mention the cooperation received from Sobhuza because there is little doubt that without it an anthropologist would not have been able to obtain accurate information on the kingship, especially its ritual, which is at the core of the traditional system. But it was necessary to draw informants from groups of varying status, or position, and who fulfilled different roles in the kingdom. Chiefs and commoners, men and women, specialists and laymen, adults and children, educated and uneducated, view their society from different levels, which together make up the social whole that the anthropologist studies. Although the majority of Sobhuza's subjects are less Westernized and less educated than he is, there are a few with higher scholastic qualifications and more radical ideas of progress.

In spite of Sobhuza's friendship—in some cases even because of it—the general attitude toward me, particularly in the early months, was one of suspicion and even fear. His mother, Lomawa, a shrewd, illiterate woman, acknowledged my presence with a formal courtesy characteristic of Swazi behavior to guests, but she allowed me entry into her huts only because of her son's instructions. To most Swazi I was *umlungu*, a White, who had to prove herself before she could be received as *umuntfu*, a person.

Anthropological field technique is designed to obtain the necessary information from its human laboratory, but its recognized instruments—genealogies, village censuses, case histories, texts, questionnaires—cannot be applied with the objective precision of a pure science. Each society requires its own approach, since each has its specific points of entry related to its structure and values. A basic requirement of all field work is an adequate medium of communication. Anthropologists have long recognized the importance of language as a means of controlling behavior and expressing ideas. One of the great barriers that had to be overcome in Swaziland was the absence of a common language. English associated with alien masters was never spoken by Swazi when on their own, even by the few who were well schooled in it. I had therefore to learn *siSwati* or the more widely recorded *siZulu*,* a language sufficiently similar to serve adequately as the medium in schools and as the official vernacular. Both Swazi and Zulu are typical of the vast family of Bantu languages made melodious by significant tonal patterns and alliterative concords that indicate, in a complicated classification of noun prefixes, a particular outlook on things concrete and abstract, on people, and on the universe itself. People laughed at Whites who spoke "kitchen Swazi" but they became interested and sympathetic when they watched me strive to acquire the "deep" language with all its nuances and melodies, and they expressed their joy when I was finally able to follow what was being said, and sufficiently fluent to take part without embarrassing my audience or myself.

In the process of mastering the language, the field anthropologist learns other

* The *si* is the characteristic prefix of this noun class.

essentials of social behavior and joins in various routine activities until he or she becomes a familiar figure whose presence is no longer disturbing. Gradually I broke through the fence of noncommunication, and field work became a richly rewarding human experience. In Swazi society I found all types of people—proud, humble, generous, mean, gentle, talkative, shy, lazy, industrious. I recognized old friends in new shapes so that the familiar became strange as the strange became familiar. The human matrix remained universally complex but the cultural imprint varied and the qualities were often differently rated. The Swazi themselves have a number of ideal personality types, and, with an increasing differentiation between the traditional and the modern, these types sometimes conflict with each other.

Since anthropology became a recognized discipline over a hundred years ago, there have been many approaches to the study of society, each making a contribution, no one really definitive and final, each stimulated by ideas current at a particular period. The following analysis is primarily influenced by the structural and functional approaches developed mainly by British schools of anthropology. The presentation of the material would have been different had I used a purely ethnographic, or a more comparative, or a psychological approach. Though much material has been omitted, what has been selected covers the main aspects of Swazi life—political, economic, legal, religious, and social—as expressed in interacting institutionalised systems of behavior and belief.

The Swazi had no script by which they could transmit their past to paper, and their approach to time was episodic rather than chronological. Famine, wars, epidemics were remembered in isolation. The major unit of time is a reign, the duration of which is obviously not as accurate a measure as a decade or century, but is an index of social time. In the reign of some kings very little occurred; under others there were major events and crises. Thus the reign of Bhunu, Sobhuza's father, was brief (1889–1899) and turbulent while that of Sobhuza was long (1921–1982) and relatively peaceful. Sobhuza, who was only five months old when Bhunu died, lived for 83 years during which time there were radical changes but relatively little violence. In the original study, Sobhuza was the paramount chief in a colonial bureaucracy, though to his people he was always the *Ngwenyama*, the Lion. In Part II he achieved international recognition as both the *Ngwenyama* and as head of an independent multi-racial state.

1/From clan to colony

TRADITIONAL HISTORY

There are several versions of traditional Swazi history because tribal historians, generally old men interested in the past, frequently contradict each other and themselves. Anthropologists are concerned less with the accuracy of remembered details or speculative reconstruction than with the way the past is perpetuated and sanctions existing institutions.

Kingship is hereditary in the proud Nkosi Dlamini clan, and Swazi historians recall the names of some twenty-five kings, though there is agreement on only the last eight, beginning toward the end of the eighteenth century with Ngwane II, the first king commemorated in modern ritual. For a reason no longer remembered, he and a small group of kinsmen and retainers left their home on the east coast and moved inland across the mountains, an achievement recorded in the royal song of praise "Nkosi Dlamini—You scourged the Lubombo in your flight." They finally settled in what is now southeastern Swaziland, known to the Swazi as Shiselweni, the "Place of Burning," a name that some informants say refers to signs of previous habitation. There Ngwane died, and annual pilgrimages have ever since been made to the cave in the tree-covered hill where he and his royal male kin lie buried in state.

Swazi have no flag or national emblem by which to rally group sentiment, but the names of kings and such other verbal symbols as songs of praise and anthems serve a similar purpose. A limited number of royal names are given in irregular rotation, and the names of the old capitals are also repeated, serving as links with tradition.

Ngwane's grandson, Sobhuza I, came into conflict over garden lands with a powerful neighbor, Zidze, of the Ndwandwe clan, who was also building up a following. Sobhuza is remembered as a strategist who, at all costs, tried to avoid pitched battles against powerful opposition. Rather than fight against the Ndwande, Sobhuza moved northward with his group and established himself finally in the midlands at the foot of the Mdzimba Mountains, which remain to this day the area of most royal villages. The people who accompanied him are described as the "pure Swazi," "those who broke off with the Nkosi Dlamini at The Place of Burning," and are the nucleus of the Swazi state.

The country they entered was already occupied by people of both Nguni and

Sotho stock. The Sotho spoke a somewhat different language and practiced slightly different customs, but they were not organized for warfare and their level of culture was the same as that of the Nguni invaders. From all these people, described as "The Found Ahead," Sobhuza demanded allegiance. Some came humbly, offering tribute of food and maidens; others were defeated and plundered, but once their loyalty was assured, they were allowed to continue under their own recognized clan heads subordinate only to the Dlamini king. At least one group simply moved beyond his reach. "The Found Ahead" who remained and survived were incorporated as a second group into the growing state. From them, the Dlamini ruler acquired, among other things, new and powerful magic for rain, war, and cultivation, which bolstered his military conquest by extending his range of ritual. He further consolidated his position by diplomatic marriages, and sought as his main wife a daughter of his erstwhile enemy, Zidze of the Ndwandwe. He also sent two of his own daughters to the powerful Shaka, founder of the Zulu kingdom, and maintained his neutrality even when the Swazi princesses suffered the fate of all Shaka's queens and were killed when they became pregnant. On Sobhuza's death, he left his successor a strong kingdom, respected and feared by neighboring tribes, with a centralized political system controlling several thousands of people scattered over areas reaching far beyond the boundaries of modern Swaziland.

Throughout southern Africa in the late eighteenth and early nineteenth centuries, small tribes linked by kinship were being organized into strong military states under ambitious rulers. This important change in the structure of the traditional political units is primarily related to greater economic pressure on the land. Being peasants, their existence depended on the soil, and they moved when the yield was considered too low or the area too limited. But the tribal population was increasing, and land to the south, formerly open to African expansion, was being taken by the Whites. Conflict between the tribes and between Africans and Whites became inevitable.

Sobhuza's heir, Mswati, by his main wife, Zidze's daughter, was the greatest of the Swazi fighting kings. Probably influenced by the successful Zulu, he reorganized his army, which before had been on a local kinship basis, into centralized age regiments, and equipped his men with the short stabbing spear in addition to the long but less controllable throwing spear. To keep order over his vast domain, Mswati established royal homesteads as mobilizing centers for men in outlying districts, and these also served as military outposts from which to launch attacks on independent tribes. His armies' raids reached Southern Rhodesia (now Zimbabwe), and the name of Mswati was the terror of the north. The warriors brought their plunder to the king, who redistributed most of it, giving preference to the heroes. Important captives were sometimes exchanged for Swazi prisoners of war. Destruction of the fighting forces of an enemy did not necessarily result in the permanent extinction of the vanquished group, or in their lasting hostility to the victors. The Dlamini king emphasized the sanctity and power of hereditary leadership, and as long as a chief or the heirs of a defeated people survived, he acknowledged him as a foundation on which the conquered groups might be rebuilt as part of the Swazi state. Thus, Mswati reinstated heirs whose allegiance was assured in the district of their fathers, and in this way both extended his domain and made staunch allies of once-powerful enemies.

The disruption of rival kingdoms magnified Mswati's power. Many survivors fled to his "armpit" for protection. His fame also attracted distant relatives of established tribesmen who were anxious for a protector in this period of inter-tribal conflict and unrest. Some were humble and insignificant and others were powerful; Mswati established loyal groups in sparsely populated districts under their own chiefs, and he placed royal princes and nominees from commoner clans in control of clans that he trusted less. The immigrants became known as "Those Who Arrived After" and form a third category in the state. Of the clan names, totaling over seventy, approximately one fifth are regarded as "True Swazi," one seventh are "Those Found Ahead," and the remainder are "Those Who Arrived After." About 70 percent of the clans are Nguni, 25 percent Sotho, and 5 percent Tonga. Every clan has its history, and the combined history of all the clans gives the mandate of superiority to the Dlamini conquerors.

The Nkosi Dlamini did not attempt to enforce their culture, and even today there are local differences in dialect, architectural style, dress, food, utensils, and ritual. But considerable uniformity resulted from the method of absorption and the participation in national affairs granted to all subjects. The groups have inter-married, all are entitled to protection, to land, to bear the national mark—a slit in the lobes of the ears—to wear Swazi costume on state occasions, to serve to-gether in the age regiments, and to speak in the council. These privileges and responsibilities of citizenship are conferred on everyone owing allegiance to the "twin" rulers—mother and son—and cultural homogeneity is greatest in the areas closest to these central authorities.

THE PAPER CONQUEST

The initial relationship between Swazi and Whites was friendly and cooperative. Informants relate that Mswati's father, Sobhuza I, was forewarned of their arrival in a dream, even before cloth, beads, and guns substantiated their existence and before news of bloody battles between them and tribes to the south spread to his people. Early in Mswati's reign, which lasted from 1839 to 1865, Boer farmers from the Transvaal came in search of better grazing for their cattle, British traders from the east coast bartered their wares for ivory and skins, hunters shot the wild game that abounded in the bush veld, and an English missionary worked for a while in the south. Several white men visited the king himself, who received them courteously.

Though the Whites came as individuals, they were not isolated. They were members of two separate and antagonistic political communities—the Boer and the British—each struggling to establish itself in a country predominantly in-habited by Africans. Initially, the Swazi were prepared to treat either or both white groups as allies, and Mswati appealed to the English for protection against the raids of the Zulu and sent an army to help the Boers defeat a hostile Sotho tribe to the north. In return for 150 breeding cattle and services (unspecified) he also signed his cross on two documents presented him by officials of the Boers; though these documents had no immediate effect, they ceded virtually his entire country to the Whites and were the precursors of the spate of concession that led to the final subjugation of his people.

Mswati's death in 1865 was followed by a period of internal strife, centering on disputed succession. Rivalry between princes for the kingship had become part of the dynamics of traditional politics, but it gave Whites the opportunity to further their economic ambitions by political intervention in the guise of "promoting peace." Mswati's heir, Ludvonga, was a minor and Mswati's mother (the daughter of Zidze) and one of his half brothers were acting as regents. Ludvonga died suddenly and mysteriously and suspicion fell on the male regent, who was clubbed to death. Ludvonga's mother had only the one son, and his half brothers, sons by Mswati's other wives, wrangled and fought for the throne. Finally one group of princes agreed to appoint the motherless Mbandzeni in Ludvonga's place to rule together with Ludvonga's own mother. Thereupon the Boer Transvaal Republic sent a commando force of 400 men to Mbandzeni's installation; after the ceremony the leader of the Boer troops had Mbandzeni make his cross on the document ratifying the concessions granted by his father Mswati.

Boer and British expressed different interests in Swaziland. The Boers were predomiantly farmers searching for good arable land and also for a route to the coast which would enable them to establish their own port and avoid all contact with the hated British at the Cape. They were therefore anxious to annex Swaziland. On the other hand, Britain, following the loss of her American colonies and the rise of free trade, wanted to consolidate her empire rather than expand it, and had no desire to assume added financial responsibility. Britain was, however, reluctant to let the Boers gain control of a country of unknown promise or divert trade from her own southern ports. Her nationals were mainly interested in mining and commerce. In 1882, gold was discovered in the northwest and hundreds of European fortune hunters entered the country. They sought personal interviews with the king, to whom they gave cash, blankets, dogs, horses, guns, gin, and other products of the "civilized" world in return for the mark which he was asked to make on the documents they placed before him.

From the time of his selection, Mbandzeni's own position in the tribe was insecure. Hostility developed between him and the queen mother and culminated in a short civil war in which he sent his regiments against her. She fled with the rain medicines, but was captured and throttled. In her place, the king's supporters appointed another wife of his father, carefully choosing a woman with the clan name of his (Mbandzeni's) own deceased mother, and with no son of her own. On two subsequent occasions, Mbandzeni executed princes whom he found plotting against his person. Neither the British nor Boer governments had legal authority to restrain him, having guaranteed the independence of the Swazi in two conventions (1881 and 1884). But the internal tensions expressed in the rebellions were intensified by the presence of Whites. They were in the country of the Swazi king, but were not his subjects; they did not serve him, yet they employed his men as their servants; their conspicuous wealth overshadowed his possessions and he complained that each white man behaved "like a king."

Though the sovereignty of the Swazi was frequently asserted, Mbandzeni had no constitutional control over Whites and a few lawless individuals, by-products of many a frontier situation, were a threat to all sections in the country. In an attempt to deal with the situation, Mbandzeni appealed to the British High Commissioner for assistance; when his request was refused he made use of a principle of government already developed among his own people: hereditary privileges in a trusted family. He turned to Sir Theophilus Shepstone, a proven friend of Swazi kings and a man who had supported the institution of chieftainship among the defeated Zulu, and asked him for one of his sons. Thus it came about that "Offy" Shepstone, who turned out to be a young adventurer, was installed by the Swazi king as paid "Resident Advisor and Agent" of the Swazi nation, with power to negotiate all matters affecting the Whites. Swazi recall with great bitterness that it was during the period of his office that the majority of concessions were granted and validated.

The concessions were economic weapons representing a type of warfare beyond the traditional system. They included laws of land ownership that clashed with rights of customary usage, claims to minerals not yet exploited, the industrial developments of a machine age, the commerce and banking of an expanding capitalist economy. A leading councilor complained: "We hold the feather and sign, we take money but we do not know what it is for."

To assist him in his economic negotiations, "Offy" also introduced into Swazi government the principle of elective, as distinct from hereditary, representation, in which special interest groups, rather than the state as such, held the balance of power. He organized the concessionaires into a committee represented by fifteen elected property owners, with five additional members as king's nominees. To this committee, Mbandzeni gave, somewhat reluctantly, a charter of self-government, expressly reserving for himself the right to veto any decisions, emphasizing that he was "still the king." But in actual fact he had lost many of the powers associated with that position and when he was near death he mourned, "Swazi kingship ends with me."

Several textbooks blame Mbandzeni for the chaos that resulted from the indiscriminate granting of concessions, and condemn him as weak and dissolute, but he is remembered by his own people as a king of peace duped by unscrupulous Whites. Judgments of personalities generally involve an element of self-identification. And it is left to the more impartial observer to point out that economic and political forces are more powerful than the qualities of any single individual in shaping the course of a country's history.

The death of Mbandzeni in 1889 was followed by a period of national unrest that was intensified, although superficially restrained, by the presence of Whites. Swazi attribute death to sorcerers, and it was customary on the death of a king to kill all suspects. The British and Boer governments, despite their verbal recognition of Swazi sovereignty, had previously protested against this royal prerogative; when Mbandzeni died, the Swazi queen regent requested to be allowed "to destroy for just one day the evildoers who had murdered the king." Permission was refused, and this time the national leaders "resentfully submitted to the British queen's detestation of the practice." After heated discussion, but without bloodshed, the council selected as main wife and future queen mother Gwamile Mdluli, a woman of unusual intelligence and ability, whose eldest son Bhunu was a headstrong youth of sixteen years. A rival candidate was sent far from the capital. Sporadic violence continued. Stories of Swazi atrocities were headlined in the settlers' newspapers. There was a recognized increase in crime. To responsible Europeans settled in the country or with interests there, the necessity for a single administration became urgent. The white committee failed to exercise control, and was followed by a provisional government representing Boer, British, and Swazi, with "Offy" as the Swazi nominee. Torn by national and personal rivalry, it muddled along for over three years, during which period it "confirmed" 352 out of 364 concessions, but it had neither the organization nor support for effective executive action.

In 1894—without consulting the Swazi though knowing well it was entirely against their wishes—the two white powers, Boer and British, concluded a further convention whereby the country became a "protected dependency" of the South African Boer Republic, and powers of traditional rulers were circumscribed by the formula that they should be recognized only "insofar as they were not inconsistent with civilized law and customs." Among the powers the Republic bestowed upon itself was the right to impose a hut tax on the Swazi, a technique deliberately introduced in many parts of Africa to coerce peasants who had no cash crops into the labor market. Swazi objected to paying "money to keep the white man in the country," and as the time for collection approached, there were rumors that they would resist by force and that their rulers had summoned specialists in war magic to fortify the army. Tension was high when a leading councilor who was sympathetic to the Whites was executed at the capital. The Republican authorities summoned the young king, Bhunu, to appear on a charge of murder. The nation mobilized. Bhunu himself sought protection from the British magistrate in Zululand. "I have fled my country," he said simply, "because Boers are invading it and bringing in arms to kill me. I have stolen no sheep and shed no white man's blood." The British intervened and after a lengthy correspondence and a most unusual trial, Bhunu was fined 500 pounds sterling (approximately 1400 dollars) and reinstated; at the same time a protocol drawn by both white governments radically curtailed criminal jurisdiction of future Swazi rulers. The "paper conquest" represented by concessionaires, but ultimately backed by superior military force, was complete, and the Swazi were no longer recognized as an independent state. When, in the following year (1899), the Anglo-Boer war broke out, the Swazi nation remained officially neutral.

THE PERIOD OF ACQUIESCENCE

In 1902, Britain reluctantly took over Swaziland as an added liability of a bitter military victory. Bhunu died during the war and his mother Gwamile and a younger brother, Malunge, acted as regents. The future queen mother, Lomawa, was chosen from among Bhunu's widows because she was of the same Ndwandwe clan with which Sobhuza I had made so successful a marriage alliance. Lomawa had one baby boy, who had been named Mona (Jealousy); once she was appointed, the boy was given the royal title of Sobhuza II.

The Swazi anticipated that the British would restore their sovereign rights and expel the troublesome concessionaires, but these hopes were soon shattered. However, in course of time, through economic and political developments, the Swazi recognized the Whites as a vital part of their world and the years of friction merge with a period of interdependence and reluctant acceptance of British control. The machinery of a modern administration developed slowly, starting in 1902 with a little police force whose primary duty was to restrain the hostility of the Swazi and collect tax. Its personnel and duties were steadily extended. In 1906 Swaziland was placed under the British High Commissioner for South Africa, and, in 1907, a small administrative staff with a resident commissioner at the head and experts for different activities was appointed.

The government realized, however, that before there could be development or security in the new multiracial milieu, it was essential that the concession issue be finally settled. So the British appointed a commission and used its findings to proclaim that one third of every land concession be set aside for the sole and exclusive use of the Swazi and that two thirds remain with the white concessionaires who could compel Swazi living in their area to move after a period of five years. Partition was organized by a skillful white administrator who divided the "Native Areas" into twenty-one separate blocks, but drew the boundaries in such a way as to create a minimum of disturbance in the more densely populated areas. The Swazi protested verbally and without effect. All arms and ammunition were taken from them.

Whereas Mbandzeni had attempted to control the Whites by techniques established in the traditional system, Gwamile and Malunge strove to regain the rights of their people through methods introduced by the Whites, within the framework of a domination they realized they could no longer overthrow by force. Gwamile openly expressed the belief that money and "books" were keys to the white man's power, and she imposed a cash levy on the Swazi for a fund to try to buy back the land, and also started a school for princes and sons of leading councilors, bringing in as the first teacher a colored man from the Cape. From the little local school she later sent Sobhuza II, together with a small clique of agemates and a sister to cook and sew for him, to a mission school in the Union (now Republic) of South Africa. Here he studied, until at the age of twenty-one she publicly announced him ready to assume the role of "Paramount Chief of Swaziland and King of the Swazi nation." In a letter written on her behalf in 1921 to the Resident Commissioner to inform him that she had handed over the reins of government, we read, "This is the day I have always longed for. It has now come at last like a dream which has come true. King Mbandzeni died in October, 1889, thirty-two years ago. As from that day my life has been burdened by an awful responsibility and anxiety. It has been a life full of the deepest emotions that a woman has ever had. Bhunu died after only a very short life, leaving me with the responsibility of bringing up his infant son and heir. I rejoice that I now present him to your honor in your capacity as head of the administration of Swaziland. He is very young as your honor can see. He shall constantly require my advice. I and the nation have every confidence in him. I have brought him up as a Swazi prince should be brought up. His spirit is in entire accord with the traditions and feelings and aspirations of his countrymen, and what is more, I have given him the opportunity to obtain the very best training which any native youth can obtain here in South Africa. Sobhuza II gets his name, title and position by the right of inheritance from his ancient house and kings who have ruled over the Swazi nation from time immemorial."

Sobhuza II's first national duty was to contest the concessions in the law courts of the white rulers. In 1922, soon after his installation, the nation sent him to London to make clear the stance he would take on the issues of Swazi sovereignty. A special court of Swaziland gave judgment against him. When the case went on appeal to the Privy Council, the Swazi state lost on a technicality. He was accompanied on this mission by a few illiterate elders, his private ritual specialist, an English-trained Zulu advocate, and a representative of the Swaziland administration. In his judgment Viscount Haldane stated "this method of peacefully extending British Dominion may well be as little generally understood, as it is, where it can operate, in law unquestionable." The Swazi did not understand, but had to acquiesce.

Though much of Swazi history is unique, the general outline for the past seventy-five years has been set by the wider economic and political interests of colonialism. Modern Swaziland is the meeting ground of two separate policies, that of the adjacent Republic of South Africa and that expressed by the British Colonial Office. The South African policy of *apartheid* is openly dedicated to the maintenance of white domination; the British proclaim the priority of African interests in their own territory. Provision has existed since 1910 for the transfer of Swaziland to South Africa, and the local Swaziland administration has been strongly influenced by economic pressure from the Republic and by the presence in the country of white settlers who have the colonial attitude toward the "natives."

Within the framework of white domination, a distinctive Swazi way of life persists. The imposition of the colonial system does not automatically eliminate an existing system of kinship or kingship. On the one hand, opportunities and inducements to change have been restricted by the Whites; on the other, a conservative monarchy has attempted to resist the loss of its tradition-based identity.

White Swazilanders to whom I spoke in 1961 considered that the position of the Swazi had "improved considerably" in the postwar years. They mentioned development in communication, agriculture, mining, and industry and increasing investments in education, health, and welfare. Superficially, indeed, it seemed that the Swazi were better off and more Westernized. Nearly all the men and women wore Western dress, few were in traditional clothing or in ragged castoffs, a common sight in the urban areas two decades ago. At Lobamba the administration had installed a new office and taps for (cold) water. More families owned beds, chairs, and sewing machines and several had battery-powered radios.

But what of the attitude to the bearers of these gifts? Swazi appeared to show no corresponding increase in good will. There was less superficial courtesy and more openly expressed criticism. Very few gave the customary greeting and the open acknowledgement "we see you," accompanied by the hand raised in salutation, a greeting which before had been extended to anybody, white or black, along the roadside. Old friends who felt they could speak freely complained that the Whites still held most of the good jobs, even though some of their own people were equally qualified. Although the administration, acting on instructions from England, was trying to hammer out a new political constitution, a section of the Swazi were becoming politically more aggressive (or progressive?) and anti-White.

The implication of the Swaziland situation is clear: economic aid alone, given without understanding of the society, may create greater antagonism than friendship and more destruction than construction. Effective control of the reaction of the people requires a knowledge of their past as well as present society and a recognition of what the people themselves want for their own future. Change is a process that may take a number of different directions; the anthropologist can offer no single formula for progress and must recognize that "happiness" is the most elusive of evaluations.

2/Kinship and locality

CLAN, LINEAGE, AND FAMILY

In the previous chapter we observed the historical process whereby people of different clans were welded into a centralized state, a political unit, by a conquering Nguni aristocracy. In this chapter we shall consider the working of the kinship system. In most small-scale personal societies, kinship by descent and ties by marriage influence behavior in a great number of situations; they determine where and with whom a person lives, his range of friends and enemies, whom he may or may not marry, the positions to which he is entitled.

The clan is the furthest extension of kinship, and when two Swazi meet for the first time they soon ask, "What is your *sibongo* [clan name]?" This is a major initial identification. Every Swazi acquires by birth his father's clan name, even if his mother is not legally married and her child is cared for by her own people. Women retain their paternal clan name on marriage but may never transmit it to their children.

Swazi clanship regulates marriage and, to some extent, political status. I will deal with the political aspects first, as I have already indicated that a centralized monarchy replaced the heads of autonomous clans. In the process of centralization, members of the royal clan spread throughout the territory and most clans are no longer distinct local groups.

Clans are graded roughly according to the relationship they have with the kingship and the position their members hold in the state. At the apex is the Nkosi Dlamini, in which the lineage of the king is pre-eminent and the closer the blood ties with kings, the higher the status of individuals; next in rank come clans described as "Bearers of Kings," that is, clans that have provided queen mothers who were as a rule chosen because they were the daughters of powerful chiefs. Third in rank are clans with their own local areas and hereditary chiefs, which have not yet provided queen mothers. Slightly below them are clans from which officials are selected for special ritual or administrative functions, and finally come clans with no coordinating clan ceremonies, no local centers, and no recognized national representatives.

The grading of clans is neither as precise nor as static as a caste system. Grading does not depend on differences of custom or occupation and is not maintained by endogamy (in-group marriage) or sanctioned by the concept of ritual pollution. On the contrary, differences of customs are tolerated, there is no clan specialization of occupation, exogamy is the rule, and interclan contact is free and intimate. But the upper limits of promotion are set by the royal Dlamini clan.

Clanship is of primary importance in regulating marriage and succession. Marriage with a person of one's own clan is prohibited except for the king, the only man permitted to marry a clan sister. Inbreeding to the point of incest is a royal prerogative in many aristocratic societies; among the Swazi, incest between the king and a sister is both openly hinted at and condemned in one of the most moving of the sacred songs sung at the annual ceremony of kingship. At the same time, clan exogamy is recognized as an effective way of extending and creating social ties, and the king is expected to unify and centralize his position by taking women from all sections of his people. When he marries a clan sister, her father is automatically removed from the royal Nkosi Dlamini clan, and becomes the founder of a separate subclan. This also limits the number of Dlamini; a nobility always tries to maintain itself as an exclusive minority.

Subdivision of clans is a widespread process, dating from the early period of migration when brothers hived off, each with his own small group of followers who identified themselves through the name of their new leader or with an incident in their more recent history. The link between them and the parent clan is retained in extended praise names (*tinanatelo*) in which the name of the common ancestor reappears; intermarriage between linked clans is prohibited. Only among the Nkosi Dlamini do we find the deliberate creation of separate subclans for the purpose of intermarriage, but the king's clan sister will never be selected as his main wife; the future queen mother is always chosen from an outside clan.

Each clan contains a number of lineages in which direct descent can be genealogically traced over three to eight generations. Swazi lineages define legal rights and claims to various state positions, but do not provide the framework for the political structure as they do in certain segmentary societies, which have no centralized rulers. Kinship reinforces local ties but the two are not identical. Evidence of an original local basis to the clan and the lineage is found in the changing meaning of the word *sifunza*. In reply to the question "What is your *sifunza?*" Swazi usually give the *sibongo* (clan name), but when asked "Who is the chief of your *sifunza?*" they generally name their political chief, though his *sibongo* is different from their own, or they give the name of the man they consider the direct successor of the founder of their clan, even though he lives in another locality.

Swazi clan and lineage structure emphasizes the agnatic* kin as distinct from the elementary family, in which relationship with both parents is recognized. However, kinship always involves some theory of descent, some explanation of conception. Certain matrilineal societies deny the physical role of the male, and interpret birth as the result of a sort of immaculate conception, or impregnation by a clan "spirit" or totem. This is not the case with the Swazi, who stress the physiological

---

* Agnatic (noun agnates) is kinship through the male line only; sometimes termed *patrilineal*.

link between father and offspring and state emphatically that a child is "one blood with its father and its mother." The king in particular must have in his body "the blood" of kingship through the male line. The biological tie between father and child must be confirmed by law and ritual, for the physiological father (genitor) is not automatically the sociological father (pater).

Rights of fatherhood are acquired through *lobola*, the transfer of valuables, especially cattle, from the family of the man to that of the woman. If no *lobola* has been given or promised, the child remains with the woman's family while she, herself, may be separated from her offspring and given in marriage to a man other than the genitor. But the child retains the clan name of the genitor, the physiological father, who may among the Swazi—but not in neighboring tribes—*lobola* his offspring, even if he rejects its mother.

When a Swazi woman is in labor, she is asked the clan name of the baby's genitor. If she is not married she gives the name of her lover and the matter is fairly straightforward—either he gives *lobola* and takes her and/or the child, or the child remains with her parents and she is married elsewhere. But if the woman is married and she knows that the begetter of her child is not her legal husband, she must still confess. Otherwise it is believed that birth will be hard and may even prove fatal, for the child belongs "by blood" to the clan of the genitor, but by law to the man who gave the marriage cattle. Adultery by a woman was formerly punishable by death of both guilty partners, partly because it was a violation of the husband's basic rights over his wife and partly because it was a threat to his group to "mix the clan names" through a woman acquired by the group.

The most important daily interaction takes place in the family environment of the homestead, where children are born and cared for, play and learn, and adults lead their private lives. The structure of the homestead is more flexible than that of clan or lineage and its composition fluctuates with births and marriages, deaths and migrations. Swazi distinguish between kinship ties and homestead ties. The homestead is an area of common living, and though ties of kinship and membership in a homestead usually reinforce each other, kinsmen trace connections through blood or marriage.

In control of the homestead is the patriarchal headman (*umnumzana*), whose prestige is enhanced by the size of his family and the number of other dependents. A conservative homestead may include the headman, his wives, his unmarried brothers and sisters, married sons with their wives and children, and unmarried sons and daughters, as well as more distant relatives. Among all southern Bantu, polygyny is regarded as a social ideal rather than a sexual extravagance, and because of the importance of payment of *lobola*, only the aristocrats and wealthy (and often elderly) commoners are able to achieve many wives. The king has the royal prerogative to take by force (*qoma*) girls he desires who are not yet betrothed, but he must exercise his privilege with restraint. In 1936, Sobhuza, then thirty-five years old, had some forty wives; by 1961 he had married eight additional women. Girls chosen by the king are publicly recognized as future queens with political potential. Many wives are primarily symbols of status, and their children build up the lineage of the father and the size and influence of his homestead.

THE HOMESTEAD PLAN

The traditional homestead is built according to a definite plan that reflects the main interests of the occupants and their status relationships. In the center is a heavily palisaded, unroofed cattle pen, *sibaya*, and, if the lay of the land permits, its main gateway should face the rising sun, a symbol in family and national ritual. Men and boys have free access to the sibaya but women may only enter on special occasions. Dug into the sibaya are deep flask-shaped pits for storing the best grain from the fields. Informants state that the pits were devised in the days of tribal warfare to hide food from the enemy, and the fenced sibaya served also as a stockade against attack. Siting the main granaries in the sibaya enables the headman to keep some check on the food supplies used by the wives.

The king's homestead follows the same basic principle as that of any established polygynist but is on a larger scale and has a greater elaboration of ritual symbols. The enormous sibaya at the state capital is the meeting place of all the people, and at the upper end is a sanctuary where the king is periodically "doctored." This doctoring ensures his status—it bestows on him the requisite personality, described by the word "shadow," and the ingredients required for the king are more potent (and secret) than those permitted to any subject.

Grouped round the western end of the sibaya are the living quarters. Among many southern Bantu there is a rigid placement of wives in order of rank, but this is not the case among the Swazi. The only fixed point is the main enclosure with the "great hut" (*indlunkulu*) under the charge of the mother of the headman, or, if she is dead, of a sister co-wife, or, in special cases, a wife who is then raised to the status of "mother." The "great hut," often decorated with skulls of cattle sacrificed to the headman's ancestors, is used as the family shrine; in the rear, the headman offers libations of beer and meat. Places and things that are sacred must not be approached by any person who is considered ritually "unclean"; among the Swazi, menstruating women, people in mourning, and adults "hot" from sexual intercourse are never allowed to enter the *indlunkulu*. The shrine is specifically dedicated to the headman's senior paternal relatives, a category of kin toward whom younger female in-laws in particular must show stereotyped respect. In some of the more conservative homes, the wives of the headman make a detour to avoid passing in front of the doorway, or they deliberately avert their eyes and drop their voices when they approach. Though they may not enter the sacred hut, they are made conscious of its presence and of their own exclusion each time they gather in the yard of the "mother" (their mother-in-law) to perform common chores and discuss domestic routine. While daughters-in-law must avoid the "great hut" out of respect, their children may even sleep in it, entrenching the legal and religious distinction that is drawn between the patrilineal in-group and the women brought in from outside. The "great hut" at the capital, a magnificent structure, is periodically repaired by materials contributed by tribal labor and retains in its framework ropes and mats handed down from one reign to another. Inside, hidden by a reed screen, are sacred relics, including types of grain no longer grown; the huge dome is supported on heavy poles of ritually treated wood, and above the doorway are tiny holes through which the king spits in times of special celebration, symbolically radiating creative essence. Here, he and his mother speak to the royal ancestors on behalf of their subjects and perform the rites to bring rain.

Distinct from the huts of the "mother" are the quarters of the wives. In ordinary large homesteads, after a period of service to her mother-in-law each wife is given her separate sleeping, cooking, and store huts, which are shut off from the public by a high reed fence. Within her enclosure, spoken of as "the hut of So-and-So," she leads a certain private existence with her own children, who, although legally bound to the patri-kin and an integral part of the wider homestead, are emotionally most closely identified with their own mother, whom they describe as "the mother who bore me." She is also allotted her own fields, and, if possible, cattle for her use, so that her "hut" is a semi-independent social and economic unit. Legal and ritual restrictions on a woman's rights are to some extent compensated for by the recognition of her economic and personal importance. A conservative headman uses his mother's hut as his daytime base and is expected to divide his nights equally between the wives. A modern headman generally has his own hut, to which he calls the women when he desires them. Among the co-wives there is frequently jealousy for which the Swazi, as other southeastern Bantu, have a special term—*ubukhwele*.

The arrangement of "huts" of the different wives facilitates the subdivision of a polygynous homestead. A headman may establish a smaller homestead for one or more wives, especially if they have grown sons, in order to obtain a wider choice of garden land, or to prevent friction between the women or (and this applies particularly to chiefs) to extend political influence. The mother's enclosure, with the "great hut," remains the main homestead, the place of ritual.

The king's wives are distributed at several royal homesteads that are strategically placed throughout the country. At the capital they live in a communal enclosure with a single narrow gateway in the high surrounding reed fence; instead of each wife having her own huts, a number of senior queens share their huts with attached junior co-wives. At the entrance of the royal harem is a hut associated with the king's marriage to his first two official wives—"the wipers away of his boyhood dirt." Like the shrine hut, this hut has been transformed from a profane to a sacred building by elaborate ritual, and it is also used as a guardroom by a trusted man especially appointed to look after the queens. The king has a personal sleeping hut deep in the harem, to which he summons his queens when he visits the capital.

Special sleeping arrangements are made for children in the homestead to conform with the expressed norm that the sex life of brothers and sisters and of parents and children must be kept separate. Young children sleep with the grandmother. Adolescent girls move into huts behind their own mothers and their brothers build barracks at the entrance of the homestead. A room of one's own is considered antisocial, and unattached individuals are always accommodated with people of their own age and sex. At the capital, the majority of the population consists of unrelated dependents who live in a double row of huts surrounding the quarters of the queen mother and of the queens. The inner row is occupied by men of rank and special office, the outer mainly by ordinary subjects who pay allegiance direct to royalty. Protecting all the civilians of the capital are men permanently stationed in regimental barracks.

Homesteads are so closely identified physically and spiritually with the occupants that the idea of selling or renting to strangers is new and repugnant to traditionalists. When a headman dies, he is buried at the entrance to the cattle byre. After a lengthy period of mourning the old site is abandoned, but the family home is revived (literally "awakened") in the vicinity by the main heir, whose duty it is to perpetuate the patrilineage. The old huts, apart from the death hut, are physically transferred to the new site and the spirit of the deceased is brought to the new family shrine. The old site, with its beacon of gravestones, becomes a treasured and fertile field for cultivating crops, which the new headman and his mother will disperse in hospitality.

Here is one example from the homestead of the late Prince Ndabankulu, an important chief in the south of Swaziland. In 1936, he had ten wives, six of whom were in his main homestead, Ehletsheni ("The Place of Whispers"), three at Mpisamandla ("Strength of the Enemy"), and two at Enkungwini ("In the Mist"). Ndabankulu's mother was dead, but a co-wife of his father was in charge of the great hut. The women at Mpisamandla included Ndabankulu's first wife and her married son, but all important occasions were commemorated at Ehletsheni. Enkungwini was established to "waken" a homestead of Ndabankulu's own father, when one of his (Ndabankulu's) married sons wanted to move from Ehletsheni in order to obtain more land for cultivation. It was considered natural that the boy's own mother, La Simelane, one of Ndabankulu's senior wives, move with her son and daughter-in-law, and that they cultivate the fertile site of an ancestral homestead. Ndabankulu sent with La Simelane a younger wife, a full sister who had been "put into her marriage cattle" and given by the parents as *inhlanti* (junior co-wife) to her older sister. Ndabankulu died a few years ago and I am told that the council chose the senior Simelane sister as his main wife. It will behoove her son to send some of his wives to "waken" Ndabankulu's other homesteads should they be left without close members of the family.

The king, in particular, must "waken" the main homesteads of his royal predecessors as well as inaugurate a series of his own. He perpetuates the old homesteads by sending some of his wives to live there, and one of their sons will become the chief prince of the area. In each reign the village of the ruling queen mother is the capital of the state; in relation to it, the king's personal homestead is described as the men's quarters or the "barracks."

The search for a site for a new homestead is guided partly by material considerations, the availability of adequate land, water, and wood, and partly by social factors. A Swazi seeks friends, preferably kinsmen, as neighbors, and also seeks a chief with a good reputation. Should he find that he has chosen badly—as indicated by the unaccountable failure of crops or the sudden illness of his children, or unnecessarily frequent demands for his service—he will move with his family and his property to a more congenial social environment. Although his physical needs are important, it is equally essential for him to live among people whom he trusts. He does not necessarily sever his connection with the main branch of his kin, and he recognizes the heir as representative of the lineage, with the right to appeal to the ancestors on behalf of all its members.

Throughout Swazi areas, homesteads are said to be decreasing in size, partly because there is no longer the need for physical protection against man and beast and also because new interests, economic and religious, are cutting through the relatively closed and self-sufficient domestic groups of patri-kin. But the homesteads of aristocrats still tend to be larger than those of commoners, and the homesteads of non-Christians larger than those of Christians. In a sample area in the middle veld, the average number of occupants was over twenty-two in the homes of aristocrats and seven in commoners' homes. The largest homestead is obviously the queen mother's; the smallest I saw belonged to a Christian widow, living with two unmarried sons, far from their nearest kin. Such an isolated group, not even a single complete family, is a modern phenomenon. It is unusual, except in urban townships, for an elementary monogamous family to live on its own without contact with kinsmen in nearby homesteads. Similarly, it is only in European employment centers that unattached Swazi live anonymously outside a domestic circle.

TYPES OF MARRIAGE

Swazi marriage is essentially a linking of two families rather than of two individuals, and the bearing of children is the essential consummation of wifehood. Swazi marriage is of so enduring a nature that should the man himself die, the woman is inherited through the custom of the levirate by one of the male relatives of the deceased to raise children in his name. Similarly, since the production of children is the essential fulfillment of the woman's part of the contract, should she prove barren her family must either return the cattle or, following the custom of the sororate, provide her with a relative, preferably a younger full sister, as junior co-wife to bear children to "put into her womb." For the second woman, no extra *lobola* need be given.

The bridal party of a Swazi princess, 1936.

A royal bride in traditional wedding dress supplied by her kin before receiving the apron of a married woman. 1936.

Divorce is rare in Swazi society and it is particularly difficult for a woman to be legally permitted to marry a second time. The reason for this is not to be sought in the amount of *lobola* but in the institutional complex of patrilocal marriage and the power of the patrilineage expressed through such customs as the levirate and sororate. High *lobola* is a symbol, not a cause, of the permanence of marriage. The amount of *lobola* varies with the woman's status. Twenty years ago, it ranged from twelve head for a commoner to as many as sixty for an important princess. Several hundred cattle are contributed by representative headmen throughout the country for the woman who is chosen as the main wife of the king.

Lobola is a controversial issue in modern Africa. Uninformed administrators and missionaries regarded it initially as "the buying and selling of women" and attempted to abolish it by law, but the tenacity with which Africans, including Christians, have retained the custom has led to a reinterpretation of it at a deeper sociological level. *Lobola* is generally translated as "bride price," but it is clear that a woman is not regarded as a commodity by the people involved. On the contrary, she is a valued member of the community, and her past status and future security are symbolized in the transaction. By giving *lobola*, her children are made legitimate and become entitled to the benefits of the father's lineage; by accepting *lobola*, her people are compensated for the loss of her services. Their emotional ties and ritual obligations toward her do not cease, and should she be ill-treated or find herself and her children destitute, she may appeal to the recipients of the cattle, who will be legally, as well as morally, obliged to assist her. The husband does not acquire a chattel, but a wife for himself and a mother for his children, and he and his kin owe her definite obligations of support and protection. In urban areas of southern Africa, money is being substituted for cattle; the mercenary aspect of the negotiations is being exploited by some unscrupulous parents who marry their daughter to the highest bidder and who, because they are remote from the extended kin, do not fulfill their traditional parental obligations. But even many educated urban women are not prepared to be married without the passing of token *lobola* in addition to Christian or civil marriage rites.

Swazi practice several types of marriage, and these are important in determining succession and inheritance in polygynous families. Selection of the successor, who is also the main heir, depends primarily on the rank of the women in the harem. Among the Swazi aristocracy the first wife is never the main wife. Seniority in marriage brings certain advantages during the headman's lifetime, but upon his death other factors are considered. The most important is pedigree, and the daughter of a king or leading chief generally takes precedence over all other wives. There are also marriages with specific kin, of which the most important in Swaziland is marriage to a woman who has the clan name of the man's own paternal or maternal grandmother. The reasons for this will appear later.

These so-called preferential marriages are generally arranged by the parents, and arranged marriages, which are not necessarily forced marriages, always bestow a higher status than those based solely on individual choice. Swazi, however, recognize the power of personal attachment, and if a man informs his parents that he wishes to marry a particular girl, they may willingly send a representative "to beg a fire" from her people. Should they agree, the full marriage ceremony is performed, and her character may win her recognition as the main wife. The woman who has least chance of being selected is one who "makes love for herself" and runs to the man's home against her parents' will. Though the man's group claims her openly as a daughter-in-law, she is at a disadvantage because of the fact that her family opposed the marriage. If they did not accept any *lobola*, she may be given as wife to another man. Sometimes a grown son gives *lobola* for his own mother in order to legalize his status in the wider patrilineage.

The traditional marriage ceremony dramatizes an underlying tension between the two intermarrying groups and the necessity to create certain permanent bonds between them. Throughout the elaborate and formal series of rituals, the woman's family must display its reluctance at losing her. Her mother weeps and tells her to behave with restraint in the husband's home though she be subject to unaccustomed restrictions and accusations, and her father asks the ancestors to protect and bless her in the midst of her in-laws. She leaves her home accompanied by a group of supporters, including "brothers" and responsible elders appointed by the parents, who remain behind. The man's group receives the bridal party with warmth and friendliness, but the girl must neither smile nor respond. In one of the most dramatic moments of the ritual, she stands in the cattle byre of her husband and mourns in song the loss of her girlhood freedom and cries to her "brothers" to come and rescue her from her fate. They have been hiding and rush to her assistance in a demonstration of family loyalty and unity. In a mock battle carried out with much apparent fierceness, they rush off with her in their midst. But the girl knows, and they know, that she must finally accept the role of woman as wife and mother, and she returns when her future mother-in-law calls her back with a promise of a cow. Later she is smeared with red clay, signifying the loss of her virginity, and a child from her husband's group is placed in her lap as a promise of future motherhood. In the end, she ceremonially distributes gifts of blankets, mats, and brooms brought from her home to the various in-laws whose favor is so necessary for her future happiness.

The marriage ceremony, which lasts several days, culminates in a feast at which an ox provided by the groom's group is divided, each family receiving half. When the bride's group returns, they leave with her a young girl to ease her initial loneliness, and the new wife is gradually introduced to the responsibilities of her new status. The following winter the groom's people bring the cattle for her marriage; her people pretend to drive the cattle back, but after this mock demonstration they make the "in-laws" welcome and may even promise to send a second daughter as a junior co-wife. Once the bride has borne her first child, she is more often called "mother of So-and-So" than by her own distinctive clan name.

BASIC BEHAVIOR PATTERNS

It is in the homestead that the main members of the Swazi family, husband and wife, parents and children, grandparents and grandchildren, brothers and sisters play out their roles in dynamic interpersonal relationships. Their behavior is patterned by the mating and kinship system; these—and not any psychological quality per se—account for the differences in the behavior prescribed for a Swazi father or mother and a father or mother in other societies.

Swazi classify kin into a limited number of broad categories, embracing with a single term relatives who, in more specialized and isolating societies, are kept distinct. Thus, the term "father" is extended from one's own father to his brothers, half brothers, and sons of his father's brothers. Similarly "mother" embraces his own mother, her sisters, her co-wives, and wives of his father's brothers. The children of these "fathers" and "mothers" are his "brothers" and "sisters," and their children are grouped in the same category as his own grandchildren. The use of a common term does not mean that a particular key relationship is unimportant. Indeed, within the category there are usually accurate descriptions of degrees of closeness. "The father who bore me" is distinguished from "my big father" (my father's older brother) or "my little father" (father's younger brother), but one's behavior toward all "fathers" is modeled on a single pattern.

A Swazi soon learns to separate in word and action the relatives of the father from those of the mother. They are two distinct legal groups, and so strong is the identification through one or the other parent that the word for father's sister is literally "female father," and the mother's brother is "male mother." Toward the "female father" a Swazi behaves with the respect and obedience associated with the word "father," and toward the "male mother" with the affection and familiarity evoked by "mother." The children of my "female father" and "male mother" are included in a single term which can be translated as "cousins," and they are treated in a different way from "brothers" and "sisters." Each kinship term is thus like a mnemonic, reminding the person with whom he or she may sleep, eat, or joke, who must be respected and who avoided.

Implicit in the system of terminology is the assumption that kinsmen covered by a single term share a common social identity and, in some situations, can serve adequately as substitutes for each other in case of need, an assumption tenable only in societies where specialization is limited and where greater importance is attached to the kinship group than to the individual. This is the reality behind such customs as the levirate, in which brothers are regarded as equivalents, and the sororate, in which sisters may replace each other to fulfill specific wifely functions.

No equality is expected or desired between Swazi husband and wife. He is the male, superior in strength and law, entitled to beat her and to take other women. She must defer to him and treat him with respect. But a Swazi woman is not an abject and timid creature; she claims her rights as "a person" as well as "a wife." Should her husband maltreat her severely, she has no hesitation in berating him and, if necessary, running off to her people; she may, and very occasionally does, lay a charge against him before the "white man's court." Her people generally send her back for they are not prepared to return the marriage cattle, but they do inflict a fine on the husband for his offense. His behavior is also largely controlled by the constant supervision of his senior kinsmen, who are interested in the security and extension of their lineage, and by the pressure of his own mother, who depends on the services of her daughters-in-law. There is generally severe censure by a woman's kin as well as by her in-laws if she complains to the alien law of the Whites.

An outstanding feature of Swazi kinship is the father's authority over his children. The term "father" is associated with someone who is both feared and respected. The headman is the "father" of the homestead. The king is the "father" of the country. The most direct and permanent power is wielded by a father over his own sons, who are legally minors even after marriage, until they establish separate homesteads, and formerly could not marry unless he provided the cattle for their wives.

Swazi men may never treat their sons as equals, even if they should wish to do so. Between father and son there is a conflict of institutionalized interests. A son is consciously recognized as a potential threat to the father's position, though, at the same time, he is necessary to perpetuate the father's name in the ancestral cult. Perhaps their relationship contains an element of the classical Oedipus complex, the unconscious rivalry for the woman as mother and as wife. The complicated rules of succession attempt to regulate the conflicting interests of father and son. The first son of a polygynous home is seldom the main heir. He is his father's confidant and helps him maintain authority. His mother takes precedence over later wives in such matters as distribution of food, but her son should never be allowed to challenge the father's position or to replace him. In polygynous families the heir is never publicly appointed until the father is dead. Conflict between the father's and son's generations impinges at the deepest levels—sex and life itself—and in many patrilineal societies there are institutional devices for minimizing contact. Among the Swazi, married sons are expected to live in the homestead of the father, but between the sons' wives and their father-in-law there is the strictest avoidance. They must not look each other in the face or use each other's names, and the women must use a special language of "respect" in order not to mouth any word with the name or even with the main syllable of the name of the father-in-law or of other senior male in-laws.

The legal authority of the father is in contrast to the more indulgent relationship with the mother, for whom Swazi men express affection and appreciation, as well as respect. A well-known riddle runs "If your mother and wife were drowning, which one would you save?" The right answer is "My mother. I can get another wife but not another mother." Swazi say "The desires of men are satisfied by women but the satisfaction of women comes through their children."

In this patrilineal patriarchal society, there is even less personal intimacy between a father and his daughters than between him and his sons. Not only are they separated by sex and age, but a daughter leaves the home upon marriage and produces children for another lineage. The legal and economic aspects dominate the father's behavior, whereas the mother, herself an outsider, is said to "feel for," and to "share the sadness" of the girl and is expected to intercede on her behalf, both before and after marriage. In recognition of the mother's services, the family that is benefiting by her daughter sends with the *lobola* cattle a special beast known as "the wiper away of tears." This is the mother's private property; it is given for each daughter and is inherited by the mother's youngest son, a stereotyped darling.

Behavior between siblings, as this last point illustrates, is influenced by seniority and sex. Older siblings take precedence over younger, males take precedence over females. This is shown in the laws of inheritance. The main heir, who is always a male, inherits the bulk of the family property, including the cattle attached to the great hut, but the eldest son of each independent wife takes the *lobola* of his own sisters—except for the animals which belong to the youngest brother. Middle sons may inherit nothing, but they must be helped with marriage cattle before their juniors. The marked inequality of inheritance frequently causes rivalry between brothers and half brothers. Girls, who can never inherit family property, are less directly involved in family disputes. Swazi men have nothing to fear from their sisters and much to gain from them. It is their cattle that enable the boys to obtain their own wives; hence, when a sister visits her married brother, she must be treated as a most privileged guest and must be waited on by his wife, her sister-in-law, whose possessions she may use freely. The brother's children are told to fear this woman, the "female father," more than their own mother.

In addition to parents and siblings, grandparents are also integrated into the intimate world of the Swazi child. They teach the young to respect their parents, but their techniques are proverbially more lenient. Grandparents "scold by the mouth," parents "more often with a stick." Because marriage is patrilocal, children frequently grow up in the homes of the paternal grandparents, but, especially in cases of illness or tensions, children may be sent to stay for long periods with the mother's people. Lineage obligations are reinforced by the paternal grandfather, the man whom the father himself must obey, while emotional protection is expected from the maternal grandparents who express their interest in the daughter's child, described as the "child of the calf," by a series of ceremonial gifts.

The conflict inherent in the parent-child generations is absent between grandparent and grandchild. Grandfather and grandson are, in fact, recognized as allies with mutual interests in curbing an overambitious and authoritarian individual, the son of the former, the father of the latter. Grandson and grandfather are culturally removed from sexual conflict, and the grandson is, to some extent, identified with his grandfather and given authority to regenerate him. The most highly rated marriage, for social and economic reasons, is one which is arranged for a man to a woman of the clan of his paternal grandmother (*gogo*).

We have already indicated that behavior between blood kin is different from behavior between in-laws. Patrilocal marriage separates a man from his wife's relatives, who live in their own homestead; but toward his senior in-laws, particularly his mother-in-law, he must show respect and avoidance, comparable to restrictions imposed on his own wife toward his senior male relatives. He may not eat, swear, or relax physically in the presence of his mother-in-law; but, being a male, he has certain privileges denied to a woman, and he is not restricted in language and movements to the same extent. On the rare occasions when he visits the village of his in-laws, he is treated as a distinguished guest and provided with all possible delicacies.

Behavior toward other members of the in-law group depends largely on whether they will be prohibited from marriage or permitted to marry. Thus, in sharp contrast to the avoidance enjoined between a man and his mother-in-law or his wife's brothers' wives, who are potential mothers-in-law, is the familiarity demanded of him toward his wife's sisters. Swazi say that the love between sisters overcomes the jealousy between co-wives; to take a wife's sister as a junior wife is provided for in the marriage ceremony itself.

In traditional Swazi society, kinsmen provide an ever-increasing network of social relationships, and in different situations people behave in stereotyped ways set by ties of blood or marriage. In the urban areas, where Swazi are isolated from the wider circle of kinsmen, they are still intensely aware of the need for people of "one blood" to assist in such crises as illness, accidents, or funerals. Clan brothers may then become substitutes for real brothers, and fictional kinship may be built up with people who come from the same neighborhood. The specialized interests that form the basis of association in more complex societies are still few in Swaziland, and it is mainly relatives who cooperate in work, ritual, and government.

3/Political structure

The Swazi were not conquered by force, and though the functions of traditional authorities were changed, the political system with its network of kinship was ostensibly allowed to continue under the British administration. It is only in very recent years that a deliberate effort has been made to integrate the dual monarchy into a Western democratic framework and to develop a single government for the entire territory of Swaziland.

The traditional statuses of the king and queen mother remain conspicuous in their daily routine. Both receive elaborate deference: their subjects crouch when addressing them and punctuate royal speeches with flattering titles. He is "The Lion," "The Sun," "The Milky Way," "Obstacle to the Enemy." She is "The Lady Elephant," "The Earth," "The Beautiful," "Mother of the Country," and so forth. Compared with them, the highest tribal officials liken themselves to "stars" and "ant heaps," and the average commoner speaks of himself disparagingly as "a dog," "a stick," "a nothing." The rulers are always accompanied by attendants and are set apart by unique regalia. The queen mother wears a crown of dark-brown wooden pegs, topped with a bright red feather of the flamingo, the rain bird, set between two lucky beans; around her ankles and wrists are tied small pouches of animal skin containing royal medicines. The king has less conspicuous insignia, except on special occasions when he appears in dazzling and startling robes. Both are regularly treated with "the medicines of kingship" to give them "shadow" (personality). The well-being of the nation is associated with the king's strength and virility, and he must neither see nor touch a corpse nor approach a grave or a mourner. The major episodes in his life—birth, installation, marriage—are heaviliy ritualized. Death ceremonies, which always reflect the social status of the deceased, vary from the insignificant burial accorded the child of a commoner to the elaborate state funerals of rulers. The king, and the king alone, is embalmed by a primitive method known only to a clan that "broke off" with the Dlamini at the original home, the "Place of Burning."

The traditional Swazi constitution is complex, and, in some respects, extremely subtle. Superficially, all powers—legislative, executive, administrative, and religious —center in the *Ngwenyama* and *Ndlovukazi*, but tyrannical exercise of their powers is restrained by their own relationship, by a hierarchy of officials whose positions depend on maintaining kingship rather than on supporting a particular king, by a developed system of local government, by councils of state, and by the

Two Methodist missionaries bring gifts to Lomawa (in leopard skin costume) during the Incwala of 1936.

pressure of subjects who formerly could transfer their military strength and support to rivals. Among the neighboring and more military Zulu, hereditary succession was tempered with assassination. The structure of Swazi kingship restrained despotism.

The first check on the abuse of power and privilege by rulers is contained in the dual monarchy itself. The king owes his position to a woman whose rank—more than his own personal qualities—determined his selection for kingship, and between the two rulers there is a delicate balance of power. He presides over the highest court, and, formerly, he alone could sanction the death sentence, meted out for witchcraft and treason, but she is in charge of the second highest court and the shrine hut in her homestead is a sanctuary for people appealing for protection. He controls the age-regiments, but the commander in chief presides at the capital. He has power to distribute land in the "native area," but together they work the rain magic that fructifies it. Sacred national objects are in her charge, but are not effective without his cooperation. He is associated with "hardness," expressed in thunder, she with the "softness" of water. He represents the line of past kings and speaks to the dead in the shrine hut of the capital; she provides the beer for the libations. He is revitalized in the annual ritual of kingship, which is held at her home. He is entitled to use cattle from the royal herds, but she may rebuke him publicly if he wastes national wealth. In short, they are expected to assist and advise each other in all activities and to complement each other. In the past, when the nation was more homogeneous and both rulers were "illiterate," their duties were evenly distributed, but today the king is educated and shoulders more of the administrative responsibilities, letting the burden of ritual fall primarily on the queen mother.

Conflict between the king and queen mother has always been recognized as a potential menace to national security and well-being, and certain rules, not always obeyed, have been formulated over the years in an attempt to minimize tension. Temperamental differences are appreciated in a society built on a personal kinship basis, and as the king is chosen by virtue of his mother's rank, there is a possibility that she might favor another son more than the heir. To avoid this, the rule for royalty states "A king is not followed by blood brothers," that is, the queen mother should have only one son. Once appointed, no matter how young she may be, the queen mother is prohibited from bearing additional children; and when her husband dies, she is excluded from the custom of the levirate that applies to all other widows. Direct conflict is also avoided by the compulsory spatial separation of the king's village from the capital. The queen mother is not allowed to move far from the national shrine, and she may spend weeks without a visit from the king. Diplomatic intermediaries carry messages between them, eliminating friction that might be engendered by face-to-face arguments.

Swazi assert "A king dies young." His mother is expected to train her successor and hand over power when the new king reaches maturity. According to Swazi idiom, "The pumpkin plant lasts beyond the fruit"; that is, the queen mother outlives the king. In the present reign, this did not happen. Sobhuza has lived longer than most Swazi kings. His own mother, Lomawa, died in 1938 and was replaced by Nukwase, her full sister and co-wife. When Nukwase died, in 1957, the tribe was in a dilemma, and the councilors finally appointed one of Sobhuza's own senior wives from the same clan as the two deceased "mothers." This woman is now called "mother," and is removed from all wifely relationship with him. Every society must adapt to the unexpected; it does not simply cease to function because of unforeseen difficulties.

In the previous chapter, we showed that the elaborate system of successsion was partly a means of protecting a man against the competition of his sons. The first son of a king is never his successor, and if he marries a woman of such high rank that she will obviously be the main wife, he only takes her when he is well on in years. Guardianship, as a means of transferring power from one generation to the next, is institutionalized at the national level in the regency.

Rulers maintain their position by delegating authority to trusted officials, related and nonrelated. Nepotism, the granting of privileges to kinsmen, is an accepted principle in Swazi government, and power radiates from the king to other members of the royal lineage, who are described as "children of the sun," "eggs of the country." The more important princes are sent to districts as chiefs and serve as members of the inner council of the state. They are expected to build up the prestige of the monarchy, to report significant rumors of dissension, and to see that subjects respond to summons to national services. But Swazi history repeats a tale familiar from the cycle of English kings: where hereditary monarchy is the accepted political system, the royal lineage itself provides rivals for kingship. Important princes should never settle too near the king and their ambition should be satisfied by granting them limited local autonomy. In Swazi idiom, "There is only one king." Not only should he have no full brother, but, in this polygynous society, he must be wary of half brothers by other wives of his late father. The princes may never enter the enclosure of the king's wives, may never touch his clothing, eat from his dishes, or use the "medicines of kingship." Their relationship with him is thus essentially ambivalent. On the one hand, it is in their interest to build up the Dlamini kingship and on the other to prevent the king from becoming too powerful. His senior male relatives, particularly his uncles and older half brothers, are among his main advisors and supporters, and also his most outspoken critics.

Protecting the king from royal rivals and other enemies are ritually created blood brothers known as *tinsila* (literally "body dirt" or "sweat"). The *tinsila* are always drawn from specific nonroyal clans. The first two *tinsila*, the most important, are roughly the same age as the king, and are chosen soon after his appointment so that they may participate with him in the ordeal of puberty, in the first marriage, and other rituals marking his growth in status. Some of the king's blood, together with special magical substances, is rubbed into incisions made on the bodies of these two men, and blood from their bodies is similarly transferred to him. Thereafter, these *tinsila*, who are also metaphorically described as the king's "twins," may touch his person, wear his clothes, and even eat from his dish. The two senior *tinsila* are called "father" by the people, including the princes, who may appeal to them to intercede with the king in personal difficulties.

"Blood brotherhood" is widespread in Africa but need not be symbolized by actual blood transfusion. It is frequently accompanied by acts of commensality and oaths of mutual help. Among the Swazi the medicated blood is sufficient, but the relationship it creates is not symmetrical: the *tinsila* benefit the king more than the king the *tinsila*. Swazi believe that any attack by evildoers against the king will be deflected by the *tinsila*, whose bodies serve as his "shield." He runs less risk of being endangered by their enemies because their position is less coveted. Yet, so close is the identification of the *tinsila* with the king that should they die before him, they are not recognized as sociologically dead, and their widows, who had been selected by the royal council and married with cattle from royal outposts, may not mourn their loss till the king himself dies.

In addition to the first two *tinsila*, a series of junior *tinsila* are appointed at different times to carry out routine and intimate ritual associated with the person of the king. Thus we have a series of individuals, drawn from commoner clans, who are brought into fictional kinship ties with the king to protect him from close physical contact with members of the royal lineage.

The female relatives of the king are political and economic assets and should be judicially handled as investments. The more important female relatives (paternal aunts, sisters, and daughters) are given in marriage to foreign rulers and to non-Dlamini chiefs, in whose homes they are recognized as main wives. However, because they live in the homes of their in-laws, they are able to take little active part in the central government.

Although the political structure emphasizes the male agnates of the king, the close relatives of the queen mother also influence national affairs. Her brothers, who are the king's "male mothers," usually receive posts in the central administration, if they do not already hold them, and act as intermediaries for the maternal line in certain situations of crisis. On the appointment of a new king, the maternal relatives of his predecessor may lose their direct influence—which is largely due to affection and not demanded by law—but they retain their social prestige and a connection with the princes. The wives of the ruling king are recognized as "mothers of the people," but they lead fairly secluded lives during the lifetime of their husband, though their families constitute his important group of in-laws. The harmony of royal homesteads depends to a great extent on the king's treatment of such relatives and their friendship toward him.

Swazi emphasize that the king's allies are unrelated commoners. A basic principle of Swazi government states "A king is ruled by *tindvuna*" [councilors]." In each reign there is a *big* (that is, leading) *indvuna* with a special title, translated by educated Swazi as the traditional prime minister, who generally resides at the ritual capital where he hears cases, announces court judgments, advises on the temper of the people, and acts as their representative. The position tends to be hereditary in the senior lineage of a limited number of commoner clans, but the state appointment is not restricted to the main heir. The quality required of *tindvuna* is "respect for people," and though an appointment rests with the king, the big *indvuna* may be dismissed only by the king in council. Through his position, the big *indvuna* obtains so deep an insight into state secrets and so great a hold over national resources that he is drawn into a web of fictional kinship with the ruling clan and treated in some respects as a senior prince, and therefore as one who requires restraint. He is entitled to eat from the dish of princes and is not allowed to marry into the royal clan. His behavior to the queen mother is closely observed, for in the past he sometimes collaborated with princes and with the queen mother against the king, and sometimes with the king against the queen mother. But the big *indvuna* himself can never aspire to kingship: he is without the legitimizing claim of royal blood. Leading councilors have younger officials, also of commoner clans, to assist in the execution of the more physically arduous tasks.

Wisdom in tribal precedence and skill in debate are important qualifications for civil appointments, but the head of the military organization must above all be able to maintain discipline. Since intertribal warfare has been stopped, the number of military personnel has been limited and civil authorities exercise more authority over the age groups that formerly constituted the regiments. In dealings with Whites, Western education is recognized as an asset and young men with this qualification are being appointed to civil posts.

The final group of traditional officials considered essential for national security are the *tinyanga* (specialists in ritual), who are drawn from selected clans and are required to fortify the rulers and the nation as a whole. There is no single high priest or medicine man able to challenge the king, whose inherited ritual power is enhanced by the training and knowledge contributed by the *tinyanga*.

Swazi traditional officials, civil, military, and ritual, normally hold office for life and are only dismissed for treason or witchcraft. Incompetence, habitual drunkenness, stupidity, or weakness of character are criticized, but as long as a man is considered loyal, he retains his post, and the only way to counteract his defects is to appoint capable men as his assistants. No salary is attached to any traditional post, but the men receive sporadic rewards for their service and may make claims on the rulers for certain specific requirements.

In addition to individual officials, two organized traditional councils guide and control the rulers. The inner council (*liqoqo*) is a development of the family council (*lusendvo*) and hence is predominantly aristocratic. Here, senior princes, together with the great councilor, have an opportunity to vent their opinions and direct policy. The number of members is not fixed, and rulers must continue with the *liqoqo* of their predecessors, occasionally adding a member of their own choice. The people have no say in and do not know of these appointments, and it would be indiscreet of them to inquire who the members are or their qualifications. There are no regular sessions and no compulsory reports on activities. The rulers may consult individual members privately, but when an important decision is essential they are expected to summon the full *liqoqo* and abide by its decision.

The second council is the *Libandla lakaNgwane* (Council of the Ngwane nation), a larger and more representative body composed of all chiefs, leading councilors, and headmen. Other adult males (not females) are entitled to attend but are not obliged to do so. Chiefs who cannot come in person are supposed to send deputies who act as their "eyes" but may not commit their superiors.

The National Council, which meets in the *sibaya* of the capital, is opened by a spokesman for the *liqoqo* who tells the people why they have been summoned; otherwise there is little formality—no agenda, no order of speakers, no time limit, no political parties, no vote. Speakers who make good points are applauded, others are heckled and may be told to sit down. There is considerable freedom of speech, and the aim is to reach agreement, not to break up into closed, opposing factions. The sanction of the *Libandla* is required on all matters brought to it from the *liqoqo*, but neither council has any specific platform and there is no sharp cleavage of interest between the two. Both developed in a society where

Mpundla Maziya, a chief of the old order, 1937.

communication was slow and life sufficiently unchanging not to require many sessions, new decisions, or trained technicians. It is only in recent years that different occupational groups have arisen to put forward sectional interests and that a radical political minority has advocated a policy influenced by different political concepts.

LOCAL GOVERNMENT

Tribal territory is divided into a number of districts, each of which is organized on principles similar to those underlying the central government. At the head is a chief (*sikhulu*), who is either a prince, a nominee of the king, or a hereditary head of a non-Dlamini clan. In his area, he centralizes law, economics, and ritual; if his mother is alive, she shares with him the responsibilities of control and is in charge of the main section of the homestead. The elaboration on this basic pattern varies with the historical background of each district, and ritual, in particular, is most conspicuous among chiefs who were established because of their own hereditary lineage.

Within each district there is a weighting of power between relatives and non-relatives of the chief. Paternal kin living in the chief's district provide him with his local and family councils and, in turn, benefit from his position; his *tindvuna* on the other hand are outsiders and represent the majority of his subjects. There is always a main *indvuna* who attends to law cases and supervises district labor, and minor officials who vary in number with the size of the district and population. Local headmen, some of whom are more active than others, constitute the *Libandla* of each chief and may also attend the national council.

The districts are attached to the main royal villages, either directly or indirectly, through *tindvuna* of the royal homesteads. In each case, the arrangement depends on political considerations and not on geographical proximity. Local affiliations are evident in legal disputes, in the granting of land, in the acceptance of new subjects, and in the organization of labor. Chiefs who come directly under the king or queen mother may have considerable local autonomy, but their powers over their subjects are restricted by their own officials who can, if necessary, appeal to the rulers for assistance, and who are expected to report subversion. There is no formula in Swaziland comparable to the "destooling" (deposing) of a chief found in West Africa, but a chief who flagrantly abuses his position may be reported to the king and told "to rest," and another member of the lineage appointed in his place.

Knowledge of the principles involved in government is acquired by every adult male as part of his domestic experience. In the homestead, the smallest local unit recognized in the political structure, the headman exercises toward the occupants rights and obligations comparable on a smaller scale to those of the chief. As their legal head, he is responsible for the torts of the inmates. As trustee-owner of homestead property he controls the distribution of cattle and the allocation of land for cultivation; as councilor he represents his dependents in local politics, and as lineage senior he appeals on their behalf to the family gods. When he considers it necessary he consults senior kinsmen, who constitute his family council.

The relationship between a chief and his subjects, like that between a headman and his dependents, is essentially personal—albeit not intimate. The term "father," extended from the family to the head of the homestead and to the chief of the district, conveys in all these contexts a combination of authority, responsibility, protection, and ritual continuity. The chief is expected to know all the families on his lands and is related to many of them. Every birth, wedding, and death is reported to him. He mourns at the funerals of his subjects and drinks at their feasts. He does not live in a different type of home nor does he attend a different school or church. His power is paternalistic, not despotic.

Swazi political authorities are criticized by their subjects if they are aggressive and domineering. Qualities such as ability in debate, efficiency in organizing work, and knowledge of the law are admired, but they are not considered essential for a chief because it is expected that his councilors will provide them. He is constantly reminded that his prestige depends largely on the number of his followers, and he is aware that they have the right to migrate from his district if he does not fulfill demands that they consider legitimate. On the other hand, his followers realize that existing bonds should not be lightly broken. Before moving elsewhere they must take a formal farewell, thanking their "father" with a substantial gift for benefits they have received. Especially at the present time when land is limited, a chief is careful to investigate newcomers who offer allegiance (*khonta*) and may refuse to accept men with bad records.

A subject is not a slave (*sigcili*). Formerly in a category different from that of ordinary subjects (*tikhonti*), who offer voluntary allegiance, were *titfunjwa*—mainly children captured in war. *Titfunjwa* were taken into the homes of the rulers and leading subjects, who were described as their "owners," but *titfunjwa* could not be sold or killed. Moreover, there was no barrier to intermarriage, and there is no section of the population today that bears any stigma of "slave descent." *Sigcili* is a term of contempt; *Sitfunjwa* is a person without the security of a kinship group and with limited independence.

Swazi make no mention of slave raiding in their traditional history, although Arab slavers on the east coast influenced much of African history before the arrival of Europeans. Chattel slavery was part of the economic structure of early white colonists in southern Africa, but it was abolished before the white man settled permanently in Swaziland. The closest existing analogy is the control exercised by white farmers in the Republic over squatters on their land, a control that stops short of the actual selling of a person and is more similar to feudal serfdom. The squatter must perform compulsory service for a set period, and has no freedom of movement. Freedom to move is a primary characteristic of the traditional legal rights of Swazi citizenship.

LAW AND JUSTICE

Like all southeastern Bantu, the Swazi have a highly developed legal system and a graded hierarchy of courts that coincide roughly with the political structure. Swazi stress the importance of "the law" in regulating social relationships. Private matters ("dirt of the home") are dealt with by the headman, his mother, and his senior male kinsmen; disputes between unrelated people are discussed in the first instance by the family councils of the litigants; if they cannot reach a settlement, the complainant reports to his chief, who sends him with a representative to the chief of the defendant and the case is tried in public. If this court does not settle the matter satisfactorily, either party may appeal to a higher political authority. Certain cases may go directly to the capital, others to the highest tribal court, presided over by the *Ngwenyama*. In every court, each man acts as his own advocate and any male present may take an active part in cross-examination and so influence the decision. Precedents are frequently quoted, but the main concern is to unravel the complicated interplay of interests involved in each dispute and arrive at a satisfactory settlement. No oath is administered, but a man may voluntarily swear by the name of a kinsman or a ruler, and perjury is a recognised offense.

Swazi distinguish between private wrongs, for which compensation must be given to the injured party, and cases "with blood," in which compensation is given to the king as representative of the state. Theft, slander, adultery, and property disputes fall into the first category and are punished with fines; murder and witchcraft belong to the second, and usually carry the death penalty. The death sentence is immediately executed and the possessions of the deceased confiscated ("eaten up"). An offense against the rulers, through their person or property, is more heavily punished than one committed against any ordinary subject.

Contact between Swazi and Whites is accompanied by an efflorescence of new legislation that penetrates even the more routine activities. Not only are crimes and civil offenses that were formerly covered by traditional law formulated in terms of the dominant white culture, but also regulations are required for an entirely new range of situations—taxation, licensing, wage employment, fencing of land, inoculation of cattle, et cetera, et cetera! Some laws and regulations apply only to Whites, some only to Swazi, others to both, and, since justice itself is relative to a particular culture and is never absolute, the same laws sometimes receive different interpretations. Liquor offenses, tax evasions, breach of masters' and servants' contract constitute the highest proportion of Swazi convictions by the courts of the white administration, but these acts are not morally condemned by the Swazi. Moreover, the diviner, or witch-finder, the superior detective of criminals in his own society, is himself defined as a criminal under the Witchcraft Ordinance and can be arrested as a murderer (see Chapter 7). Case records reveal points of social tension, and legal statistics indicate the extent of social maladjustment. Breach of law occurs in every society, and some form of social sanction is essential for the maintenance of an established order. In Swaziland—as in other colonial societies—law is also used to perpetuate and enforce racial pluralism.

Two distinct legal systems, traditional and Roman-Dutch, are administered through a series of parallel courts, which interlock at certain levels. In some cases, Swazi litigants may exercise choice of court; in others, the limits of jurisdiction are defined. The superiority of white courts is not automatically accepted. Disputes over property, eviction from land, and complaints lodged by women are believed to receive more sympathetic (but not more equitable) hearing in courts presided over by white magistrates. This can be illustrated by a summary of one of numerous cases I recorded in 1936 in the court of Chief Ndabankulu. An elderly woman, Velepi Hlatshwako, and a man, Alpheus Shongwe, were brought before the chief's court, charged with "soiling the law," and fined. It appeared that about twenty years before, Velepi had been given in marriage to a man named Isauk Mabuzo (who was also present). The marriage had been unhappy: he accused her of misconduct and laziness; she accused him of ill-treatment. After a particularly violent dispute, he had "tied up her kit" and sent her from his home. This did not necessarily mean that he was relinquishing her altogether, but it was a demonstration of the extent of his displeasure: he wanted either the return of his cattle or the assurance that his wife would reform. Instead of returning to her father and reporting what had happened, in which case every effort would have been made to reunite the couple, Velepi "stole herself" and went to Alpheus Shongwe, who had been her lover before she married Mabuzo. Shongwe, the present defendant, was eager to keep her and sent a message to her parents offering bride price. They refused, saying they could not accept *lobola* twice. Her father (since deceased) and other members of his family council tried to persuade her to return to Mabuzo, but in vain. At that stage, Shongwe could have approached Mabuzo with an offer of cattle "to break the stomach" (that is, break his [Mabuzo's] relationship with Velepi), but instead Shongwe and Velepi moved to another district and let the matter ride. Mabuzo himself made no further effort to regain his wife until her daughter, fathered by Shongwe, was ready for marriage; then Mabuzo claimed both women under the terms of his original marriage payment. Shongwe, Velepi, and their daughter had become converts to the Wesleyan church, and, on the advice of the minister, went to the district commissioner to "state their case." The commissioner, a young man, summoned Mabuzo to the court house and publicly rebuked him for his "mercenary approach." Mabuzo went back to his chief, Ndabankulu. The chief and his court summoned numerous witnesses and unraveled the intricate details. This court agreed that Mabuzo was morally as well as legally in the right. Velepi had disobeyed her father and her husband, and she and Shongwe had gone "over the head of the chief" by appealing to the district commissioner. It was obvious that Mabuzo was entitled to any marriage cattle for the girl and that women like Velepi "soiled the law."

Knowledge of tribal law and court procedure is part of the normal experiences of most Swazi men, who are expected to attend discussions held in the yard of the chief's homestead, and to "talk cases" with friends and acquaintances. The formality and technicalities of the European court present a sharp contrast to tribal procedure; conservative Swazi have stated that in the former, the question of wrong and right is of secondary importance, that "the only way to win" is to have a smart lawyer.

CHANGING ALIGNMENTS

The traditional Swazi constitution, which grew organically and is verbalized by elders, is deliberately being replaced by a new written constitution. Deliberate constitution making is not a fundamental innovation, but is restricted by the limits of a society in which there is no separate legislature and most changes come about unobtrusively through court judgments arising from specific conflicts. Swazi laws, rooted in precedents drawn from a relatively static society, are validated by reference to the past: "They were in the beginning" or "They were from the ancestors." Contact with the more heterogeneous society of Whites created what has been described as "a legal vacuum" and formulae are required to deal with new situations in politics, economics, education, and health. This is part of a familiar pattern of social change in which a small-scale society, characterized by inter-personal relationships, must adapt to a more complex and anonymous outer world that requires greater specialization at both the local and international level. In all colonial systems power moves downward, and British policy in Swaziland is directed from the Commonwealth Relations Office in Britain through a high com-missioner (representing the Queen) in South Africa, to a local resident com-missioner, who acts as the link between the Swazi on the one hand and the settlers on the other. From this point, power is divided between district commissioners and traditional chiefs, each with their associated personnel. Not until the late 1950s was there an effort to integrate the traditional authorities into a single bureaucracy.

The entire territory, occupied by Whites as well as Swazi, is divided into three major districts and subdistricts. Unlike tribal subdivisions, these are units of ad-ministrative authority that have no essential political cohesion or loyalty, and their boundaries can be altered without consulting the inhabitants. The administrative officer in charge has no permanent roots in the country and no land to distribute to kin and followers. When he is transferred he leaves his house and his office to an unknown successor and relinquishes all ties with the people and the place. His office duties are both more general and more specific than those of tribal chiefs. He acts as a magistrate, revenue officer, tax collector, coordinator of various technical departments in the area, and as liaison officer between traditional authorities and white settlers. His post requires nontraditional qualifications—a relatively high standard of education, a knowledge of written law, a minimum of clerical efficiency, and administrative ability. Promotion depends mainly on individual achievement (academic or legal qualifications and some fluency in the vernacular) and not on claims of kinship and pedigree. Swazi draw a sharp distinction between "chiefs of the office" and their own "chiefs of the people." In Swaziland, "chiefs of the office" are white, and therefore—the argument runs—speak differently, act differently, live differently, and think differently from "the people," but not from "other Whites." The majority of Swazi do not realize that even if the conspicuous difference of color did not exist, the duties and qualifications written into the position of "chief of the office" would create a bureaucratic officialdom distinct from the traditional chiefs.

Africans employed in the white-controlled bureaucracy have an ambiguous status and often conflicting roles. A few Swazi, mainly men of tribal standing, have been specifically recommended by the traditional rulers to serve as assessors to the "white" courts or as advisers to the district commissioners. They are paid by the administra-tion, but their field is limited to matters affecting their own people and their primary loyalty is to the traditional society whose mores they must explain to the Whites. In a separate category are clerks, teachers, agricultural demonstrators, cattle guards, and other technical staff that are selected, appointed, and paid by the white administration; their qualifications are formulated by Western standards, with the emphasis on education, training, and efficiency. Although these individuals derive their positions from the Whites, their color keeps them outside the world to which their white colleagues return as the sun sets. Some accept this, but an increasing number resent it, and are among the more articulate of the emerging opponents of colonial rule.

Conflict is inherent in changing societies where hereditary chiefs are used as representatives both by their own conservative subjects and by the new administration, each of which represents different values. In other parts of Africa, the position has at times become sufficiently tense to prompt the colonial government to depose chiefs who expressed the opposition of their own people. In Swaziland there has been less arbitrary action, but the position of the Swazi king cum paramount chief has long been the focus of opposing systems. In the first period of contact the Whites exaggerated his rights and powers to obtain concessions for themselves; later, they curtailed the substance of traditional authority but used the king indirectly to act as the primary agent in bringing about his people's acceptance of innovations. At present, Sobhuza is still expected to be the first to improve his stock, use new agricultural techniques, employ demonstrators, encourage creameries and dairies, patronize schools and hospitals, and so forth. Until the early forties, he alone had regular and formal contacts with senior members of the white administration; these gave him a greater semblance of power than he actually wielded, with the result that his subjects tended to blame him for legislation for which he was in no way responsible and about which he was sometimes not even consulted. He and his mother were the only two members of the traditional hierarchy who were paid by the administration. He received 1250 pounds sterling (approximately 3000 dollars) per annum and she 500 pounds sterling (approximately 1200 dollars), which amounts were obviously inadequate for any national undertaking, but described by some Swazi as an attempt to "buy the kings."

During the war years, an effort was made to introduce the Swazi into fuller administrative, judicial, and financial control. The model selected was Nigeria, under the policy of indirect rule, and three basic proclamations—the Native Authorities Act, the Native Courts Act, and the Native Treasury Act—were eventually passed. But the Swazi situation was fundamentally different from that in West Africa where the European or white population was virtually restricted to an administrative cadre. In Swaziland, the country was owned largely by Whites, and even when additional powers were granted to the Swazi by the British government, the white settlers remained a distinctive elite, with entrenched economic privileges, high status, and close ties to white officialdom.

4/Work and wealth

THE WORK CYCLE

Swazi are traditionally peasants who cultivate crops, keep cattle and other domestic animals, hunt, and gather numerous wild fruits and vegetables. The main crops are corn and millet; in addition, every Swazi homestead produces subsidiary foods—peanuts, gourds, sugar cane, and pumpkins.

Economic activities follow the rhythm of the seasons. The women begin by hoeing and sowing small plots along the river banks where the soil is generally moist and seeds germinate quickly. With the coming of the rains in September, men and women move to large inland fields which the men prepare with ox-drawn plows. Heavy rains are expected in the summer months, from November to January, and the last gardens must be planted. In midsummer, agricultural work is intensified and communal work parties, especially for weeding, are frequent. During the day, the homesteads are emptied of able-bodied adults, and even the young children toil in the fields, often returning home in the late afternoon. In autumn, from February through March, women cut the ripe corn and tie it into bundles, then carry it home on their heads, or the men cart it on ox-drawn sleds, the main means of transport. In winter, from April through July, after the last corn is harvested and the millet gleaned, the scene of activity changes again from the fields to the homes. Men and women rub and beat the corn from the cobs and thresh and winnow the millet, reserving the best quality for storage in the underground pits and using the inferior grain for immediate consumption and to reward workers with beer.

Other activities are fitted into the agricultural cycle. When the harvest is in, people have more leisure and sociability increases. Women take the opportunity to visit their parents and headmen attend more cases at the chief's courts or relax with beer-drinks. Only in the dry season, once the danger of lightning is past, may new huts be built and old ones repaired. Winter is also the hunting season, and the time when government officials go on their tax-collecting tours—with a resulting increased exodus of recruits to white labor centers.

Many Swazi live at a precarious subsistence level; their food supplies fluctuate annually between plenty and a scarcity bordering on famine. Winter is the time of general satisfaction and physical well-being, but in summer, before the new crops ripen, comes the moon named "to swallow the pickings of the teeth." Corn and millet, the staple cultivated foods, are the main commodities purchased from trading shops; it is estimated that at least 25 percent of the Swazi do not grow enough for their domestic needs. Milk and meat are also prized, but the milk yield of Swazi cattle is low; milk, preferably soured and thickened in gourds, is eaten primarily by children; beer from sprouted grain is the substitute in adult life. Beer and meat are considered an ideal combination, but cattle are seldom slaughtered. A wide range of wild leaf vegetables, roots and fruits, and various types of insects are enjoyed, but these are unreliable additions to the starchy diet. A few nutritious items of food are culturally excluded from the entire population or from specific sections thereof. Fish is never eaten by conservatives; specific birds and a few animals are taboo to associated clans; eggs must not be eaten by females; and a married woman may not take milk in any form in the husband's home unless a special beast has been allotted her. Christians do not follow the traditional food taboos and many women converts eat eggs, buy fish, and are prepared even to take milk in public; but on the whole, the diet is unimaginative and, according to Western standards, badly balanced. There is no difference in the quality of food available to different status groups and the desire is to feel (and *look*) replete.

Formerly, the Swazi were entirely dependent on the land for their livelihood, and the power the rulers wield over their subjects is still referred back to their rights to allocate land. Swazi say that land, the basis of subsistence, is "served" to the people by their political overlords, and every man has the right to eat. Individual ownership through freehold and leasehold are alien concepts; rights are secured by allegiance and usage, not purchase or rental. Should the subject leave the area for several years, his land reverts to the chief, but if their mutual relationship was good, it may be reclaimed when he or his sons return. In most of southern Africa, Africans are prohibited from buying land, and there is developing a class of landless peasants who live and work on white men's farms, or whose homes remain in native areas but who obtain their food requirements with money wages. In Swaziland, it is still relatively easy to find adequate building sites, but there is an increasing scarcity of fertile, arable soil. Land is open for purchase, irrespective of color, though so far most purchases have been made by the nation, through a special fund. The majority of Swazi are still reluctant—or afraid—to own land individually and to exercise a power associated with chieftainship.

Swazi have a limited knowledge of agriculture, and, compared with the peasants of Europe or some of the Bantu tribes in central Africa, are unenterprising farmers. They recognize different types of soil, but are not very careful in their selection, and though they realize that cow dung fertilizes the ground, they do not bother to carry it to the gardens; they do not rotate crops or practice irrigation, and "doctoring of seed" and shifting cultivation are the limits of technological effort. Cultivation is not a prestige occupation, and, as among all southern Bantu, is left primarily to the women, whose main garden tool is still the iron hoe. The introduction of the plow was probably as radical an innovation into southern Africa as that of the horse among the Plains Indians. Since handling cattle is taboo to women, the plow drawn by oxen directly involved men in the essentials of cultivation, changing the division of labor and, in some areas, the attitude to agriculture itself. Swazi have begun to grow cash crops, especially tobacco and cotton, and to form farmers' associations. Group and areal differences in response to agricultural improvements can be related to both personal and structural factors, including the character of the local chief (conservative or "forward looking"), and the relationship with the local representatives of the agricultural department, especially the agricultural demonstrator. Land allocated to and cultivated exclusively by women is not regarded as a source of cash income.

Swazi have no objective measure of area, and the size of the plots attached to each homestead depends primarily on the supply of resident labor. Women, who receive their gardens from their husbands upon marriage, may obtain occasional assistance from work parties of kin and neighbors. The rulers have several "gardens of kingship" in different localities, cultivated for them by chiefs in the area, and they are also able to command the service of regimental age-groups stationed at royal homesteads, a privilege shared by district chiefs over local contingents.

Sites for building and for cultivation are individually allocated, but grazing lands are communally used. The general approach of conservatives is that land which has not been specifically altered by the efforts of man remains under the control of the political authority for the use of his people as a whole. Hence, such materials as reeds for fencing, grass for thatching, and indigenous trees for firewood are available to all people in the district. Hunting lands are similarly controlled by chiefs, who organize communal hunts.

Cultivation provides the staple food of the Swazi, but pastoralism is more highly rated. Swazi have the so-called "cattle complex" typical of many tribes in eastern Africa: cattle, in addition to their direct value as a source of food and clothing, serve as potent symbols in a wider range of situations, both economic and ritual. They are the conservative's closest approximation to currency, his highest reward for service, his means of ratifying marriage, the medium for propitiating ancestors, and essential requirements in various treatments for health and prosperity. Their physical presence is necessary for most national and family rituals; a man without cattle is therefore considered poor and insignificant and has been likened by informants to "an orphan without kin." The slaughtering of a beast, its division and preparation, is one of the most important social situations in which status and kinship bonds are literally carved in the carcass. Each portion of the animal is allotted to set groups of individuals in terms of sex, age, and relationship; there is no personal preference permitted for choice parts. The distribution and consumption covers several days, generally culminating in the cooking of a special dish made from the blood mixed with grain and shared between men, who eat it in the *sibaya*, and women, who sit in the yard of the hut of the headman's mother. The overall importance of cattle is reflected in the language, which is rich in terms for hides of different colors, horns of many shapes, and organs of animal anatomy. Men are referred to in terms of cattle and cattle are praised with the praises of men. The king is "The Bull" of the nation.

Cattle are unevenly distributed, and although every Swazi has a claim to land, he has no equivalent claim to livestock. Men obtain cattle thorough inheritance, or the marriage of sisters or daughters, or as gifts in return for particular services.

Rich men may lend beasts to people in need, who may use the milk and be rewarded with a calf when the other animals are required by the owner. At present any wage earner may gradually accumulate a herd, but the cattle of kingship, the cattle of the nation, still far exceed those of any single individual. This national revenue is derived from several sources—inheritance, death dues for important headmen, gifts accompanying requests for rain, "thanks" for favors received, fines, and especially the marriages of princesses, and also of daughters of unrelated subjects (often royal warriors) whom the king previously assisted with their marriage cattle. I calculated (in 1936) that the royal cattle numbered over 3000; the total cattle owned by Swazi was counted as 334,000. Through its compulsory "dipping" against specific diseases, the white administration keeps accurate vital statistics of cattle (more accurate than of the human population), but the records do not reflect actual ownership; cattle of kingship are often registered in the names of special headmen, and poor men are registered as "owners" of borrowed cattle. In the past, national revenue was mainly derived from loot in warfare or from the "eating up of the *sibaya*" of wealthy and ambitious subjects condemned as traitors or wizards. Several royal cattle posts were established by previous kings and represent capital investment of a premonetary period. Each cattle post has its own name, history, and place in government. The animals are used to feed the people at national gatherings, to obtain wives for princes, or to provide beasts for national sacrifices. There is one sacred herd to which mystical properties are attributed and which provides fat used only for anointing the king, his mother, and his first two ritual wives.

Cattle circulate primarily through marriage, and cattle and wives together are the traditional hallmarks of status and the indices of wealth. In Swazi society, wealth follows the curves of natural increase and may fluctuate considerably in a man's lifetime, not through the artificial manipulation of the exchange or as a result of training, concentration, thrift, and industry, but through "good luck" or "bad luck." Death and sterility are economic as well as social threats. Swazi political leaders, because of their favored position in a polygynous and aristocratic society, have more opportunities than their subjects to recuperate from economic misfortunes. The white administration, through its veterinary department, is attempting to reduce the numbers and improve the quality of Swazi-owned cattle by experiments in pasturage, cattle culling, and organized cattle sales. Some Swazi are responding, but conservatives remain reluctant to commercialize cattle. The conflict between the traditional and Western attitudes is subtly expressed in the remark of a fairly educated Swazi: "I only like to sell cattle when I speak English." In addition to cattle, Swazi also keep sheep, goats, dogs, chickens, and, in some areas, horses, but these have not the same importance in the ritual or economy. Informants state that their forefathers had fat-tailed sheep as well as cattle before the Whites arrived, and it is significant that sheep is the animal that is taboo to all members of the royal clan. Animal husbandry in general is carried on at the expense of agricultural development. Until recently, approximately 75 percent of native area was devoted to grazing and only 10 percent to cultivation; the remaining 15 percent was not suitable for either purpose.

DIVISION OF LABOR

Tribal (peasant) economy has little room for specialists, and the main criteria for division of labor are sex, age, and pedigree. Every man, irrespective of his rank, knows how to build, plow, milk cattle, sew skins, and cut shields; every woman is able to hoe, thatch, plait ropes, and weave mats, baskets, and beer strainers. Swazi attach value judgments to activities over which one or other sex claims a monopoly by reason of assumed psychophysical attributes. Specific "masculine" tasks that carry high status include warfare (possibly the raison d'être of original male mastery), animal husbandry, and hunting. Men are also the important public figures, the orators and councilors, and the family priests. A woman's life is restricted by domestic activities, the rearing of children, and the regular chores of grinding grain, carrying water, cooking foods, smearing the floors with cow dung. Men and women cooperate in agriculture and building, but the man's share is more spasmodic and energetic, the woman's more monotonous and continuous.

Age has a less defined influence on the division of labor. Children are encouraged to do the same work as adults and relieve their mothers of certain tasks in the home. It is only in relation to ritual that age becomes a primary qualification. Immature girls are required to help in the national rain rites and in the ceremonies periodically organized to drive pests from the crops; old women are similarly considered ritually pure and given specific tasks.

Rank by birth cuts across distinctions of age and sex so that every Swazi does not participate to the same extent in manual labor. Aristocrats and leading councilors are responsible for providing suitable conditions for the success of the efforts of others rather than their own labor. They arrange for specialists to treat the land and seed; they summon men and women for work parties in district and national enterprises; they supervise the feeding and entertainment of workers when a task is complete. They are not, however, exempt from work with their subjects, and most of them perform a certain amount of service for the rulers. On occasion some chiefs have displayed long fingernails with obvious pride, but even the most noble women, including the queen mother, are expected to take part in cultivation.

Close personal relationship between the workers and the rulers as well as between the workers themselves contrasts sharply with the legal and economic behavior of employer and employee in Western industry. There are no fixed periods of work, no regular hours, and no stipulated pay. An age set may be summoned for several days in succession, but sometimes weeks will elapse without any demand for its services. No man is forced to work, though if he consistently shirks his obligations, his peers may reproach him and belabor him with sticks. It is frequently impossible for members of a homestead to do all the work required for their subsistence without extra help; as there is no special class of laborers, they rely on kinsmen and neighbors, organized into temporary labor associations. When members of both sexes are present, they are divided into two competitive groups, spurring each other to greater achievement. Swazi generally sing as they work, their movements coordinated through music and rhythm. Every joint economic activity has its own sets of songs, and the song leader is the closest approximation to a foreman or timekeeper. The number of work parties and their size depends on status and, to some extent, on the nature of the undertaking. There are occasional large-scale national enterprises, which require considerable planning and foresight and involve as many as a thousand workers on specific days. For the organizer, a work party is both an economic venture and an occasion for the enhancement of prestige. He or she—for women may also initiate the enterprise—must calculate whether supplies are sufficient to feed the workers. The reward of communal work in conservative homes is always food, beer or meat, eaten at the home of the host. This is as integral a part of Swazi economy as money payment in European service. But the host, unlike an employer, offers sporadic hospitality, and the food is not regarded as a wage or a means whereby people hope to support themselves. It is a way of expressing thanks, a reward to be shared among the workers according to rank, age, sex, and locality. Individual effort or piecework is not considered. Some workers come early, others late. There are well-known shirkers who enjoy the feasting without having contributed their labor, but they are aware that if they shirk too frequently, they, in turn, will not receive assistance. The work party is, in some respects, the antithesis of a trade union, and an administrative instruction from the British government to introduce trade unions into Swaziland met with the criticism from conservatives that this was a device to compel laborers to work for a definite period of time at a fixed rate instead of on a personal and voluntary basis. Traditionally, there is no sharp division between employer and employee, and reciprocity was the most powerful sanction in maintaining Swazi economic organization.

SPECIALIZATION

As a result of the economic homogeneity of Swazi society, each individual plies a number of crafts, but recognition of individual aptitude has led to a limited specialization within the general skills expected of each person. Some men are better than others at tanning the hides (used for shields and for skin skirts and aprons worn by conservative married women), and some women are more skilled than others at beadwork, basketwork, and plaiting mats, and so may be asked to produce these, at a price, for the less skilled. There is a marked tendency for all goods to be commercialized at the present time. Prices vary, and bargaining is not part of the Swazi convention of exchange, as it is in oriental communities. The main source of income for women who have no special skill and do not have outside employment is the sale of home-brewed beer, on which the profit may be as high as 100 percent, but the smallness of economic venture is indicated by the fact that the capital involved, if the grain is bought, is seldom more than 30 shillings (less than 5 dollars!).

The term *tinyanga* is applied specifically to specialists in ritual—medicine men and diviners—but may be extended to smiths, woodcarvers, and potters, whose crafts tend to be specialized and hereditary and involve unusual "power," and risks requiring ritual protection.

The roles of medicine men and diviners and their relationship to the supernatural will be more fully discussed in Chapter 5. Here we are concerned with the economic aspect, for these *tinyanga* have the greatest opportunity of acquiring wealth by individual achievement. Payment varies with qualifications and the nature and success of the treatment. A medicine man of good repute receives an initial gift of a goat, spear, or other articles to "open his bags," and a further payment to make the medicine "shine." During treatment he receives the hide of any beast that is slaughtered, and he is liberally provided with meat. If the patient recovers, a cow is given in thanks, but if no cure is effected, there is no final fee. For other services, such as the "pegging down" of a homestead against evil-doers or the purification of a homestead after lightning has struck, payment may be a goat or a bag of grain. A diviner's fee depends on his technique and the seriousness of the situation, but generally specialist services receive no regular stipulated payment. Sometimes the amount is decided in advance; at other times new requests are made in the course of treatment. Not to pay an *inyanga* is dangerous because of the supernatural powers he may evoke if angered. As in other societies, payments incurred by illness can cripple a family for life, while successful medicine men flourish. The amount of time *tinyanga* devote to their practice depends on personal interest, but Swazi do not regard even this exclusive profession as a substitute for peasant farming.

Smithing, which includes both smelting iron from the rock and forging it into shape, was formerly the most exacting and remunerative of the crafts. The finished articles, especially iron hoes, knives, and different kinds of spears (the main weapons of war), were in great demand and short supply. Smithing was a hereditary occupation requiring long apprenticeship and surrounded by taboos. The smithy, with its flaming forge and elaborate bellows of goatskin, was built a distance from the homestead, and women were not allowed to enter. Rich iron deposits west of Mbabane are at present being exploited by white mining companies, and Swazi smiths find it more convenient to use scrap iron and to repair old articles rather than create new ones, which can now be bought at trading stations. Certain iron instruments are sacred, and these are kept for state rituals.

Swazi claim that at one time they also had specialists in copper and brass. Substantiating this are the large brass beads, handed down from one reign to the next, that adorn the skirts of the first ten wives of the king, and a copper bracelet that is also part of the royal insignia. But if the process of forging copper was once known, this knowledge has been lost.

Wood carving is limited to essentially functional objects, especially headrests, milk pails, meat dishes, and spoons. There are no masks or sculptured figures, though the bush veld is rich in indigenous timber. The carver has no special status comparable to that of medicine men or even of smiths, nor is the apprenticeship in any way restricted. Woodcraft is encouraged in the schools and a small tourist trade is being developed.

Pottery making survives as a special craft of women who, using the coil technique, produce different sizes and shapes of drinking and cooking vessels of considerable beauty and symmetry, decorated with simple geometrical designs. The kiln is a hollow in the ground, covered with dry brush; because it is difficult to control the heat, breakage is high. As in other situations where there is an element of risk and technical control is limited, the Swazi potter resorts to various magical aids.

Markets comparable to those found in West Africa do not exist in Swaziland, but a certain amount of internal trade follows the irregular distribution of raw materials. Wood carvers, especially, are concentrated in bush country, and some of the best clay is found in riverbanks in the northwest.

With Westernization, a range of new, full-time occupational situations have been introduced. Some 12,000 Swazi males are employed mainly as unskilled laborers in farming, mining, building, and transport, and some 1000 women are also in farming and domestic service. A much smaller number (under 500 men and 200 women) are teachers, clerks, and messengers, and there is a growing number of Swazi, mostly men, in "self employment" as shopkeepers, butchers, and "agents." New jobs associated with school education carry more prestige and a higher standard of living than those that do not require "writing." But as yet there is no economic class division, and the few educated men and women in financially good positions have not cut adrift from the extended family; the majority of their kin are both uneducated and unskilled peasants, and are often migrant laborers.

WEALTH AND STATUS

Accumulation of wealth is not conspicuous in traditional society, where rulers and subjects live in the same type of home, eat the same kind of foods, and use the same limited range of utensils and implements. The perishable nature of most Swazi products as well as the limited range of choice make generosity the hallmark of achievement and the primary virtue of *buntfu* (humanity). From infancy, children are taught not to be greedy or to take too large a portion of food from the common pot, and they, themselves, soon enforce the rule of sharing. A mother who hides food for her own offspring will be insulted by co-wives and suspected of witchcraft, and the character of a headman is judged by his hospitality. A donor must always belittle his gift, while the recipient must exaggerate its importance and accept even the smallest article in both hands.

Begging has a connotation different from that expressed in the European milieu. Among conservatives it carries no shame. To beg is a sign of deference and to give is a token of superiority, enhancing status. It is the person who refuses a request who should suffer; to avoid inflicting shame, borrowers express their requests through intermediaries and the refusal should be couched in self-deprecatory terms. Something given in response to a request is a favor and need not be returned. It is totally different from objects that are specifically borrowed and also from those that are bought and for which there is an obligation to pay at a later date. A person is thanked for a favor by the further request "Do the same tomorrow."

Inequality of wealth has always been acceptable but only within the aristocratic framework. Commoners who acquired too many wives or cattle were in danger of being "smelt out as evil doers," for whom death was the penalty and whose property was legally "eaten up" by chiefs. These drastic measures are prohibited by modern law, but in the rural areas there is still considerable restraint on ambition and ability. Rich conservatives divide their homesteads, lend out their surplus cattle, bury their grain in underground pits, and hide their money in the ground. The fear of witchcraft acts as a check on economic enterprise, and it is safer to plead poverty than to boast of wealth.

Although display of wealth is limited in traditional circles, a large range of trade articles has made economic differences more conspicuous, and a new, white-controlled, economic milieu has redefined status. Smart suits, record players, Western furniture, and sewing machines are the prized possessions of self-styled "progressives" while Sobhuza demonstrates a new "high" in aristocratic living. But the major obvious disparity in wealth is not between traditional and progressive or aristocrat and commoner, but between Whites and Swazi.

5 / Age and education

TRAINING THE YOUNG

In every society age is a social, not an absolute, concept, measured by artificial standards correlated more or less directly with the major physiological changes of infancy, prepuberty, adolescence, maturity, and the menopause. Generally speaking, in preliterate peasant societies increasing age carries increasing responsibilities, and elders, as "repositories of tradition," exercise considerable influence and command corresponding respect. The authority of age characterizes all Swazi behavior, and age is the main factor in group association.

Swazi distinguish, linguistically and ritually, eight periods of individual growth, from birth to "almost an ancestor." Until the third month of life a Swazi baby is described as "a thing." It has no name, cannot be handled by the men, and, if it dies, it may not be publicly mourned. It is recognized as being very weak and vulnerable (infant mortality is tragically high), and the parents perform various rituals to protect it against dangers emanating from animals, humans, and from nature herself. In the third month, the infant is shown to the moon and symbolically introduced to the world of nature. It is entered into the category of persons, and is given a name, which may be sung to it in its first lullaby. It remains a "baby" until it has "teeth to chew" and "legs to run." This stage, which lasts roughly three years, is traditionally terminated by the act of weaning. Until then the baby remains most closely attached to the mother, who carries it everywhere in a sling on her back, feeds it when it cries, and tends it with devotion. Other people, including the father, may also fondle it and deliberately try to teach it basic kinship terms and correct behavior.

Obedience and politeness are inculcated from the beginning of awareness. Little achievements meet with warm encouragement and such stereotyped praise as "Chief," or "Now you are really a man"—or "a woman." Toilet training is generally achieved within the first two years without much apparent conflict. The mother abruptly removes the baby from her back when she feels discomfort, but occasional lapses are treated with tolerance. Weaning, enforced, if necessary, by the mother's rubbing bitter aloe or some other unpleasant-tasting substance on her nipples, is a symbolic as well as a real separation from maternal care.

The baby now becomes a toddler, who must begin to be independent and associate with his peers. When the mother goes to work in the fields or to gather firewood, she may leave him for many hours in the care of children not much bigger than himself, who play with him, sing to him, and teach him accepted rules of behavior. Disobedience or rudeness may provoke a sharp slap, but, as a rule, less drastic teaching by the play group appears sufficient to produce conformity. The threat of a beating is constantly uttered by both adults and older children for various "mistakes," but is seldom carried out.

Discipline becomes more strict and punishment more physical as the child grows older, but the overall impression is that Swazi children are reared with unselfconscious indulgence relatively free from constant adult supervision. They also learn unconsciously through riddles and verbal memory games, said to "sharpen the intelligence," and there are songs and dances to "make a person grow into a person." Most of the play of children is based on the activities of the adult world. Small boys model clay oxen (today some model automobiles) and indulge in stick fights. Girls pretend to grind and cook and do each other's hair. Children of both sexes build miniature huts near the homestead and act out the roles of kinsmen. In the evenings, the old women in whose huts they sleep after weaning recount tales and fables which, though ostensibly meant to entertain, frequently point out a moral. Legends dealing with clan and tribal history are recalled on specific ritual occasions.

At about the age of six, Swazi children have a small slit made in the lobe of each ear. They are no longer protected toddlers; they are now held more responsible for their own actions. Control of tears and laughter is part of the stereotyped process of growing up, and though the ear-cutting operation is quite painful, the children must bear it bravely. Thereafter they are encouraged to participate in economic and social activities insofar as their physical strength permits. The education of boys and girls is differentiated in accordance with the male and female roles in this society. The training of boys is directed toward hardening them physically and bringing them into public life. They must be severed from the womenfolk and "must not grow up under the skin skirts of their mothers." They go in small gangs to herd the calves in the neighborhood and are later promoted to the herding of the cattle, during which period they spend much of the day away from their homes, acquire a knowledge of nature, and learn to fend for themselves. The girls, on the other hand, are allowed less freedom of movement. They accompany their mothers or agemates to draw water or gather wood, or plant in the fields, and much of their time is spent working in the home where they help with the cooking and smear the floors. But a Swazi girl, like a Swazi boy, has an easy life before marriage, with much time for singing and dancing, recognized essentials of social life.

The attainment of puberty is a major landmark in individual development but is not publicly celebrated. Group circumcision of boys was practiced until the reign of Mswati, when the custom was abandoned. It appears that the mortality was high and the military needs of the nation were considered more important than the ritual of personal transition. A symbolic circumcision, however, is still performed for the king as part of the ritual of his installation. There are no initiation ceremonies for girls, but menstruation imposes certain taboos on their public behavior and there is a conspicuous cultural difference between "little girls" and "maidens ripe for lovers." After puberty boys and girls are expected to enjoy sexual experiences, stopping short of full intercourse, before finally assuming marital responsibilities. Sexual morality is strictly defined as virginity, not chastity. Formerly, if an unmarried girl were found by her husband to have broken the law, her shame was indicated in a public ritual and the number of her marriage cattle was reduced. Today the ritual is discreetly modified, but there may still be a reduction in the number of her cattle, particularly if she has already borne a child.

The period of relative sexual freedom is shorter for a girl, who is expected to marry a man several years her senior. The end of girlhood is marked by appropriate clothing and a change in hairstyle. A man should only marry when his age group receives permission from the king. Formerly, this was overtly symbolized by sewing on waxen headrings, but this was abandoned for the present king, whose grandmother, the Queen Regent Gwamile, considered it an unnecessary token of manhood for those who "put on hats" and had Western education. Very few head-ringed men survive, but marriage is still essential for the attainment of full tribal responsibilities and privileges. The married woman gains demonstrably in status with the birth of her first child, and reaches her highest position in the home of her married son. In old age, both men and women are entitled to veneration and care from the young; elders supervise the education of the young and lead the rituals.

REGIMENTAL AGE GROUPS

Against these general age categories, individuals refer their own ages to important social episodes—wars, famines, epidemics, the arrival of important personalities, public celebrations—and, particularly in the case of men, to their age groups, or regiments (*emabutfo*, sing. *libutfo*).

The announcement of a new *libutfo* is made by the king when there is a representative gathering at the capital; it is the duty of those present at the gathering to inform others in their districts. The nucleus of the new group exists in the growing youths who already live in royal homesteads. A new *libutfo* should be formed every five to seven years, when the last group is considered ready for marriage. The main dividing line between those groups permitted to marry and youths who may not yet "spill their strength in children" is drawn for purposes of ritual. When, in 1935, after a lapse of some fifteen years, Sobhuza II inaugurated the Locust Regiment at a public meeting, many in the "bachelor set" had already taken wives or given their lovers children. He later sent his messenger to collect a fine from these men for breaking the law, but the Christian Swazi, backed by missionaries, successfully objected to "interference" by a polygynous king in their private lives. This was one of the many situations in which the traditional political structure, sanctioned by ritual and ethics, conflicted with a new individualism and foreign religion.

Unlike other tribes in east and central Africa, the Swazi have no compulsory period of barrack life for every male. Each man is automatically recruited into a *libutfo*, but only a certain number reside more or less permanently in the public barracks attached to royal homesteads. These royal warriors (*emabutfo*) are distinguished from the rank and file (*emajaha*) who remain for the greater part of their lives in their own homesteads, or even in the homesteads of local chiefs, and who come to the royal centers only to perform specific services. *Emabutfo* have special titles, ornaments, songs, and dances indicative of their higher status, and it is from this group that the king selects his most trusted messengers and attendants. Formerly men—especially if important—were eager that at least one of their sons should stay at state headquarters for some years, and family councils sent the heir to be educated in the etiquette and ways of the court. In addition to princes and sons of chiefs, poor commoners, who could derive few benefits from their own parents, offered their services to the rulers with the expectation that they would be suitably rewarded. The decision to become a "king's man" rests mainly with the individual; he need not obtain the prior consent of a father or guardian, for no one can prevent a subject from working for the king, the "father" of the nation. Thus, although every Swazi is automatically a member of an age class and there is no sharp distinction between civilian and soldier, the system makes a markedly different impact on individuals depending on whether or not they reside in a royal village.

Regiments are organized into distinctive units. The smallest is the squad (*siceme*) of eight to twenty men who stand together in the dance, an essential part of group activity, and form a recognized working team. Several squads join together to make a company (*lichiba*), led by a prince, and each company has its own name, war cry, and decorations. The princes are subordinate to the regimental leader, or commander-in-chief—a commoner chosen by the king for his ability to maintain discipline, his military knowledge, trustworthiness, and loyalty. On national occasions he assumes control of all local contingents.

Age groups cut across the boundaries of local chiefs and across the bonds of kinship, incorporating individuals into the state, the widest political unit. Between members of the same regiment, and particularly those in permanent residence, there is a loyalty and camaraderie. They treat each other as equals, eat together, smoke hemp from the long hemp pipe that is part of their joint equipment, work together, and have a central meeting place or clubhouse in the barracks. They call each other "brother" or "my age mate," "my peer," and the ties between them are said to be stronger than those between kinsmen of different generations. Toward other age sets there is often openly expressed rivalry and occasional fights, usually provoked by disputes over beer or women. Young regiments resent the marital privileges of the older men who, in turn, attempt to keep the young from monopolizing as lovers girls old enough to become wives. To prevent feuds between the regiments national policy dictated periodic action against an external enemy.

Warfare was an essential function of the age groups, a clue to their former importance and present impotence. The Swazi, however, were never as aggressive as the Zulu in the period of military conquest, and though warfare offered the main opportunity for the display of individual courage and strength, Swazi leaders did not encourage reckless loss of life. When necessary, the regiments did not hesitate to retreat into their mountain caves; in battle formation the older regiments were strategically placed to control the younger and more foolhardy. The indoctrination of the army before it left for battle stressed both fierceness and cunning, and there were rituals for both national success and personal safety. Warriors who achieved a kill were decorated with medicated necklaces, and mimed their grand achievements in solo dancing at public gatherings. But they and their weapons were "cleansed of the blood" to prevent them from being infected with an obsessive urge to destroy.

Warfare was controlled so that it did not disrupt normal existence; the men usually left for battle only after they had completed the main work in the fields, and reserves always remained behind for economic and ritual duties. The regiments took no large quantity of food with them; they staved off hunger by smoking hemp and relied on obtaining meat from cattle looted from the enemy. During the warriors' absence, a strict supporting discipline was imposed on those who stayed behind. Wives and lovers in particular had to behave with special decorum, in the belief that if they were rowdy, drunk, or sexually "hot" they would subdue or "burn up" the strength of the warriors.

Death on the battlefield was considered a national sacrifice. Kinsmen were not allowed to mourn their dead who had fallen in battle and the king did not demand a beast for purification. Although warfare was extolled, the taking of life was considered fearful and dangerous. On its return, the army was "doctored" in a not always successful attempt to guard against the vengeful spirits of the dead. Warfare was considered an outlet for individual ambition and aggression but could not be allowed to become a menace to the peace of the state.

The last time the regiments functioned as traditional units was in the reign of Sobhuza's grandfather, but since then the Swazi have been indirectly involved in three major wars—the Anglo-Boer War, and the two world wars. In the Anglo-Boer War, the Swazi as a group remained neutral; in World War I, a small contingent served in France. In World War II, nearly 4000 were recruited by Sobhuza and sent to the Middle East, where they built roads and fortifications, acted as stevedores, stretcher bearers, drivers, mechanics, and machine gunners. The Whites have not, in practice, attacked militarism; they have not shown that fighting is bad, bloodshed in battle brutal, nor that nationalism is dangerous. They have increased rather than decreased the importance of armed strength as a source of national unity and individual security, but they have monopolized the power of force. Compared with the armaments of modern warfare, the traditional weapons (knives, spears, knobkerries, and shields) are antediluvian and the methods of using them have not even the superior strength of barbarism. A Westernized Swazi commented, "The Whites have crushed intertribal war but they have introduced a false security of life and have stamped into Swazi culture the cheapness of individuals in an industrial economy."

Certain observances connected with warfare have been transferred to situations created by Western industry, especially deep-level mining. In conservative Swazi homes, women whose men work in the gold mines of South Africa follow the ritual precautions for protecting men engaged in battle; if a miner is killed in an underground accident his kinsmen do not have to pay death dues to the king. This transference of custom does not signify an identification of the value of death in the mines with that of death on the battlefield but an association of the two ways of dying through physical danger and attacks by hostile aliens.

The age sets were more precisely organized in the days of intertribal warfare than at present, but much of the structure survives for other than military purposes, which they continue to fulfill. When the regiments were not fighting they served as labor battalions, particularly for the aristocrats, and this remains one of their major duties. Their most intensive work depends on the agricultural routine of plowing, weeding, guarding the corn against the birds, reaping, and threshing; they may also be summoned to gather wood, cut leaves and poles for building, move huts, drive locusts off the fields, skin animals, run messages, fetch and carry. No matter how arduous a task may be, work begins and ends with the *hlehla*, a dance song in the cattle pen. During the performance, which always attracts children and often the women of the homestead, individual workers dance out of the group and sing short songs of their own composition, boasting of some achievement or exhibiting their artistic virtuosity.

During their period in royal homesteads, warriors are responsible for their own subsistence, but the rulers are expected to provide them periodically with beer and meat. Formerly, when cattle were raided from hostile tribes the men were better fed; the present rulers are less able to support financially a large permanent retinue, and this is one of the main reasons for the decline in the numbers of *emabutfo*. Those who stay lead a precarious hand-to-mouth existence, relying largely on the generosity of the women in the neighborhood for whom they do occasional jobs in their spare time, and wandering from beer-drink to beer-drink. Moreover, money has become a necessity since every male over the age of eighteen is required to pay an annual "poll tax," ranging from 35 shillings (roughly 5 dollars) for the unmarried to 90 shillings (roughly 13 dollars) for men with four or more wives. The king pays the tax for a few selected warriors, but most of the others are driven to work for Whites; for the younger generation, the prestige derived from living at court is challenged by the opportunities and excitement of the new urban and industrial centers.

The age classes are, however, still required for state ritual, and at the annual ceremony of kingship, designed to rejuvenate the king and strengthen the people, separate duties are allocated to the oldest regiments, to the regiment of men in full vigor of manhood, and to the youths who are considered sexually pure. Ritual is part of the educative process, a symbolic affirmation of certain social values, and in traditional Swazi society where specialized formal educational institutions are nonexistent, the age classes serve as the main channels for inculcating the values of loyalty and group morality. The emphasis is less on the content of a curriculum and the acquisition of new knowledge than on traditional values. In the past, special "old people" were appointed as instructors; teaching was not a separate career and learning was a gradual and continuous process of consolidation. The warriors are expected to master the main skills associated with adult life—in the barracks they even perform tasks normally left to women—and to develop the qualities of "manhood," specifically those related to the code of sexual morality. When a girl accepts a lover, she and her friends are expected to visit his barracks in special courting dress, which is brief but elaborately decorated with beads, and to sing and dance to make the relationship public. Should she on a subsequent visit find him absent, it is the duty of his agemates to try to see that she remains faithful to their friend. They find her accommodations and provide her with food. Lovers of other regiments are considered fair game, but the man who steals a girl of his own agemate is beaten and ostracized. In some other societies, sharing of women is a right of group membership; among the Swazi the emphasis on sexual monopoly over a particular lover is related to the ritual obligations placed on each member of an age group. In the main annual ceremony of the state, every individual of the unmarried regiment is responsible for contributing "pure strength" to kingship. At the present time, lover relationships are often not public and participation in state rituals is frequently evaded.

Education has, in fact, become secularized—to the extent that it has been taken from the control of the Swazi state with its particular framework of ritual and transferred to the education department of the Western administration. At the same time 90 percent of the schools in Swaziland are mission-controlled, and mission institutions are by definition opposed to traditionalist values. The conflict between Christian churches and the Swazi state is producing a cleavage in the Swazi people between Christians and traditionalists, a cleavage that does not necessarily coincide with the division between the educated and uneducated. In 1936 Sobhuza attempted to bridge the gulf by suggesting the introduction of a modified age-class system in all the schools. The idea, investigated by anthropologists, met with the approval of the (unorthodox) head of the local administration, but the missionaries, who obviously could not support a system directed by a polygynous king, head of a tribal religion, offered the Pathfinder Movement (Black Boy Scouts) instead. Sobhuza's scheme was finally applied in three schools and maintained and financed by the Swazi nation itself. For various reasons, however, it failed to achieve a unity—which the Swazi state itself no longer represented. I mention this experiment in misguided "applied anthropology" because it illustrates these points: first, the awareness of tribal leaders of the conflict between traditionalist and Western values; second, the extent to which these values are deeprooted in social institutions such as chieftainship or church; third, the interaction of institutions in a wider power structure—the military nation as compared with a colonial government with limited authority over Whites as well as Africans. The Swazi age-class system represents a passing social order. It grew with territorial expansion and the need to maintain political independence and internal security. Its weapons proved ineffectual against conquest, symbolized by monopolistic concessions, Western industry, counterreligious institutions, and a bureaucratic colonial system.

Swazi women are also organized into age sets of married and unmarried, but these are less formal than those of the men and do not extend under a common name throughout the nation. They are essentially local work teams that engage in

Girls carrying reeds for annual Umhlanga ceremony.

specific tasks for district or national leaders. Women are never stationed in barracks, and the age of marriage for a girl is sanctioned by her parents and her friends, not by the rulers.

Sometimes a group of teenagers are brought together under the patronage of unmarried princesses or daughters of chiefs into a temporary association, for which they lay down laws regulating clothing, food, language, and morality. No member may be "touched by a male," a regulation from which not even the king is immune. Violation of the code is punished by fines, imposed and collected by the girls, and also by organized songs of ridicule. The association, which begins and ends with tribute labor, lasts from one winter to the next, and the older girls are then publicly recognized as ripe for marriage.

In tribal society a person is a meeting point of identities—the identity of siblings, the identity of the lineage, the identity of the age group. The modern Western system gives greater scope to the individual, male or female, young and old. When conflict breaks out in conservative homesteads between parent and child generations or between older and younger siblings, it is not a conflict of ideologies but of personality. Sons may covet the power of the father, but when he dies, they hope to exercise over their own sons the authority they themselves once resented. Young people are anxious to possess the privileges of their seniors, not to abolish the privileges of seniority; young brides may rebel against the way particular in-laws abuse the rights of age, but they agree to the principle that age and sex are entitled to those rights. At the present time, the social structure which gives power to the older generation is challenged by the money economy, a new legal system, and schooling for a literate society. A son is still dependent on his father and ultimately on his chief for the land on which to build his home, but he is legally permitted to move for working purposes into the European town and support himself on cash wages. The manual occupations opened by Western enterprise require physical strength, for which the old are rejected, while the young and fit are in demand and able to contract in terms of their personal legal status. Formal education weakens the claim of the uneducated that the possession of the greatest knowledge is obtainable only through age. Books and classes, quick roads to learning, contradict the system of gradual education in which the major phases of physical development are correlated with responsibilities associated with the group of peers.

6 / The supernatural

THE SPIRIT WORLD

Swazi culture sanctions enjoyment of the material and physical: food, women, and dancing. It does not in any way idealize poverty or place a value on suffering as a means to happiness or salvation. To deal with the hazards of life— failure of crops, unfaithfulness of women, illness and ultimate death—the culture provides a set of optimistic notions and positive stereotyped techniques that are especially expressed through the ancestral cult, the vital religion of the Swazi, and through an elaborate system of magic. The ancestors sanction the desires of their descendants; magic provides the techniques for the achievement of these desires.

In the ancestral cult, the world of the living is projected into a world of spirits (*emadloti*). Men and women, old and young, aristocrats and commoners, continue the patterns of superiority and inferiority established by earthly experiences. Paternal and maternal spirits exercise complementary roles similar to those operating in daily life on earth; the paternal role reinforces legal and economic obligations, the maternal role exercises a less formalized protective influence. Although the cult is set in a kinship framework, it is extended to the nation through the king, who is regarded as the father of all Swazi; his ancestors are the most powerful of the spirits.

Swazi believe that the spirit or breath has an existence distinct from the flesh. When a person dies, both flesh and spirit must be correctly treated to safeguard the living. Mortuary ritual varies with both the status of the deceased and his or her relationship with different categories of mourners. The more important the dead, the more elaborate the rites given the corpse; the closer the relationship through blood or marriage, the greater the stereotyped interest demanded by the spirit of the mourners. A headman is buried at the entrance of the cattle byre, and his widows, children, siblings, and other relatives are constrained to undertake different demonstrations and periods of mourning. The widows shave their heads and remain "in darkness" for three years before they are given the duty of continuing the lineage of the deceased through the levirate. A wife is more expendable; the deceased woman is buried on the outskirts of her husband's home, and the mourning imposed on him is less conspicuous, less rigorous, and of shorter duration. The social order regulates overt demonstrations of grief, irrespective of the depth of personal emotions. Death, more than any other situation in Swazi culture, exposes the *social* personality of man, woman, and child in the fullest context of kinship. The living must, in turn, adjust to the loss by building new bonds on established structural foundations.

The spirit of the deceased is ritually "brought back" to the family in a feast that ends all active mourning; the spirit continues, however, to influence the destinies of kinsmen. It may manifest itself in illness and in various omens, or it may materialize in the form of a snake. Mambas are associated with kings; harmless green snakes are associated with commoners and women; and certain snakes are excluded from the ancestral realm because they "never come nicely." An ancestral snake does not show fear and moves with familiar sureness within the hut. It is a bad omen if such a snake comes in and quickly leaves. The body of every Swazi is believed to have at least one snake, which is associated with fertility and health. It is somehow connected with the spiritual snake, but is not conceptualized in any elaborate theory of transmigration or reincarnation. The existence of an ancestral snake is simply stated as fact, with the emphasis on practical implications.

Illness and other misfortunes are frequently attributed to the ancestors, but Swazi believe that *emadloti* do not inflict sufferings through malice or wanton cruelty. The mean husband, the adulterous wife, the overambitious younger brother, the disobedient son may be dealt with directly or vicariously by the spirits, acting as custodians of correct behavior and tribal ethics. Ancestors punish, they do not kill; death is the act of evildoers (*batsakatsi*), who are interested in destroying, not in perpetuating, the lineage or the state. If an illness originally divined as sent by the *emadloti* later becomes fatal, evildoers are assumed to have taken advantage of the patient's weak resistance.

While each specific death is interpreted as an act of witchcraft, death is also recognized as universal and inevitable. In a myth, widespread throughout the southeastern tribes, death was imposed by the arbitrary and inconsistent nature of *Mvelimqanti*, "The First to Appear," the Creator or "Great Ancestor." He sent the chameleon to mankind with a message of eternal life, then changed His mind and sent the lizard with the message of death. The chameleon, with its peculiar mottled and changing skin color and its markedly protruding eyes that turn in all directions, is quite distinct from the ordinary lizard, which glides along without changing color and has sleepy eyes that look only straight ahead. The lizard arrived before the chameleon, who had stopped to eat of tasty berries growing by the wayside. When the chameleon arrived and delivered his message, he was driven away—death had already become part of life. Christian missionaries introduced the word *Nkulunkulu* (Great Great One) as a translation of the Biblical God, but the ideas underlying the two deities are worlds apart.

Ancestors have greater wisdom, foresight, and power than the rest of mankind, but no spirit of a deceased ever reaches complete deification or is regarded as omnipotent. Swazi ancestors are approached as practical beings; there is no conflict between the ethics of the ancestral cult and the mundane desires of life. Swazi desire the ends they say the *emadloti* desire for them. Swazi are not concerned with the life led by the dead, but with the way the ancestors influence their lives on earth. No one inquires from a diviner if the *emadloti* are happy and satisfied, till they show they are unhappy and dissatisfied. Ancestral spirits, like witches and sorcerers, are thought of most when comforts are few and troubles are many.

Swazi have no class of ordained priests, and the privileged duty of appealing to the *emadloti* rests with the head of the family. The father acts on behalf of his sons; if he is dead, the older brother acts on behalf of the younger. In this patrilineal society, ancestors of a married woman remain at her natal home; they are approachable only by her senior male kinsman, but they retain a protective interest in the woman who has provided cattle through her marriage, and in her children who consolidated her position as a wife. Contact is usually made through the medium of food, meat, or beer; the dead, who are said to be often hungry, "lick" the essence of the offerings laid at dusk on a sacred place in the shrine hut and left overnight. The family head addresses the dead in much the same way as if they were alive; appeals to them are spontaneous and conversational, interspersed with rebukes and generally devoid of gratitude. Recognition of the holy, as distinct from the profane, is, moreover, expressed on certain occasions through sacred songs. Each clan has a special song and there are a number of anthems reserved for rituals of state.

Each family propitiates its own ancestors at the specific domestic events of birth, marriage, death, and the building and moving of huts; in addition, the royal ancestors periodically receive public reognition. Every year before the rains are due cattle are sent from the capital to the caves in two tree-covered groves, where dead kings and leading princes lie buried in order of seniority. The groves, described as frightening and awe-inspiring, alive with the sound of majestic voices and the movement of great snakes, are in the charge of important chiefs in the vicinity. They must see that no one enters without permission, and there is a current mythology concerning the doom of unfortunates who unwittingly intruded into the domain of the sacred. The ruler's emissaries report the affairs of the country to the dead and appeal for prosperity, health, and rain. Some of the cattle are sacrificed; the others are brought back to the royal village, where various taboos have been imposed on normal behavior. The cattle are brought in on a night when the moon is full, and the ordinary people are ordered to wait in their huts in silence while the king and his mother meet the returning pilgrims. Together they walk through the great cattle pen chanting a sacred song associated with major developments of kingship. That night the gates are left open, so that the ancestral cattle may wander freely through the village. The following day, there is the main sacrifice, in which each animal is dedicated to specific dead and eaten in a sacramental feast. So close is the identification between the animal and the human that kinsmen who would have practiced avoidance of the person in life are prohibited from eating of the flesh of the sacrificial victim.

Subordinate to the ancestral cult, suggesting a separate cultural influence—another layer of tradition—is the recognition accorded the forces of nature. The sun, moon, and rainbow are personified, and though they are not appealed to directly, they are drawn into the orbit of human destiny. Swazi believe that the earth is flat and that the sun, the male, crosses the sky in a regular path twice a year. Each night he sleeps and wakens again strong and refreshed. The moon is the woman who dies periodically and is connected with the cycle of fertility. The rainbow is the sign of the "Princess of the Sky," associated with spring. All major rituals are timed by the position of the sun and moon. Ancestral spirits are most active at dawn and dusk, and ceremonies to mark an increase in status are generally performed when the moon is waxing or full; ceremonies that temporarily isolate a man from his fellows take place when it is waning, or "in darkness."

As previously stated, rain is in a different category from most other natural phenomena. It is believed to be controlled by medicines associated with kingship and is interpreted as a sign of ancestral blessing and good will. Knowledge of rainmaking is secret to the queen mother, her son, and three trusted assistants, but every subject is aware that at certain times the rulers are "working the rain." The techniques they use increase in strength with the month and general climatic conditions, and move, if necessary, over a period of time from minor to more elaborate rites. Failure to make rain come has many explanations: disobedience and disloyalty of the people; breach of taboos; hostility between the rulers themselves and other actions that evoke the prohibitive anger of the royal ancestors. The efficacy of the medicines is not doubted—rain eventually falls—and the belief in the rulers as rainmakers, a belief held even by many Christians, remains one of the strongest sanctions of traditional Swazi power. Lightning, on the other hand, is associated with the "Bird of the Sky," which lives in certain pools and can be controlled by particularly powerful evildoers. There are special lightning doctors to treat homesteads and people with antilightning medicines.

A rich body of folklore relates various places, plants, and animals to the world of men, but the Swazi have no store of sacred oral literature. The world of nature is of much the same order and quality as the world of man, and the animal kingdom in particular provides characters and situations that illustrate the aspirations, contradictions, and conflicts experienced by humans. No special tales based on the ancestral world or nature are accredited to divine inspiration. In the hierarchically structured but kinship-oriented society of the Swazi, articulate revelation is restricted to medicine and divination.

SPECIALISTS IN RITUAL

In all situations requiring "deep" (esoteric) knowledge, Swazi consult medicine men (*tinyanga temitsi*) and/or their colleagues, the diviners (*tangoma*), the main specialists in Swazi traditional society. Medicine men work primarily with "trees" (roots, bark, leaves) and other natural substances, and enter the profession of their own accord; diviners diagnose the cause rather than direct the specific cure and rely on spirit possession for their insight. Within the two major categories of ritual specialists several grades are distinguished on the basis of training and technique.

Every Swazi has some knowledge of "medicines" for common ailments and other misfortunes (poor crops, failure in love, sick cattle) and the lowest grade of ritual specialist includes people who, usually through personal experience, have picked up remedies for specific purposes and are not prepared to disclose their secrets without reward. They claim no inspiration from the ancestors and no tradition of belonging to a family of doctors. Behind their backs they are spoken of contemptuously as "crocodiles"—the quacks—and they are said to be increasing in number since they have had the opportunity of acquiring medicines from men outside the country and from Western drugstores. Informants say that some of these self-taught specialists are skillful enough but insist that the ancestors must subsequently have agreed that their work meets with success.

More highly rated are the medicine men whose careers are destined from birth or sanctioned by the powerful dead. Knowledge of rituals and medicine bags are retained in certain families as an important part of the inheritance. The owner imparts them to a favorite son, a younger brother, or close kinsman, who is "pushed by the heart to learn" and need not be the main heir. Once qualified, he calls on the "father spirit" in each situation and periodically renews the power of the bags in ritual reaffirmation of his spirtual dependence.

Some *tinyanga* specialize very intensively and will treat only a single illness or misfortune; others have a very diversified practice and offer panaceas for an extensive and varied range of difficulties. Added tension and insecurity have multiplied the situations for which medicines are desired, and many illiterate Swazi apply the same principles to get better jobs, make profitable beer sales, or "sweeten the mouths" of men brought before magistrates for breaking the "white man's laws." Specialists in ritual, unlike specialists in handicrafts, effectively resisted change, and while many mundane objects were easily replaced by trade goods, the range of "medicines" has been extended.

In Swazi "medicine" the material ingredients are emphasized more than the verbal spell. These ingredients are frequently chosen on the familiar principles of homeopathic magic—like produces like, and things once in contact retain identity even when separated by distance. Their names may indicate the purpose of the rite for which they are used and serve as abbreviated spells. Thus, in a love potion of a leading *inyanga,* the main ingredient is a resilient, everlasting leaf named "disobey her mother"; for the medicine to secure a homestead against evildoers, "pegs" are cut from a tree that remains firm in the thinnest soil on a precarious slope. In the treatment for success, instructions given by an *inyanga* must be implicitly obeyed and any pain he inflicts must be stoically endured. Most doctoring for even indirect benefits (household safety, protection against lightning, as well as personal quandaries—love, ill health) involve techniques such as injections, inhalation, and purgatives. In all but intimate sexual affairs, all people in the homestead must take part, for each member is recognized as interacting with others, and correct adjustment of social relationships is considered essential for a successful result.

The Swazi have no association of medicine men. Each *inyanga* works alone, drawing on a common stock of traditionally "proven" remedies to which he may add his own findings. Each *inyanga* is conspicuous by his "bags"—pouches, gourds, and charms—and when consulted he proudly displays their contents and expatiates on their "strength." Success is also attributed to the innate "power" (personality?) of the practitioner, whose own life conditions should support his professional claims. Renowned medicine men are themselves men of substance, and the profession provides the main opportunity for the individualist of traditional society.

The diviners, often people of outstanding intelligence, are the most powerful and respected of specialists. Their nonconformity is sanctioned by the spirits. The first symptom of possession is usually an illness that is difficult to cure and frequently follows terrible physical or emotional experiences. The patient becomes fastidious about food, eats little, complains of pains in various parts of the body and strange sensations between his shoulder blades and in his head. After sacrifices and medicines have proved useless, an already established diviner may diagnose that the sufferer is troubled by a spirit that must be made to express itself. Inarticulate noises and wild behavior indicate possession by the wandering ghost of a stranger or of an animal, and treatment is directed to its expulsion, or exorcism, by "closing its road." On the other hand, possession by friendly humans, most frequently kinsmen, is considered socially beneficial and the patient is encouraged to become a diviner. This involves long and arduous training during which he wanders over the countryside, eats little, sleeps little, is tormented by fearful dreams—of snakes encircling his limbs, of drowning in a flooded river, of being torn to pieces by enemies: he becomes "a house of dreams." These dreams must be interpreted to forestall misfortune to himself and others. He is also purified with special potions and various medicines to enable him to hear and see the spirit that is guiding him. Each novice composes a song and when he sings it, villagers come and join in the chorus to help him develop his powers.

A master diviner may have several novices living at his home for varying periods, forming an embryonic ritual school. When he considers them to be fully trained he puts them through a public graduation ceremony. Spectators hide articles for them to discover and they are also expected to throw hints to selected members of the audience about their various predicaments. As in many transition rites, each novice is said to be "reborn" and is honored with gifts of goats, special clothing, and beads to mark the change in status.

Despite the prestige and power of diviners most people do not wish to become possessed. The reasons given express socially inculcated attitudes to this type of greatness. It is best to be normal, not to be limited all one's life by the special taboos on sex, food, and general behavior that are imposed by the profession, not to be exhausted by the demands of a spirit greater than oneself, not to have to shoulder responsibility for the life and death of others. There are men who therefore try to stop the spirit even in cases of ancestral possession, but on the whole such tampering is considered dangerous since it may leave a person permanently delicate and deranged, an object of spite by the spirit he has thrust from him and of neglect by others, angered at the reception given to one of their kind.

Although very few Swazi women practice as herbalists, more women than men appear to be "possessed," and there are a large number of well-known women diviners. The difference in number of women herbalists and diviners is a consequence of the sexual division of labor and the relative statuses of male and female. A woman's duty is the care of home and children. A herbalist who must wander around the countryside to dig roots and collect plants is brought into intimate contact with strangers, and this is contrary to the norm laid down for female behavior. As a result, girls are rarely taught medicines by their fathers, the

Girl dancing in a trance of spirit possession, 1937.

heir to the family bags is always male, and no husband encourages a woman to practice medicine. Possession, however, is in a different category. A woman does not fight against the spirit of an ancestor that wishes to "turn her around," and even her husband is afraid to interfere and must submit to her "calling."

Political leaders and other aristocrats are positively discouraged from becoming either medicine men or diviners, for this would interfere with their administrative duties and does not fit into their ascribed status. At the same time, they employ *tinyanga* of all types to bolster their powers, and the *Ngwenyama* is himself believed to have "deeper" knowledge of medicines than any of his subjects and to be able to detect evildoers without preliminary possession by virtue of his unique royal medicines.

In most séances the clients sit in a semicircle on the ground, chant songs, and clap their hands while the diviner, in full regalia, smokes *insangu** and dances himself into a high pitch of excitement. He asks no questions but makes statements to which the audience replies "We agree." Each statement is a feeler, a clue whereby he builds up his case, piecing together the evidence from the emotion behind the responses, until finally he gives the desired information. Diviners, often shrewd judges of human nature, have a wide knowledge of local affairs and their

---

* *Insangu* is a potent drug, similar to marijuana.

interpretations generally, perhaps unconsciously, confirm the suspicions or crystal-lize the unspoken fears of their clients. It is, however, often considered desirable to consult other diviners who may use different methods. An increasing number of modern diviners "throw bones," a technique associated with Sotho and Tonga influence. The "bones" may be the astragali of goats, cowrie shells found on the East Coast, or oddly shaped seeds. The diviner, pointing to the different pieces, interprets the combination of positions. Exceptional divinatory devices include the "talking calabash" (a ventriloquist trick), a rattle that shakes of its own accord, and a magic wand. Public séances to "smell out evildoers" are prohibited under the Witchcraft Ordinance, but continue secretly in the frontier regions. In Namahasha, high in the Lubombo between Mozambique and Swaziland, I have seen a diviner in full regalia, "smelling out" with a magically impregnated hippo whip as he danced in front of a tense audience that had come from a homestead some fifty miles away to learn the "cause" of a sequence of misfortunes and deaths. The poison ordeal may be administered as the ultimate test: the in-nocent will not be affected, but the guilty will writhe, vomit, and confess. The poison is collected in Mozambique; as a rule, diviners from that area are asked to assist in its preparation, but its use must be sanctioned by the *Ngwenyama*.

Over the years new techniques of divination have been introduced and integrated with traditional modes of thought and behavior. Allied to the traditional diviner are "prophets" who belong to certain Separatist churches and claim to be possessed by the Holy Ghost, in which guise they carry on both divination and exorcism with less fear of "white man's law." There have also been two associations, similar to those in other parts of Africa, that have been directed against witchcraft in general, and have reaffirmed the strength of divination.

WITCHCRAFT

Medicine men and diviners, official supporters of law and authority, have as their illegal opposition the evildoers (*batsakatsi*). Swazi *batsakatsi* include witches, whose evil is both physiological and psychological, and sorcerers, who rely on poisons, conscious violence, or other techniques for the deliberate destruction of property or person. The propensity to witchcraft is transmitted through a woman to her children, male and female; a male does not pass it on to his offspring. The initial quality must, however, be further developed by injections and training, or the potential witch will be mischievous but ineffectual. Qualified witches are believed to form a permanent gang, within which they are ranked on the basis of evil achievements. They operate at night; during the day they gloat consciously on their nefarious activities. A sorcerer obtains his "poisons" from outside and acts individually in specific situations against personal enemies. To be effective he may seek assistance from a medicine man who, by collusion, also becomes an evildoer; the most powerful *tinyanga* are therefore sometimes feared as the greatest *batsakatsi*.

Batsakatsi may work through direct contact with the person by striking a victim through his food. The reality of the power of evildoers is considered self-evident; it is manifest in otherwise inexplicable misfortunes and confirmed by confessions at séances and ordeals. Moreover, at the end of every individual's life, sorcery or witchcraft turns up the trump card of death.

Murders for "doctoring" (so-called ritual murders) still take place in Swaziland, and fall into two main situational types: (1) agricultural fertility; (2) personal aggrandizement. The victim, referred to as "a buck," is innocent of any crime and is killed with as much secrecy as possible. An analysis of the European court records indicates that the characteristics of sex, age, and pigmentation of the victims show no uniformity, and that different organs are selected from the corpse. Where the accused are found guilty of murdering for "medicine" to doctor the crops, capital punishment is carried out on the principals; others involved are sentenced to imprisonment with hard labor for periods ranging from fifteen years to life; in murders for personal aggrandizement the death penalty is invariably imposed, but in certain circumstances it is commuted to a long term of imprisonment. The men employing the "doctors" are generally important headmen, sometimes chiefs suffering economic or status insecurity. The average Swazi condemns murders committed in self-interest as sorcery, and places the ritual specialist who gives the instructions in a different moral and legal category from the diviner who, in his capacity as a witchfinder, may be responsible for the destruction of people publicly revealed as evildoers. The distinction is not accepted by Western law.

Swazi complain that batsakatsi are more common now than in the past and blame the law that has made "smelling out" by diviners illegal. They argue that "the white man's law protects women and witches. Bad men flourish and those who smell them out are hanged." But, in fact, any increase in sorcery, as in other types of magic, must be sought in additional situations of conflict, feelings of inadequacy and helplessness, financial uncertainty, rivalry for jobs, competition for the favor of white employers, and personal insecurity in an alien-dominated milieu.

Witchcraft and sorcery can be directed against anyone, but because they emanate from hatred, fear, jealousy, and thwarted ambition they are usually aimed at persons who are already connected by social bonds. The social content is stereotyped by the alignments of Swazi society and indicates points of tension or friction, actual or anticipated. In the polygynous homestead, the umstakatsi is usually a jealous co-wife or an unscrupulous half brother who is ambitious of the inheritance; outside the homestead, suspected evildoers are blatantly successful and aggressive peers. Important men do not need to use sorcery against insignificant inferiors, nor are they suspected of doing so. Sorcery is an indication of status and of the ambitions for improvement of status that operate within the limits of the stratified traditional society. Thus, not all destructive ritual is condemned as the work of evildoers, nor do all "productive" medicines receive social approval. Judgment depends on the situation. It is legitimate to use retaliative medicine on the grave of a person whose death was attributed to an unidentified evildoer, or to doctor property so that a thief will be inflicted with swollen finger joints, or to inject into an unfaithful wife medicine that will punish her lover with a wasting disease. It is illicit to employ productive medicine for unlimited wealth or success. In short, the umstakatsi undermines the status quo; the inyanga struggles to maintain it. Wedged between the chief and the tinyanga on the one hand and the batsakatsi on the other, the masses are molded to accept a relatively unenterprising conservatism.

CHRISTIANITY

Traditional Swazi religion is challenged by Christianity. In 1946 nearly 40 percent of Swazi were registered as "Christians" and more than twenty different sects were listed. In Swaziland, as in the Republic of South Africa, a growing number of converts belong to Independent, or Separatist churches, which vary greatly in organization and credo but share one common characteristic—independence from white control. These churches offer new opportunities for self-expression and power; many of the founders are men of unusual personality, and some are more highly educated than the average Swazi.

Largely because of tribal status and a vested interest in polygyny, Swazi male aristocrats have tended to resist conversion from the ancestral cult, but their mothers and wives have been more responsive. The Methodists were the first to establish a mission in Swaziland. The late *Ndlovukazi* Lomawa was a recognized supporter of the church, though the National Council ruled that full conversion—including the clothing in which it could be demonstrated—was incompatible with the ritual duties of her position. She was particularly sympathetic to a Zionist Separatist church whose charismatic local leader had converted close members of her natal family, and, at the same time, had acknowledged the claims of hereditary kingship exercised by her son, the *Ngwenyama*. When she died, she was buried

INdlovukazi Lomawa (center) dressed for church; on her right is her sister Nukwase, 1937.

according to custom away from the capital in a former royal village, so that her son would not be weakened by contact with death or the dead. At her funeral—which her son was not permitted to attend—various church officials paid their respects. Despite the fact that leading councilors tried to follow traditional practices, the entire mortuary procedure was interrupted for a few hours when her sister, who later succeeded to the position of queen mother, found that the church membership cards of the deceased (described as her "tickets across the Jordan") had been left behind at the capital. These were fetched and placed beside the dead woman in a wooden coffin that had been specially shaped to hold her body, which was bound in fetal position and wrapped in a shroud of black cowhide.

The traditional religion has been influenced by Christianity, and Christianity as practiced by the Swazi has, in turn, been influenced by existing traditions. The extent of adaptation by the white-controlled churches ranges from the eclectic approach of Catholics to the rigidity of extreme Afrikaner Calvinists.* The Catholic church, which began work in 1914, later than most churches in Swaziland, increased its enrollment more rapidly than any other white-controlled church. But the proselytizing influence of all white missions virtually came to a standstill in the late 1930s, when the nativistic African Separatist movement boomed on an upsurge of nationalism. Separatist "Zionist" leaders consulted with Sobhuza and decided to form the Swazi National Church, with a flexible dogma and great tolerance of custom. Sobhuza was thus to be ritually entrenched, both as head of the traditional ancestral cult and as priest-king of a new faith, a position different from that in neighboring areas where traditional chieftanship had been deliberately broken down or where the chief himself had been converted to Christianity. At the same time, separatist movements cannot—by definition—really create lasting unity. A church, planned as a memorial to the noted Lomawa and designed by an imaginative European architect, was half-built when friction, accentuated by lack of funds, broke out between the leaders and construction stopped. So the walls remain roofless, symbolizing a religious and secular unity that is desired but does not exist in modern Swaziland.

THE ANNUAL RITUAL OF KINGSHIP

Throughout this study I have mentioned the annual ritual of kingship, the *Ncwala*, a ritual rich in Swazi symbolism and only understandable in terms of the social organization and major values of Swazi life. It has been variously interpreted as a first-fruit ceremony, a pageant of Swazi history, a drama of kingship, and a ritual of rebellion. This beautiful and complex ritual is described and analyzed in great detail in *An African Aristocracy*; here I can but outline some of the main sequences and characteristics.

The central figure is the king, the "owner" of the *Ncwala*; performance of the

---

* *Afrikaner* is the term for white South Africans who speak Afrikaans, a local language developed mainly from Dutch. Afrikaners tend to be culturally insular and racist.

Ncwala by anyone else is treason, which, on two historic occasions, cost the lives of overambitious princes. The *Ncwala* reflects the growth of the king and is thus not a static ritual. When the king is a minor, the ritual is less elaborate, the medicines less potent, the animals required for doctoring smaller, the clothing simpler. When he reaches full manhood and has his first ritual wife, the *Ncwala* reaches its peak. All subjects play parts determined by their status: the queen mother, the queens, married and unmarried regiments, princes, the king's artificial blood brothers, councilors, ordinary commoners, and ritual specialists known as "People of the Sea," all have specific duties and receive appropriate treatment.

The *Ncwala* is a sacred period set apart from the profane and mundane routine of normal life. Public rites extend for roughly three weeks of each year, and are divided into the Little *Ncwala*, which lasts two days, beginning when the sun reaches its southern summer solstice and the moon is dark, and the Big *Ncwala*, which lasts six days from the night of the full moon. In the interim period, sacred songs and dances of the Little *Ncwala* are performed in key villages throughout the territory. It is believed that wrong timing will bring national disaster that can only be circumvented by elaborate counter-ritual, a common cultural device to make people abide by tradition, yet not automatically accept calamity.

The *Ncwala* involves considerable organization and preparation. Several weeks before the ceremony the "People of the Sea" are brought to the capital for initial arrangements, and are then sent out to collect the water and other ritual ingredients. They divide into two groups, one traveling through the forests to the coast and the other to the confluence of the main rivers of the country. They must draw "the waters of all the world" and also dig potent sacred plants to strengthen and purify the king. In every homestead where the priests rest, the host provides beer and meat, and from all strangers who cross their paths they demand a small fine, which will be burnt on the last day, the day of final national purification. At the capital itself, preparations are made by the councilors, who will also be held responsible for the correct timing.

The honor of opening the *Ncwala* is bestowed on the oldest regiment. Thereafter, other participants join in, taking their places according to rank and sex. The stage is the *sibaya* of the capital, but the main rites are enacted in secret in the king's sanctuary. The public contributes by performing sacred songs and dances. As the sun sets in a moonless night, the formation of the dances changes from the crescent of a new moon to the circle of the full moon. Princes and foreigners are dismissed as the warriors chant a new song that is associated with other important events of kingship—a king's marriage to his main ritual wife, the return of ancestral cattle from the royal grave, the burial of kings. It is a key song of the *Ncwala*.

> Jjiya oh o o King, alas for your fate
> Jjiya oh o o King, they reject thee
> Jjiya oh o o King, they hate thee.

Suddenly the chief councilor commands "Silence," and the singing ceases while the king spits powerful medicine, first to the east, then to the west, and the crowd

Mandanda Mtetwa, the most senior traditional councilor at the Ncwala, 1967.

is given the signal to shout "He stabs it!" Informants explained that "Our Bull [Our King] has produced the desired effect: he has triumphed and is strengthening the earth. He has broken off the old year and is preparing for the new." This climaxes the opening of the ceremony. The people then sing a final song comparable to a national anthem, praising the king as "the Bull, the Lion, the Inexplicable, the Great Mountain." At dawn of the following day, the ceremony is repeated. Afterward, warriors go to weed the queen mother's garden, for which service they are rewarded with a feast of meat. The Little *Ncwala* is over, and the men may return to their homes until the moon is "ripe."

In royal homesteads, the songs and dances of the Little *Ncwala* are rehearsed and the sacred costumes are prepared for the main ceremony. The words of the songs are surprising to Europeans, who are accustomed to hear royalty blatantly extolled, the virtues of the nation magnified, and the country glorified at national celebrations. Most songs of the *Ncwala* have as their motif hatred of the king, and his rejection by the people. The actual words are few, mournful, and tremendously moving; they are reinforced by dancing, which mimes much of the drama. The beautiful clothing, including feathers of special birds and skins of wild animals, indicates differences in rank and also carries deep magical and religious significance.

On the first day of the Big *Ncwala*, the regiment of pure unmarried youths is sent to cut branches of a magic tree with which to enclose the king's sanctuary. Swazi believe that if the branches are cut by anyone who has violated the moral code of his age group, the leaves will wither. Such branches must be cast out and the culprit ostracized and even attacked, not so much for his sexual violations as for his willingness to endanger the well-being of the state. The tree is quick-growing, with leaves that remain green for many weeks, when cut by the virtuous. The cutting must begin as the full moon rises, to the rhythm of a new sacred song —a sacred lullaby—the theme song of the second stage of the drama. The qualities of quick growth, greenness, toughness, and fertility characterize most elements of the *Ncwala* ritual.

On the morning of the second day, the youths return, bearing their wands proudly aloft and chanting the lullaby. The councilors surround the sanctuary with the mystic greenery, behind which the powers of the king will be symbolically reborn.

The main event of the third day is the "killing of the bull," the symbol of potency. The king strikes a specially selected black bull with a rod doctored for fertitlity and "awakening," and the pure youths must catch the animal, throw it to the ground, pummel it with their bare hands, and drag it into the sanctuary where it is sacrificed. Parts of the carcass are used for royal medicine; the remainder is an offering to the ancestors.

The "Day of the Bull" fortifies the king for the "Great Day" when he appears in his most terrifying image and symbolically overcomes the hostility of princely rivals. In the morning he bites "doctored" green foods of the new year; his mother and others follow suit, their medicines graded by status. Later in the day, under the blazing sun, all the people, in full *Ncwala* dress, and with the king in their midst, dance and sing the *Ncwala*. Toward sunset the king leaves them; when he re-emerges he is unrecognizable—a mythical creature—clothed in a fantastic costume of sharp-edged green grass and skins of powerful wild animals, his body gleaming with black unguents. The princes approach and alternately drive him from them into the sanctuary and beseech him to return. Behind them the people sing and dance. All members of the royal Dlamini clan and all "foreigners" (seen as potential enemies) are ordered from the cattle byre; the king remains and dances with his loyal supporters and common subjects. Tension mounts as he sways backward and forward. At the climax he appears holding in his hand a vivid-green gourd, known as the "Gourd of Embo" (the north), the legendary place of Dlamini origin. Although picked the previous year, the gourd is still green. The king throws it lightly on the horizontally placed shield of a selected agemate, who must not let the fruit, sacred vessel of the past and symbol of continuity, touch the ground. The old year has been discarded; the king has proved his strength, and the people are prepared for the future.

Life does not immediately return to its normal routine; major rites of transition generally involve gradual readjustments. The whole of the following day the rulers are secluded and unapproachable, their faces painted dark with medicines, their bodies anointed with fat from the sacred herd. Subjects are placed in a condition of ritual identification and prohibited from many normal physical activities—sex, washing, scratching, merrymaking. There is a deep silence at the capital. The *Ncwala* songs are closed for the year.

On the last day, the ointments of darkness are washed off the rulers, who are then bathed with foamy potions to make them "shine" anew. Objects used throughout the ceremony, and which represent the old year, are burned on a ritual fire. The king sets light to the wood (which must be without thorns) with ancient fire sticks and walks naked and alone round the pyre, sprinkling medicated waters. At noon, he and his people, dressed in partial *Ncwala* clothing, gather in the *sibaya* where they perform a series of solemn, but not sacred, dance-songs. Rain —the blessings of the ancestors—must fall, quenching the flames and drenching all the participants. If no rain falls, the people fear a year of dire misfortune. But the rains usually come, and in the evening the rulers provide vast quantities of meat and beer, and there is gaiety and lovemaking. Early the next morning the warriors assemble in the *sibaya*, sing ordinary march songs, and go to weed the queen mother's special field. The local contingents are then free to return to their homes, where they may safely eat of the crops of the new season.

Now for some brief comments on certain general features of the *Ncwala*. Culturally, it is a dramatic ritualization of Swazi kingship in all its complexity—economic, military, ritual. The sacrament of the first fruits, an essential rite in a series of rites, relates the rulers to the productive cycle, and the timing links them mystically with the great powers of nature—the sun and the moon. Fertility and potency are stressed as essential qualities of social continuity and must be acquired by stereotyped techniques. Swazi (like all people) believe that the efficacy of ritual lies in correct repetition; certain changes have been made in the course of time but the tendency has been to add new items rather than discard old.

The *Ncwala* symbolizes the unity of the state and attempts to maintain it. Fighting and bloodshed are recognized as possible dangers at a time when regiments from all parts of the country are mobilized at the capital. The men are prohibited from carrying spears, the main weapons of attack; only shields and sticks are incorporated in the costume. Emotional fervor is canalized in songs and dances, obligatory acts of participation that induce the sacred pulse, the *tactus* of Swazi national life. Internal solidarity is frequently intensified by outside opposition; the king outshines his rivals and the nation is fortified against external enemies. In the past, the *Ncwala* frequently preceded an announcement of war.

The people committed to the *Ncwala* represent the social groups that accept the authority of the traditional rulers; those who deliberately refrain from taking part indicate the limitations of their present acceptance. Certain missions prohibited their converts from dancing the *Ncwala*, and those Swazi Christians who attend are mainly members of Independent churches. It is significant that, since 1937, the leader of the main Zionist Separatist sect has traveled to the capital for the *Ncwala*, thereby publicly demonstrating his support of Swazi kingship. Thus the *Ncwala* serves as a graph of status on which the roles of the king, his mother, the princes, councilors, priests, princesses, commoners, old and young are mapped by ritual. The balance of power between the king and the princes and between the aristocrats and commoners is a central theme; the ambivalent position of a Swazi king and the final triumph and sanctity of kingship are dramatized in ritual. The groups and individuals who have no set roles in the present-day *Ncwala* reflect the influence of European dominance and of a new basis of stratification.

7/Continuity in change

It has become platitudinous to state that Africa in the past decade has been swept by the "winds of change." Since the independence of Ghana in 1957, thirty-three former African colonies have been admitted to the United Nations, and even more remote areas of Africa have become foci of international interest. The details of change in the different areas and the reaction to the new developments are, however, complex and varied. In this chapter I shall briefly indicate a few major trends in Swaziland. Social change generally involves selection, and deliberate selection is always influenced by past experience. Some traditional customs and institutions adjust readily, others show a tenacity or resistance that is often difficult to explain in terms of Western motivation or rationale. But the process of integrating the new with the old cannot be locally controlled; the destiny of the Swazi, or of any small-scale society in the modern world, will in the long run be shaped by external forces, which can be structurally interpreted.

ECONOMIC GROWTH

There is in modern Swaziland increasing contact with the outside world, both economically and politically. Economically, Swaziland is booming. The geographical isolation, the safeguard of conservatism, is being rapidly and deliberately broken down. New highways are opening up the territory by connecting growing urban centers; solid bridges are replacing old ponts and narrow causeways; electricity plants are operating in areas where the candle and oil lamp were the only known artificial lighting. Trucks, vans, automobiles, buses, and taxis rush past barefoot peasants on the new roads. Small aircraft carry white executives to and from developing areas in the territory. A contract has been signed for the building of a railway linking Swaziland with the eastern seaboard at Lourenço Marques (now Maputo).

These are tangible signs of a new economic orientation. From being one of the poorer underdeveloped areas, Swaziland is being transformed into an area of promising investment through public loans and private enterprise. The local administration succeeded in raising its first general-purpose loan; the British government more than tripled its grants-in-aid; in 1961 the territory received a

77

2.8-million-dollar credit from the World Bank's International Development Association (IDA); private white entrepreneurs, apprehensive of the *apartheid* policy of the Republic of South Africa, transferred capital to Swaziland. A poll tax, paid by Africans and, in Swaziland, also by Europeans, constituted over 40 percent of the total revenue in 1946; it dropped to 5 percent by 1956. Income tax, paid mainly by Europeans, rose almost correspondingly.

The surface of Swaziland is increasingly being shaped by the use of inanimate power, an index of industrialization. In 1949 the Colonial Development Corporation purchased 105,000 acres in the lowlands for irrigation, agriculture, and ranching, and financed the building of a canal to bring water from the Komati River 40 miles away. Since then two other large and several smaller irrigation schemes have been completed, transforming the agricultural possibilities which had previously been limited to dry-land farming. A large-scale forestry industry has developed in the western and northwestern areas of the territory on land previously used for the winter grazing of sheep, which were herded across the South African border. The Colonial Development Corporation, together with the international firm of Cortaulds Ltd., has formed a pulp company with an initial capital of 5 million pounds sterling (approximately 15 million dollars). Two large sugar mills are operating in areas where wild animals once roamed freely; a citrus industry, representing considerable capital investment, is already yielding favorable revenues; rice of good quality is being grown in areas under intensive irrigation.

The enumeration of these innovations does not indicate their sociological effect. Change is not a simple movement "from the traditional to the modern." From the time of Mswati, the social context of the Swazi has included Europeans, and in the colonial situation Europeans and Africans (colonizer and colonized) interacted, borrowing from each other. But activities and benefits have been and are unevenly shared between them. It is the Europeans who, recognizing the rich economic potential of modern Swaziland, have taken the initiative in development. Traditional Swazi leaders did not press for greater ease or speed of communication with the rest of the world. When the idea of a railway was first mooted in the late nineteenth century, the Swazi spokesmen expressed opposition on the grounds that it would lead to an exodus of young people, particularly women, trying to escape family obligations and tribal restraint. The present rulers have accepted the new railway plan as part of a process of modernization, which they are unable to check, but do not necessarily favor. Nor is there any pressure by the Swazi to have highways, railway stations, or landing strips constructed near key homesteads. The main royal villages are still on dirt roads, which, particularly in rainy weather, are braved by car only by an intrepid driver.

Land for agriculture and pasturage continues to be the foundation of Swazi existence. By the end of 1959, 51.5 percent of the total territory was available for occupation by the Swazi nation. In addition to the Swazi areas described in Chapter 1, more land was purchased by the Swazi nation, and land known as native land settlement areas was purchased by the government from European owners, or set aside by the government from Crown land. Contact with white systems of land tenure, increasing scarcity of land, and such permanent improvements as fences, wattle plantations, and immovable homes, have led to a greater emphasis on individual rights; but, at the same time, the majority of Swazi still appear to consider that land should be held by the chief as the tribal representative, and that every subject should be entitled to its use in a reciprocal political relationship.

Swazi lack capital and technological training, and many are dubious of the values that are associated with Western investment. Over 90 percent of the irrigated land in the country is owned by Whites, who use it for the varied and profitable cultivation of rice, sugar, and citrus fruits. Some 1000 acres under irrigation were made available at no cost to the Swazi, but by 1961, not many Swazi had taken advantage of the offer. This does not mean that the Swazi are incapable of changing. Largely through the efforts of the Department of Land Utilization (a postwar development) Swazi are adopting more intensive and commercial methods of agriculture. Contour plowing and other techniques of soil and water conservation are more widely accepted; the purchase of fertilizers has risen, and the cultivation of cash crops—especially tobacco and cotton—has increased. Today, there are more self-supporting Swazi farmers than there were ten or twenty years ago. The *Ngwenyama* has appointed a board, known as the Central Rural Development Board, to approve schemes for land use and resettlement plans; this board serves as a counterpart in Swazi area to the Natural Resources Board that operates in freehold farms.

Why, then, have the Swazi not made use of the possibilities opened by irrigation? Is it because of fear on the part of conservatives of appearing too ambitious? Is it because of their suspicion of Whites, "who do not usually give something for nothing," or because they prefer their existing mode of agricultural techniques? Research on this and similar situations of resistance to change is required.

The purely economic advantages of individual tenure are weighted against the social and political isolation that it is assumed to predicate. A 1960 study by John Hughes revealed that a group of educated Swazi agriculture students foresaw political, economic, and social dangers in individual tenure. Politically, it would entail the loss of effective control that is vested in the traditional rulers: individuals who owned land could "behave like kings" and pay no attention to tribal leaders, nor take part in the annual rituals of national unification. Economically, individual ownership could produce a class structure opposed to the traditional hierarchy based on birth, and also give rise to a landless peasantry. Socially, it would undermine the quality of "good neighborliness" that characterizes the Swazi community, which is bound together by the sharing of land. The study stressed the widespread fallacy that "progress" and "traditionalism" must always be opposed and that "progress" inevitably means following a Western model. Individuals who have received Western education may deliberately support certain elements of traditional culture.

Animal husbandry is still a major interest of many conservative Swazi. They own more cattle, goats, sheep, horses, donkeys, pigs, and fowls than do the Whites, and many Swazi areas suffered from overgrazing. The agriculture and veterinary departments meet considerable resistance to their efforts to improve the land by restricting the number of animals. At the same time, under an order made by the *Ngwenyama* in council, cattle are regularly culled from the herds of Swazi who own more than ten head of cattle. The animals thus acquired are auctioned and a levy on the proceeds is credited to the Lifa, or Inheritance Fund, which was started in 1946, both to reduce overstocking and to purchase additional land for the Swazi people.

The economic future of Swaziland is largely dependent on the development of her rich mineral potential, recognized by Whites, as well as by Swazi, from the early period of contact. There are known deposits of gold, asbestos, barytes, iron, and coal. For many years asbestos was the most profitable investment, contributing some 50 percent of the total value of all exports. With the establishment of a Geological Survey Department in 1945 and a Mineral Development Commission in 1953, there has been a systematic attempt by the administration to stimulate and direct prospecting and further exploitation. Swaziland is being brought increasingly into the network of international finance by exports of mineral wealth to the Republic of South Africa, the United Kingdom, France, Spain, and, most recently, Japan. The domestic economy, in turn, reacts to such world trade conditions as the marketing of lower-grade asbestos by Russia and the falling off of demand for andalusite coal by Western Germany. The Swazi people do not own any of the local mines, but are affected by opportunities and conditions of employment. The question of the rights of the Swazi as a nation to mineral wealth is again under review, reviving the old issue of the interpretation of the concessions granted Whites by Mbandzeni.

Despite the economic growth, industrial conditions are still rudimentary. Legal provision for trade unions has existed in the statute books since 1942, and there is also a growing body of deliberate legislation to control the workers' safety, health, and welfare. But the first trade union was formed only in 1962 by workers in the pulp factory, and in the absence of trade unions the administration encourages the appointment of tribal representatives at all major industrial concerns. There is only the beginning of an awareness on the part of the Swazi of the need for workers in mines and factories to develop their own organizations.

MIGRATION

More skilled immigrants are coming into Swaziland; simultaneously, however, unskilled Swazi continue to migrate seasonally and temporarily to more industrialized centers. The total population of Swaziland, enumerated in the census of 1956, was 240,511, of whom 233,214 were Africans, 5919 Europeans, and 1378 Eur-Africans. The figures included 11,728 Swazi temporarily employed outside the territory and 3470 "foreign Africans" temporarily employed in Swaziland. Between 1946 and 1956 the African population increased by 51,945, of whom 4854 were new immigrants. Although non-Swaziland Africans totaled only 8048, or 3.4 percent of the African population, the number of immigrants had increased by 152 percent. Equally, if not more significant, was the increase in European immigration. Between 1946 and 1956 the European population increased by 84.9 percent compared with an increase of only 16.9 percent in the previous decade. The net natural increase remained fairly constant at between 10 and 15 per 1000, and most of the increase was therefore due to immigration; between the years

1952 and 1959, the European population doubled. But the vast majority of the population, over 90 percent, is still Swazi; it provides the "host" culture, to which the African immigrants adapt, and which the Europeans cannot ignore.

The African immigrants fall into two separate categories. First, there are those who look to Swaziland as a permanent home and seek opportunities denied them in their former place of domicile. They include teachers, progressive farmers, and traders from South Africa, anxious to escape certain restrictions of *apartheid*. Before they can be granted the use of land, symbol of citizenship, they must be accepted by the traditional rulers. Should they want to buy land, they also require the approval of the High Commissioner. In the second category of African immigrants are temporary laborers, brought mainly from Portuguese territory (now Mozambique) and subject to white employers, not Swazi chiefs. The apparently anomalous situation in which a section of the emerging educated middle class of Africans from the Republic are moving into Swaziland, while roughly 11,000 unskilled and semiskilled Swazi work annually in the Republic and roughly 3500 Africans from Portuguese territory (Mozambique) work in Swaziland, can be explained by political and economic pressures. Crudely stated, political freedom is greater in Swaziland than in either of the other territories, but wages are highest in the Republic, the strongest labor magnet, and lowest in Portuguese territory (Mozambique). For the wage earner, the economic appears to override the political factor. However, it must not be forgotten that each person is motivated by subtler drives than are revealed in gross statistics of migration.

I have not the detailed data to evaluate the political or social effects on Swazi life of the continuous process of temporary emigration of large numbers of Swazi males. Conflict in the kinship system, especially in marital relationships, may or may not have become intensified, illegitimacy may or may not have increased, political loyalties may or may not have been weakened. It is difficult, moreover, to isolate migration as a single factor from the total range of intensified pressures to which modern Swazi are subjected. However, it is clear that migrant labor has become an accepted activity; migrants often earn more than they could produce with their present agricultural facilities, and money for tax, food, and clothing has become a necessity of the times. There does not appear to be any marked increase in the number of migrants who abandon their ties with their kin and remain away indefinitely; the majority, irrespective of their employent experiences, retain their Swazi identity and return eventually to their country.

Within Swaziland itself there has developed a greater internal mobility. The highest increase in population (67.7 percent) is in the central district of the midlands, the area that has always allowed for closest settlement and is now the main center of urban development; the lowest increase (14.7 percent) is in the Mankaiana district, the least industrialized. Elsewhere in Africa the new urban and industrialized centers have produced a radical political elite. In Swaziland, with its migrant labor force, centralized political structure, and very recent industrial development, an urban-rural dichotomy is only beginning.

The major concentrations of Swazi people, however, no longer occur in traditional royal homesteads, but in centers of European settlement and development. Approximately 4 percent of the African population resides in recognized urban townships. By 1959, Mbabane, the administrative capital, had an estimated population of 5500 inhabitants, of whom some 4200 were Africans. Bremersdorp, more centrally situated for commerce, had a population of 4300, of whom some 3000 were Africans. The Havelock asbestos mine, the largest local employer of labor, housed over 1000 male Africans. Swazi rulers may still obtain the services of loyal subjects for major state rituals and economic enterprises, such as rebuilding the national shrine hut or moving a royal homestead, but the permanent residents in the capital number less than 300.

European immigrants have come mainly from other areas in Africa, particularly the Republic of South Africa and [the former Portuguese colony of] Mozambique where racial tension is threatening economic as well as political stability. It is not possible at this stage to know how many European immigrants will remain in Swaziland, or for how long; they have brought in capital and certain skills and have opened new avenues of local employment. Some have also bought land, which establishes a common interest between them and earlier European settlers, rather than traditional Swazi authorities.

POLITICAL DEVELOPMENTS

The traditional Swazi rulers find their position attacked by new ideologies. A democratic system gives greater recognition to achieved than to ascribed qualifications, and uneducated hereditary local chiefs, in particular, find their authority questioned by more Westernized subjects. New ideas of "freedom" are brought in from outside, and events in other parts of Africa have become topics of conversation in many Swazi circles. Political refugees, white and black, escaping for different periods from the repressive policy and "states of emergency" in the Republic of South Africa, have moved into Swaziland, and the country is strategically placed in the route of African independence movements.

Swaziland, like Southern Rhodesia (now Zimbabwe) and Kenya, is politically complicated by the presence of White settlers. In this respect it is different from Basutoland (Lesotho) and Bechuanaland (Botswana), where Whites are restricted to an administrative cadre and to traders and missionaries with limited land rights. The influence of the white-settler–controlled Republic of South Africa is strong, and the British government—though it has expressed its opposition to *apartheid* and supports, in principle, the ultimate achievement of African self-government— is sensitive both to the claims of white Swazilanders anxious to preserve their privileges and to the economic pressures of the white Nationalist government of South Africa.

The colonial administration has, however, struggled increasingly to adjust traditional institutions at both the central and local levels to the demands of a modern government. A great deal of the traditional power structure has been retained. The *Ngwenyama* is recognized as the main Swazi representative, and the two councils continue to some extent as before. In addition, a skeleton of the main council sits weekly, or as needed, to transact everyday matters. Close contact with government is maintained through a standing committee, appointed by the *Ngwenyama*-in-council. A new range of functionaries has been brought into existence, and the standing committee consists of a chairman, the treasurer of the Swazi National Treasury, the secretary to the nation, and six representatives from the six administrative districts, who are paid from the Swazi National Treasury. The meetings combine both traditional and modern formalities, and efficiency is not considered their main value. There is still virtually unrestricted discussion and an effort to reach unanimity; if this is not achieved, action is generally delayed for as long as possible.

Swazi legal procedure has been drawn into the more formal structure of the West. Fourteen Swazi courts, two courts of appeal, and a Higher Swazi Court of Appeal were instituted in 1950. Swazi courts are empowered to exercise civil and criminal jurisdiction in most matters in which the parties are Africans. Cases arising from the marriage of Swazi by civil or Christian rites are specifically excluded from their civil jurisdiction, and such cases as witchcraft and murder from their criminal jurisdiction. In other cases Swazi courts administer not only traditional law and custom (subject to certain restraints of Western ethics) but also new rules and regulations issued by recognized Swazi authorities under the Swaziland Native Administration Proclamation and laws authorized by an order of the resident commissioner. The personnel, procedure, and powers of Swazi courts are more clearly defined than heretofore, and all judgments are recorded.

The Swazi have been granted additional financial responsibilities through the Swazi National Treasury, which derives revenue from payments by government of proportions of various taxes, all fines and fees from Swazi courts, and various other sources. The Swazi treasury now pays the rulers, chiefs, and officers of the Swazi administration and also contributes to agricultural, medical, and educational projects. The institutional separation of administrative, judicial, and financial functions of government is a major innovation, but it must be re-emphasized that these functions themselves were also fulfilled in the traditional system. The present system of parallel administration is expensive and ineffective, as we saw in Chapter 2. Power moves down through a chain of British-appointed officials on the one side and the traditional hierarchy on the other, with conflict centered in a few leading personalities. Educated Swazi, including some of the traditional leaders, recognize the impracticability of the traditional system for reaching rapid and major decisions, but they are seeking to build on certain accepted foundations and do not want an imitation of constitutional techniques developed in alien contexts.

In an attempt to bring Swaziland into line with developments in other British territories, a new constitution is being officially formulated, and the legal expert appointed for this purpose is struggling to reconcile a number of conflicting interests. In the first place, one section of the population, the majority of Europeans, afraid to concede the democratic principle of universal franchise in a society where Africans are an unassailable numerical majority, are striving for racial protection through a qualified franchise. The Swazi themselves are divided in their reaction to the white man's fears of being "swamped" or "suffering retaliation for their previous discrimination." Some Swazi are prepared to accept communal representation as a temporary measure, others reject it outright. The party system is itself criticized by prominent Swazi, including Sobhuza, who argue that the caucus, seen as the essential policy-making instrument, is less "democratic" than the traditional system of traditional councils. Conservative Swazi do not accept the necessity of an organized opposition for political freedom and argue that no "count" should ever be made to expose the extent of disagreement. The retort of the more "modern" Swazi is that dissidents should not be treated as traitors.

Swazi, like other Africans, are beginning to experiment with the multiparty system. In 1959, a small group of Africans with white and African supporters outside Swaziland formed the Progressive party, the first "modern" political party in the territory. The local leaders were Dr. Ambrose Zwane and Mr. John Npuku. Dr. Zwane is the son of the ritual specialist who accompanied Sobhuza to England in 1922.

Dr. Zwane's bonds with the people and with Sobhuza are deep and strong. But he is acutely sensitive to the discrimination imposed by Whites on all Africans in the south, and his politics have an African Nationalist motivation and Pan-African affiliation. Mr. Nquku is a Zulu who has lived for many years in Swaziland, where he has held the post of supervisor of schools. As an educated foreigner without recognized ties of kinship or locality to substantiate his claims to loyalty, his position is more difficult and less secure. He lost considerable support in 1961, after having been accused of self-interest and dictatorial behavior. The Progressive party is in process of dividing into splinter parties.

In 1962 a new party, the Swaziland Democratic party, came into existence, with Simon Sishayi Nxumalo as interim chairman. The Nxumalo family is extremely well known and Nxumalo is the clan name of Sobhuza's own mother and paternal grandmother. The Democratic party is linked indirectly with the nonracial Liberal party in South Africa, but realizes the need to gain support from the traditional rulers of a largely conservative population. The most recent declaration of Democratic party policy decries the use of violence, of any abrupt break with the past, and affirms that it will use only legal and constitutional means to achieve its aims. It asserts its strong opposition to all forms of totalitarianism, such as communism, fascism, and *apartheid*, and its general principles include "the protection of fundamental human rights and the safeguarding of the dignity and worth of the human person irrespective of sex, race, color or creed." Its franchise policy is moderate: "the party" recognizes universal suffrage as the ultimate goal, but opposes its introduction in Swaziland before the people have had an opportunity to acquire more political experience. The party desires the "independence of Swaziland within the Commonwealth to be attained with a minimum of delay required to make Swaziland economically and politically viable." It "favors a constitutional monarchy with the *Ngwenyama* as King."

The supporters of new political movements include progressive farmers interested in individual land ownership, and teachers and skilled workmen who resent racially differentiated pay scales and employment opportunities. Though still small in number, this emerging middle class is important because it is in line with the trends toward nationalism that are observable in the rest of Africa. But in Swaziland, the new leaders are aware that the traditional Swazi rulers are still sufficiently strong to be useful allies, and they are reluctant to express open antagonism lest they drive away the mass support required for effective action.

It is clear that while the Swazi are being inducted into the strange language and ideologies of modern political maneuvering, they are still interested in conserving the key symbol of unity—the traditional monarchy—and that existing institutions and loyalties will influence future political alignments for some time. The Swazi appear to be moving toward a specific type of society, a modern nation state, distinct in organization and in goals from the clan, the tribe, and the colony described in Chapter 1, yet retaining a continuity unbroken by revolution. Swaziland is one of the very few territories in Africa in which national aspirations coincide with ethnic and cultural homogeneity, and non-Swazi in the territory are insignificant in number. In Swaziland the spontaneous but indecisive resistance to Whites that was characteristic of the earlier periods of contact has grown by fairly gradual stages into a more positive approach, expressed in modern political movements and ideas of "freedom," "democracy," and "self-determination." But experimentation with these new concepts and institutions meets with resistance from entrenched traditionalists, some of whom are Western-educated.

As in other areas where Whites are a settled and privileged group, Swazi nationalism is influenced by racialism. But the extent of racial tension is itself a variable, and in Swaziland it is not as openly acute as it is in South Africa, nor as it was in Kenya. The explanation of this must be sought in a number of factors, such as the relative distribution of land, economic security, administrative policy, political responsibility, and, by no means least important, in the existing culture and in the personality of the leaders.

In Swaziland national identity is symbolized by Sobhuza. Every individual Swazi has a number of other identities, sometimes complementary, sometimes opposed: African as distinct from European and Eur-African, commoner as distinct from aristocrat, peasant as distinct from proletariat. But African nationalism has not yet become (and may never become) the overriding identity in Swaziland. Although the main cleavage in Swazi society is still between Whites and non-Whites, the line is not completely rigid. Individual Whites have identified with Swazi political, economic, and cultural aspirations. The British government is gradually removing discriminatory practices and a few Westernized Swazi have been brought into a small multiracial circle. The new Swazi elites retain their ties with their more traditional kin and as they come to realize their own potential as Africans, are not prepared to accept patronage or tolerate discrimination. The majority of white settlers, in an effort to retain their privileged position, which they interpret as "security," are beginning to be involved in the political struggle with the more liberal metropole on the one hand and the democratic locals on the other. Although conservatives complain that they are being "sold down the river by Britain," there are a few Africans who complain that the process of liquidation is not sufficiently fast. It seems that four separate groups are engaged in the struggle for power: first, the traditionalists who are able to use the Swazi National Council as their organization; second, the nonracialist Democratic party, represented by a few educated men of both color groups; third, Swazi nationalists who, through the Progressive party, interact with other African nationalist movements; and finally, white nationalists who support the racialist policy of the Republic of South Africa. There are obviously many crosscurrents in modern Swaziland politics. The machinations of princes in the traditional society appear as pure clique politics with little relationship to any social change, and are on a different political level from the techniques of power politics deployed at the present time.

SOCIAL SERVICES

The average Swazi (like the average citizen in other countries) is less immediately concerned with political activities than with more direct personal social services, such as education and health.

There are at present some 300 recognized schools for Africans in Swaziland. The majority of these schools are still controlled by missions, subsidized by government grants-in-aid. The Swazi nation continues to maintain and finance one high school and two primary schools, with a total enrollment of over 700, and some enterprising chiefs encourage nondemoninational schools in more remote areas. The government itself has complete responsibility for nineteen secular schools. Until 1961, all schools were racially segregated. In 1961 one white school admitted non-Whites in a process that was not accompanied by any crisis.

Greater interest in education is reflected in the higher proportion of children of both sexes who attend school (approximately 55 percent of school-age children were enrolled in 1959, compared with approximately 30 percent in 1945), an increasing number of pupils in the middle and higher grades, and a growing pride and interest among parents in the children's achievements. Before 1945, little encouragement was given to promising students to strive for university degrees. Now, though the number of students may not warrant a university in Swaziland itself, selected individuals receive government scholarships to attend universities elsewhere. There is a growing recognition among Swazi leaders that the rapid expansion of education, particularly higher and technical education, is essential for the Africanization of the various departments of the administration.

In Chapter 4, I indicated that the traditional rulers are conscious of the danger of cleavage between the educated and uneducated, and between those who identify with Christian missions and those who identify with *emadloti*. The spread of Independent churches weakens the religious influence of orthodox missions and fosters a recognition of traditional ritual. Moreover, many of the princes and young chiefs, even if they, themselves, have little education, are interested in marrying trained nurses and teachers. These women, recognized as a new elite, belong, or have belonged, to Christian churches. By marrying into the aristocracy, new links are forged between traditional rank by birth and modern status by achievement, and between upholders of the ancestral cult and members of the more universalist Christian sects.

Together with educational progress, there has been increased investment in health facilities and services. Three Swazi qualified as doctors in the past ten years, and two of them are practicing in government hospitals in the territory; the third, Dr. Zwane, left the service for private practice and politics. Doctors, hospitals, medical outposts, and various health services are now accepted as part of ordinary living. But again, as in other contact situations, there is a duality in adaptation. The acceptance of new medicines and new medicine men does not automatically eliminate the use of ancient remedies, nor the belief in witchcraft, nor the inspired diagnostician and curer. Though the Western medical service, with its hierarchy of trained personnel, introduced new professional associations and institutions, Western treatment is often an addition to, not a substitute for, the traditional.

PERSPECTIVE

Modernization increases the range of choice, extends the field of individual development, and also multiplies points of potential conflict. Some localities in Swaziland have become more modernized, or "Westernized," than others through external environmental factors—the site of an industry, irrigation canal, or other technological developments—and/or the responsiveness and initiative of particular chiefs or other influential individuals.

Readiness for change rests in part in discontent with the present and in part in anticipation of future rewards, but there always remains a residuum from the past.

In the trend toward increasing complexity of social interaction, which is characteristic of small-scale societies subjected to Western impact, the residuum may make for stability, or become a focus of increasing conflict. Here a distinction must be drawn between cultural and structural persistence. This chapter has emphasized cultural persistence while indicating that there have arisen simultaneously new political tensions and realignments of interest groups. Structural cleavage between Whites and non-Whites, between radicals and conservatives, and between landowners and land users has not crystalized as sharply as in other countries where opposition to the entrenched privileges ("stubborn conservatism") of traditional ruling groups has accelerated political revolutions. The position, however, is changing rapidly, and we can anticipate that in Swaziland there will be major clashes, complicated by the presence of white settlers, and the resulting structural changes may radically undermine cultural continuity.

—December, 1962

View of Mbabane, the capital of Swaziland, 1973.

TOPOGRAPHY

HIGH VELD
MIDDLE VELD
LOW VELD
LEBOMBO MTNS

0   20
MILES

LOCATION

SWAZILAND

0   1000
MILES

PIGGS PEAK

HAVELOCK
PIGGS PEAK

ERANCHI

HLUME

BLACK
UMBULUZI   UMBULUZI

GOBA

KOMATI

M
B
A
B
A
N
E

B
R
E
M
E
R
S
D
O
R
P

S T E G I

MBABANE

LITTLE
USUTU

LOZITHLEZI

M
T
I
L
A
N
E

WHITE
UMBULUZI

STEGI

26°30'

LOBAMBA

GREAT   USUTU

BREMERSDORP

26°30'

MANKAIANA

INGWEMPISI

USUTU

BIG BEND

USUTU

M A N K A I A N A

A
S
S
E
G
A
I

MLATUZANE

MLATUZE

27°

PIET
RETIEF

HLATIKULU

27°

H L A T I K U L U

GOEDGEGUN

INGWAVUMA

R
E
P
U
B
L
I
C

O
F

S
O
U
T
H

A
F
R
I
C
A

M
O
Z
A
M
B
I
Q
U
E

GOLLEL

31°   32°

HK

SWAZILAND

INTERNATIONAL & DISTRICT BOUNDARIES

NATIVE   AREAS
NATIVE   LAND   SETTLEMENTS
ADDED   SINCE   1945
EUROPEAN   AREAS

RAILWAY

LOMATI

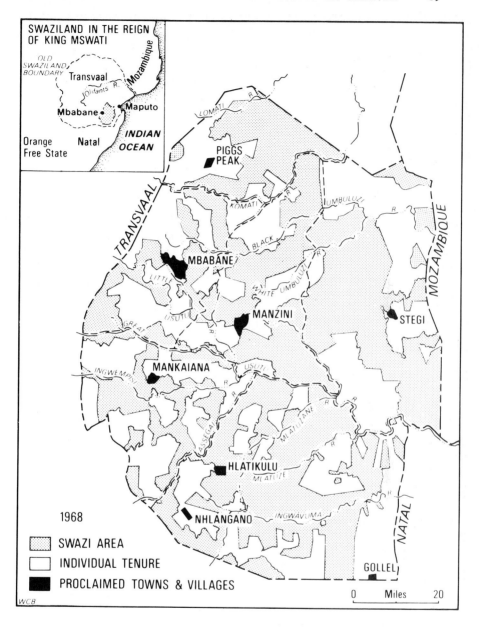

SWAZILAND IN THE REIGN OF KING MSWATI

OLD SWAZILAND BOUNDARY

Transvaal

Olifants R.

Mozambique

Mbabane•

•Maputo

Orange Free State

Natal

INDIAN OCEAN

LOMATI R.

PIGGS PEAK

TRANSVAAL

KOMATI R.

UMBULUZI R.

R

BLACK

MBABANE

LITTLE

WHITE UMBULUZI

R

STEGI

GREAT

USUTU

R

MANZINI

MOZAMBIQUE

INGWEMPISI

USUTU

R

MANKAIANA

ASSEGA

R

MLATIZANE

R

R

HLATIKULU

MLATIZE

R

1968

NHLANGANO

INGWAVUMA

R

NATAL

SWAZI AREA

INDIVIDUAL TENURE

PROCLAIMED TOWNS & VILLAGES

GOLLEL

0   Miles   20

WCB

PART TWO | From Colony To Kingdom

8/From colony to kingdom: 1960-1968

In the final chapter of the original case study, Swazi history reached a turning point: the first stage in the complex process of decolonization. Acquiescence in British rule was turning to open aggressive resistance waged by competing political factions. The *Ngwenyama* Sobhuza was in the ambivalent position of a traditional king to the Swazi but of a "paramount chief" in the colonial hierarchy. The stand he would take in different situations, more particularly the use he would make of his traditional powers, would be crucial for the fate of Swaziland.

In the early sixties it was assumed that control would rest for the foreseeable future with Great Britain. The idea of independence was remote. Britain, under a Labour government voted into power after World War II, was committed to the principle of granting its various and widespread colonies responsible government and ultimate independence but retained control of when, and under what conditions. It aimed explicitly at gradually imprinting, through a series of interim constitutions requiring patience and lengthy negotiations, a final blueprint expressing its own twentieth-century ideal of democracy through universal franchise, secret ballot, and a multiparty system with emphasis on the rights of the individual and the protection of minorities.

Swaziland was far behind most other British colonies in terms of modern political institutional development. It did not yet have a unified legislative council. Swazi acted through their traditional system represented by the *Ngwenyama*-in-council, and white settlers who had no legislative powers expressed their views through a European Advisory Council (EAC). The central administration headed by British officials, instituted from London, dealt with the two racial groups separately, so that direct political confrontation between them was avoided. At the same time, however, economic conflicts were intensifying with industrial development, coupled with problems of employment and continuing racial discrimination. Rights to land, minerals, and labor became critical issues.

A HISTORIC MEETING

Chapter 7 introduced various groups and individuals battling for political leadership and control of economic resources. Superficially, the situation appeared familiar: white settlers seeking to maintain their privileges; Blacks struggling to receive their share; a hereditary traditional African aristocracy facing the challenge of a Western-oriented elite; and a colonial administration interested in exercising influence over future developments. Observers predicted political outcomes according to the particular models of national movements they had in mind, especially Ghana and Nigeria. But each country is in many respects unique, and the process of history does *not* repeat itself. Goals, options, and techniques change over time. Individuals change their minds, groups their alliances. Even the British umpire may bend the rules of the game!

Looking through my notebooks that cover some fifty years, I am acutely aware of the relativity of events, contradictions in interpretation of motives and assessment of results, and of changes in individual situations and cultural context. When an anthropologist moves to an analysis with a perspective across time, what are observed and recorded are not objective or fixed facts but the elusive situations of historical reality. With this approach, I resume the story of the Swazi.

I begin with a meeting referred to by informants as "historic," called by Sobhuza on April 23, 1960, at Masundvwini, the Western residence, (mentioned on page 6). He had invited a few carefully selected Whites, three members of the central government, and two white settlers: one a highly respected American medical missionary and educator who had been in Swaziland since 1925, the other a self-educated successful farmer who had arrived in 1938 and paid allegiance to Sobhuza through one of the local chiefs. With Sobhuza were several of his counselors, both Western-educated and traditional. Sobhuza spoke for two hours without notes. The press was not invited.

Sobhuza explained that he had called the meeting "to discuss events in this troubled world," and more particularly "how we can remain in peace knowing we are going to live here together." He referred to "the cruel and inhuman treatment of Africans by Europeans" as "the false belief that this was a way to protect [European] interests." He suggested that the root of the troubles, including racial conflict, was fear, but stressed that it would not help Africans if Europeans disappeared, taking with them all their knowledge and skills. As a political and ethical solution he proposed the establishment of a legislative council in which Europeans and Swazi joined together on an equal basis to deal with matters of the territory as a whole. Since they had been brought up in different cultures with different ideas of democracy, he said, European representatives should be chosen by their own system of election and the Swazi according to their familiar system of consensus and appointment.

The speech raised a number of controversial questions. What did he mean by "equal basis"? Was it in numerical terms? What place would there be for non-Swazi Africans or for Western-oriented Swazi? What would be the relationship between the new council and existing institutions in the country? The need for some form of legislative council had been raised on previous occasions, but Sobhuza's initiative and suggestions precipitated action. On instructions from the British Secretary of State for the Colonies, Resident Commissioner Brian Marwick established a constitutional committee to examine the issue and formulate proposals. Marwick, a highly competent administrator whose professional contact with the Swazi extended back to 1925, was eminently qualified for the task. He was also a trained anthropologist who had gained the respect and confidence of Sobhuza and many of his people. His interest in Swazi culture, his liberal political opinions, his commitment to nonracialism, and his outspoken manner as well as his principled support of Swazi interests, had on several occasions brought him into conflict with some of the leading Whites, including Carl Todd, chairman of the EAC.

The original constitutional committee consisted of twelve Swazi appointed by Sobhuza from the Swazi National Council (SNC), three of whom were also leading officials of the Swaziland Progressive Party (SPP); twelve Whites appointed by Resident Commissioner Brian Marwick, of whom ten were actively identified with the EAC; and four officials of the British administration, including Marwick as chairman. He appointed a small working committee within the larger committee to gather essential historical background information on Swazi institutions and invited opinions from other interested parties. The committee as a whole concentrated on specific constitutional issues, including the monarchy, the local political organizations, succession, and land and mineral rights.

At the first session of the full committee held on November 4, there was obvious tension between individuals expressing different ideologies and interests. Particularly acrimonious were exchanges between the Western-educated but extremely conservative Secretary of the SNC, Polycarp Dlamini, and the more democratic leader of the SPP, John Nquku. Carl Todd supported the Swazi conservatives, arguing that comments by members should be made within the framework of the policy outlined by the *Ngwenyama*, not contrary to it, and he urged the committee not to allow "new forces in Africa" to control the situation. At the end of the meeting, Polycarp Dlamini announced that the *Ncwala* was about to begin; no further discussions could take place until it came to a formal end. Then there would be Christmas and New Year celebrations. The date of the next meeting of the constitutional committee was set for February 17.

In the period of sacred time, national priests performed *Ncwala* rituals to unite and strengthen the nation symbolized by the monarchy. But core members of the SNC held secret political discussions and members of the SPP engaged in building support through open secular activities. At a public meeting called by Nquku and held in Mbabane, the British administrative capital, the most eloquent exponent of the SPP policy (with its emphasis on universal franchise and one man–one vote) was Prince Dumisa. Young, Western-educated, and high in the royal genealogy—in Swazi terms, a "son" of Sobhuza himself—Dumisa had been conspicuously absent from among the other princes dancing the *Ncwala* at Lobamba.

The SNC conservatives reacted by agreeing in a private session to refuse to allow Nquku to represent the nation on the constitutional committee. Sobhuza reluctantly accepted their decision, and Marwick, as chairman, stated that he had no alternative but to exclude Nquku from the discussion. Dr. Ambrose Zwane and Obed Mabuza, the two other Western-oriented educated African members of the SPP appointed by Sobhuza, walked out in support of their leader. Thus it came about that in subsequent discussions three major political viewpoints dominated the meetings: that of conservative traditionalists of the SNC, that of the majority of settlers represented by the EAC, and that of Western-oriented senior British civil servants.

However, general proposals skillfully drafted by Todd indicated little divergence of opinion between the SNC and the EAC. They provided for an equal number of Swazi representatives chosen by acclamation and of Europeans elected by Western methods; and they gave support to the *Ngwenyama* and the traditional Swazi hierarchy at the same time that they protected the privileges of Whites and gave their sanction to the *Ngwenyama's* traditional control of minerals. The government officials abstained when the vote on the proposals was taken. They considered the suggestion of racial federation on a fifty-fifty basis inimical to the achievement of the ultimate ideal of a nonracial state and were critical of the exclusion from the SNC and EAC proposals of Western-oriented and -educated Africans. While recognizing the need to safeguard the position of the *Ngwenyama*, they also contended that future economic development such as control over mineral wealth required that traditional authorities be recognized by the legislature as agencies that should not be restricted in an undefined manner. When the final proposals were presented to the Secretary of State, Marwick submitted a separate "Note of reservations by the chairman and official members." The proposals together with the official reservations and a response by the Secretary of State were released on March 1, 1962.

A coolness had developed between Sobhuza and Marwick and Sobhuza avoided as much as possible meeting with him. But they had a private discussion in April, and on May 2, 1962, Sobhuza stated publicly that when, at the historic meeting, he had used the words *equal basis* he had not been speaking of numbers, since "equality is not a question of numbers." Some of his audience accepted this as an elucidation of his original statement. Others considered it a retraction that came too late, since the SNC and the EAC representatives on the constitutional committee had used equality of numbers as if they were the king's directive.

Sobhuza was shrewd enough not to interpret politics at the level of numbers of representation in government: to him, the critical issue was who would control economic resources, particularly land and minerals. Once the proposals had been submitted, Marwick considered that the constitutional committee had completed its task and was automatically dissolved, but the SNC and EAC continued to work together. On September 3, 1962, at a joint meeting without the presence of the official government members, they passed several resolutions, of which the two most significant were (1) that the *Ngwenyama* be recognized as King of Swaziland, a resolution qualified by a clause that Europeans could retain their allegiance to other governments but would respect the position of the king, and (2) that the Secretary of State be requested to withdraw conditions relating to control by the central government of mineral rights and that full control be vested in the *Ngwenyama* on behalf of the Swazi nation. Political feelings ran high and economic tensions surfaced.

AN IMPOSED CONSTITUTION AND LABOR UNREST

The next official step was taken by the British through the Secretary of State, who called a constitutional conference in London starting on January 28, 1963. He invited a wider range of representatives than had participated in the original constitutional committee and included one representative from each of three Swazi-led political parties. Sobhuza was especially invited to fly to London for the conference but refused, explaining that he could not commit his people without consulting his full council, nor did he feel that he could absent himself from his country at a time of internal crisis.

At the opening session the Secretary of State, Duncan Sandys, informed the delegation that the British had no preconceived plan but put forward suggestions as a basis for discussion. These were closer to those of the local British officials and political party leaders than to those of the EAC and SNC. The delegates reacted critically to the new suggestions, their diverse responses revealing a complex mixture of idealism, realism, sincerity, and double-talk. The meetings continued without clear direction. No one seemed prepared to change his own mind, so no one could really influence the mind of another. The speeches were often long, the arguments heated, and comments ad hominem. The deepest passions were involved—nationalism, self-interest, fear—and basic ideologies were opposed. The issue of control over minerals reflected a fundamental opposition between the British concept of a twentieth-century constitutional king and a traditional Swazi concept of sacred kingship.

After two weeks of wearying and sometime pointless discussions, the Secretary of State lost patience and, on February 12, announced that since no agreement could be reached he would impose a constitution.

The delegates returned, frustrated and angry, to report to their various constituencies. Sobhuza made no immediate public statement. On February 27, the Secretary of the Swazi National Council issued a formal summons to "the nation" to come to Lobamba to hear the SNC delegates report on the conference. Some 3000 people attended. They sat on the ground of the vast national *sibaya* facing the *Ngwenyama* and his close advisers. Sobhuza heard his representatives vigorously challenged not only by the members of political parties but also by prominent members of the broader-based SNC, councilors he trusted. They accused his men of submitting proposals without a mandate from the entire nation and of not expressing the ideals of the *Ngwenyama*.

Dissension within the country intensified. White settlers sought support for their interests from the *apartheid* government in South Africa; black and white refugees opposed to the *apartheid* regime sought asylum under the British in Swaziland. In April 1963 Dr. Zwane formed his faction of the SPP into the more radical Ngwane National Liberatory Congress (NNLC), with Prince Dumisa as secretary general. Swazi politics were no longer contained within the boundaries of a small territory. Swazi politicians moved into the international arena with appeals to the Organization of African Unity (OAU) and the United Nations (UN).

Politics became more directly expressed in economic conflict. As early as 1942 the British had introduced legislation for the registration and regulation of trade unions. But Sobhuza associated trade unions with strikes, and, with the support of white employers, appointed traditional representatives to negotiate on behalf of the workers. This system was particularly resented in industries in which there were non-Swazi or where workers had no stake in the rural areas. Leaders of the political parties recognized the potential advantages of using the legitimate grievances of workers for political ends by supporting and, in the case of the NNLC, by initiating strikes.

Between February 28 and June 30, 1963, six strikes involving 5000 workers in major towns and industrial centers shook the serenity of Swaziland. The small police force, fewer than 350 officers and other ranks, was unprepared. On June 8 the SDP had called a mass meeting in Mbabane of domestic servants, a generally poorly paid category of workers endemic to the colonial situation. The NNLC took over the platform, and on Sunday, June 10, called for a general strike. The following day some 3000 men and women, led by Prince Dumisa, demanded to see the Resident Commissioner. He agreed to talk to fifteen representatives, but no agreement was reached. That night, prisoners in the Mbabane Central Jail rioted and ten escaped. A number of white residents formed a special guard, and Mbabane was described as "a town in a state of siege."

The Resident Commissioner asked Sobhuza to send the *emabutfo* (age regiments) to help maintain law and order. Sobhuza refused. He would not use force against his own people, and felt that the British had provoked the situation through their support of political parties and trade unions. Under pressure from his own staff as well as many other white residents, Marwick cabled for assistance, and on June 13, 1963, a battalion of some 600 British soldiers was flown in from Kenya. As the planes thundered overhead thousands of Swazi converged at the ritual capital of Lobamba, where the *Ngwenyama* was already waiting. This time it was leaders of the NNLC who asked him to call out his regiments. In their view the battle was no longer between traditionalists and politicians, but between the colonial administration and the Swazi—between rulers and ruled. Again Sobhuza refused. Again, it would have meant civil war, and the end of national unity. Instead he urged "the nation" to keep the peace and advised the strikers to return to work. The strikes were broken without bloodshed. However, some 250 workers were arrested, and although most were soon released, leading members of the NNLC were kept in custody and charged with public violence.

In September of that year, Sobhuza-in-council was working on yet another petition, to be presented this time not to the British queen or the Secretary of State but to the British people through the British Parliament. It requested changes in the proposed constitution, and referred specifically to three key issues: the mode of election; the constitutional status of Swaziland, including the position of "your humble petitioner as Paramount Chief under the constitution"; and Swazi land and minerals. But the petition, presented on November 19 by Patrick Wall, a Conservative member, had no effect.

In December 1963, Swaziland's first Legislative Council (Legco) was established by an order in council issued by the British under authority of the Foreign Jurisdiction Act of 1903. The post of resident commissioner was upgraded to that of queen's commissioner, with powers equivalent to that of governors of other British colonies and with direct access to the Secretary of State. While the title of King was officially restored to the *Ngwenyama*, his powers and privileges were restrictively defined. But, at the end of the complicated document, there was a short schedule titled "Matters which would continue to be regulated by Swazi law and custom." These included the office of *Ngwenyama*; the office of *Ndlovukazi*; the appointment, revocation of appointment, and suspension of chiefs; the composition of the Swazi National Council, the appointment and revocation of appointment of members of the council and the procedure of the council; the *Ncwala* ceremony; and the *emabutfo* regimental system. Since Swazi members of Legco were automatically members of the Swazi National Council, the British assumed (or hoped) that the latter would gradually disappear, or rather merge with the more modern Western institutions and that the king himself would accept a role comparable to that of a British sovereign who "reigns but does not rule." But this did not happen, and the constitution, which aimed at integrating the Swazi and the White into a single system, in fact entrenched a structural duality.

Rumors were being circulated by political party leaders that Sobhuza had lost the support of "the nation," and that the viewpoint of British officials, personified by Brian Marwick, had the support of the majority. Sobhuza, however, had his own sources of information, and the day after the final constitution was announced he declared that the issue of national support should be decided by a plebiscite. Marwick refused Sobhuza's request for cooperation as a pointless exercise and warned him that Sobhuza would be responsible if there were any trouble. Sobhuza replied that the queen's commissioner was responsible for keeping law and order, and if he wished he could prohibit the holding of a referendum, recognized as a Western democratic way of gauging public opinion.

The referendum spoken of later as "the reindeer election" took place on January 19, 1964. The form was simple, direct, and graphic. There would be only one question: Do you or do you not agree with the petition submitted by the *Ngwenyama* to the British government? Since at that time some 75 percent of Swazi adults were illiterate, the choice was represented by two animal symbols: a lion for the Swazi king and the reindeer, a foreign animal described as "with horns on horns," for the opposition. Though leaders of the political parties, for reasons of their own, called on their followers not to vote, the turnout was remarkable and the results convincing. According to the organizers, 122,000 Swazi of an estimated voting population of 125,000 chose the Lion, 154 the reindeer. And despite criticism of the loaded symbols and allegations of rigging the results, it was clear that Sobhuza had won a major victory.

ELECTION IN TRADITIONAL PERSPECTIVE

The election of members for Legco was a different matter. The SNC was not the king, and the choice of candidates was more controversial. Marwick attempted to persuade Sobhuza not to identify himself with any one section of the population, but Swazi traditionalists argued that a Swazi king could not, and should not, be neutral. On April 16, 1964, Sobhuza announced that, in response to a request put to him by a delegation of princes and councilors, he had agreed to establish the Imbokodvo National Movement (INM), which he claimed was not a political party but would serve as the political arm of the SNC. He inter-

Prince Masitsela giving a certificate of literacy to a rural woman, 1966.

preted the name *Imbokodvo* (literally The Grinding-Stone) symbolically—it was the essential utensil required in every Swazi home to break down separate grains into a single paste for the staple food of the people. He said that the full Swazi name should be *Imbokodvo lemabalabala* (The Grinding-Stone That Brings Together Many Colors).

Electioneering by candidates of the political parties followed the essentially Western model of personal canvassing and propaganda, with each candidate extolling his own qualifications as well as expounding his party policy. The approach of the INM was different: the individual was overshadowed by the monarch, and the traditional chiefs served indirectly as electioneering officers. The choice of candidates was made through *tinkundla*, regional councils initiated at Sobhuza's suggestion in 1956. Each *inkundla* was a type of royal village under a governor appointed by the king, to whom chiefs in a defined neighborhood were attached as local contingents. *Tinkundla* thus provided a system of local government distinct from that of the central administration, with its hierarchy and bureaucracy of district and subdistrict commissioners, appointed by nonhereditary criteria and emphasizing different educational qualifications (see page 41). By 1963, twenty *tinkundla* had been established. Each sent two representatives to SNC headquarters and the final selection was approved by the king. Traditional status and record of national service, as well as experience of the Western system, was considered in the selection. Sobhuza appointed as leader of the INM Prince Makhosini Dlamini.

It was inevitable that with the racial basis of representation, Whites should develop their own political parties and factions. The more conservative members of the EAC formed the anti-British, pro-South African United Swaziland Association (USA). A few liberals joined the Swaziland Democratic Party (SDP). It was to the political advantage of the INM to form an electoral alliance with the USA to win the seats that were reserved for, or also open to, Whites.

Throughout the election, strict government surveillance was maintained, with the troops and the Swaziland police in charge of radio communications. There were heated arguments at several of the polling booths but no fighting. Each party had its symbol and each candidate was identified by a photograph and an inanimate object drawn by lot (this time no animal symbols were allowed). Sixty percent of the registered Whites and eighty-five percent of the Swazi went to the polls.

The INM and USA coalition won an overwhelming victory. The USA swept all the European-roll seats and the Imbokodvo-sponsored candidates won every seat on the National roll. The Imbokodvo received 79,683 votes, the NNLC 11,364, and the remaining three parties 2228 in all. Though the NNLC obtained 12.3 percent of the votes, it did not win a seat. Consequently, there were angry denunciations and protests after the elections, appeals to the Liberation Committee of the Organization of African Unity, and cables to the General Secretary of the United Nations, the British colonial secretary, and the British prime minister protesting the results and alleging malpractice by candidates and electioneering by chiefs in rural areas. But the attitude of the British had changed as support for the *Ngwenyama* had become increasingly apparent. The colonial office replied through Francis Lloyd, who had replaced Brian Marwick as queen's commissioner, that their redress for alleged malpractices lay in an appeal to the courts. The parties attempted to unseat fourteen Imbokodvo members, but their suit was dismissed for lack of evidence.

As king of the Swazi and head of a potentially new African state, Sobhuza began to clarify his political stance in relation to South Africa, other African countries, Portugal, and the rest of the world. He had gained sufficient confidence to formulate for himself an overall strategy and also to re-evaluate relations with white settlers. One of his first acts was to make it officially known that the INM represented the majority of all the people in his country and to deplore the fact that no Imbokodvo official had been invited to attend the meeting of the OAU, which had heard only the opinions of the NNLC. He subsequently called a meeting of the nation and also released a statement in the *Times of Swaziland*, the only local newspaper, in which he mocked at rumors that he was "planning to sell his people to Verwoerd [the then prime minister of the Republic of South Africa] or negotiating to have his country annexed to the Republic of South Africa." "What is surprising," he said, "is that while all nations are clamoring for freedom, we the Swazi nation should wish to go from one domination to another." But he was still dissatisfied with "the imposed Constitution."

The official opening of Legco was set for September 9, 1964, at the High Court in Mbabane. The British hoped that it would be a rather splendid occasion and made careful arrangements for the order of arrival and the allocation of seats. Some thousand warriors in Swazi attire who marched to Mbabane stood outside in the section cordoned off for the public; facing them, separated by police and British troops, were several hundred members of the NNLC, occasionally chanting congress protest songs and calling on the king to stay out of politics. The *Ndlovukazi* and her attendants arrived in state. But Sobhuza did not appear. The queen's commissioner announced that the *Ngwenyama* was "regrettably indisposed." Sobhuza's carefully worded speech was read by Msindazwe Sukati, M.B.E., who had held the difficult post of senior liaison officer between Sobhuza and Brian Marwick in the turbulent preconstitutional period.

Sobhuza's speech referred to disappointments and tribulations of the past but emphasized hopes for the future and expressed the determination of the Swazi to achieve their independence "calmly and fearlessly." The policy speech for the INM was made by Prince Makhosini, who stated bluntly that the first thing required was a new constitution, one which was not based on racialism and which accorded the king of Swaziland his rightful position as leader and mouthpiece of the nation. As he elaborated points put forward in the most recent Imbokodvo manifesto it became increasingly clear that the INM would no longer be subservient to white opinion. The INM would use its majority to free itself from its embarrassing alliance with reactionary members of the USA, enabling it to move closer to the national aspirations previously expressed by opposition parties.

Swazi nationals who had opposed the INM were encouraged to change their political allegiance. The first party leader to respond favorably was Sishayi Simon Nxumalo of the SDP, who had received only 147 votes in a constituency in which his family was prominent and where he himself was respected. But as a member of a political party he had been described as "fighting the king." In a letter to the press he announced his resignation from the SDP in order to work for wider national unity. Sobhuza gladly accepted his decision and sent him as his personal emissary to various African countries, as well as overseas, to explain the Imbokodvo policy. Sishayi was encouraged to play a major entrepreneurial role in Swazi political and economic affairs. Several other prominent individuals followed his lead. The Imbokodvo grew in strength, while personal rivalries weakened opponents who could not fall back on any stable institutionalized foundation, relying as they did for their main support on workers in urban centers or company towns engulfed by rural areas controlled by hereditary chiefs.

Legco meetings followed traditional British procedure: they began and ended at set times, the agenda was announced in advance, motions were then discussed, the vote taken by a show of hands, and the results announced as the ayes or the nos have it. Swazi members reported that they enjoyed the meetings and, on Sobhuza's instructions as well as in their own interests, they attended regularly. Since there were no political parties in the Legco, members debated and argued freely

Sobhuza addressing the nation in the sibaya *of Lobamba.*

among themselves, and voting showed no consistent alignment. But on several important issues there was sharp division between the Swazi and the official representatives, with USA members wavering.

For Sobhuza as *Ngwenyama* it was a strange period. Not only was greater formal authority vested in the queen's commissioner, but Sobhuza's own representative, Prince Makhosini, appeared, as leader of the INM, more frequently before the general public to express the national interest. Other close advisers and officials of the SNC met less conspicuously at Lobamba or at the traditional administrative headquarters, Lozitha. Yet everyone knew that Sobhuza was the power behind the scenes, that Swazi members dashed down the hill from Mbabane to wherever he happened to be, at all hours of the night, in response to his summons *Ngemandla* (with all power); that because of him the new secretary of the SNC was in effect as influential as the chief secretary in the central administration; that all discussions in Legco were reported to him, and that his appraisal of individual members would determine their future.

THE REASSERTION OF KINGSHIP

At first, Sobhuza had been prepared to move toward independence gradually, but he soon appreciated that this was not necessary. He had the support of the majority of his own people and of other African leaders. Makhosini had officially attended a session of the OAU in Nairobi and made a public speech for "independence now." The Secretary of State for the Colonies authorized Francis Lloyd to appoint a committee to review the present constitution and make detailed recommendations for the next stage—internal self-government preparatory to independence. This committee was composed of twelve unofficial members— eight Swazi and four Whites, chosen from Legco, and two officials in addition to the queen's commissioner as chair. It met for the first time in August 1965. The automatic exclusion of opposition invoked inevitable and predictable reactions of protest and of appeals, but the British were now committed to recognizing the legitimacy of the elected members of Legco and the leadership of Sobhuza.

The committee identified as its "fundamental problem the restoration of what the Swazi regarded as the original treaty relationship which Swaziland had with Britain and the recognition of the kingship of the *Ngwenyama*." This original treaty relationship referred to the Pretoria Convention of 1881, which was signed by British, Boers, and Swazi and recognized the independence of the Swazi under their own king. To the Swazi this was a binding charter never legally abrogated, and subsequent proclamations and conventions which denied or ignored Swazi sovereignty were described by them as "breaches of faith and broken promises." Thus the model of a precolonial, independent Swazi kingship served as a guide for the twentieth-century constitution in which Sobhuza, in his role as *Ngwenyama* of the Swazi, would also become the head of a multiracial state. But this was still in the future.

During an interim period officially termed "Self-government" authority would be vested in the hereditary Swazi king and a bicameral parliament (a House of Assembly and a Senate) elected by universal franchise and a common voters roll, but at the same time important powers of external relations, internal defense, and rights over employment conditions of civil servants were to be reserved to the queen's commissioner. Explicit recognition was again given to the SNC and its status and powers relating to Swazi law and custom and control of Swazi national land. The *Ncwala* and the *emabutfo* were mentioned specifically.

This complex constitutional document, published officially in siSwati and in English, was being discussed when I arrived in Swaziland in August 1966 to study the process of adaptation of an African monarchy to recent political innovations. Many of the objections against the "imposed constitution" of 1963 had been removed. The *Ngwenyama* was recognized by Whites as well as Swazi as king of the country, and former British crown land as well as Swazi nation land was to be transferred to him in trust for the Swazi nation. Only one major issue was holding up the final draft of the independence constitution, an issue ostensibly centered in control of rights to minerals and mineral royalties but fundamentally revealing the subtle distinction between the British interpretation of the role of a king and the Swazi concept of kingship.

Approaching the *Ngwenyama* as a British-style constitutional monarch, control over mineral assets could correctly be vested in him, but he would be obliged to act on advice of the cabinet, representing the elected parliament. But from the traditional Swazi viewpoint, rights to minerals, like rights to land, should be vested in the *Ngwenyama*, who would then appoint his own committee, independent of cabinet control, which would allocate revenues it received in accord with what the *Ngwenyama*-in-council considered the interest of the nation.

The right to control revenue from minerals was clearly a highly controversial issue of political as well as economic importance. It brought to the fore the dilemma of integrating two political systems in a country in which, following the colonial regime, wealth and special technical skills were still largely monopolized by Whites, many of whom were not citizens of Swaziland. The reluctance of the British to accept the Swazi viewpoint was interpreted by the Swazi as an indication of the lack of trust in the *Ngwenyama* as head of a multiracial state. In principle, the British acknowledged the commitment of the Swazi to traditional institutions they considered significant for their future identity as an indepndent nation, but, as a colonial power, Britain was not able to reconcile these with its own economic interest or political concept of democracy. The final constitution, described by the Swazi as the Westminster Constitution, was published as an Order in Council in February 1967. It represented "the considered opinion of British legal experts." Rights over minerals would be vested in the king but controlled through Parliament, and independence was promised not later than 1969.

In the last session of Legco (February 16 to March 7 1967), members dealt with twenty-one bills relating to such vital issues as immigration, irrigation, citizenship, and education. Beneath the formalities and courtesies there were deep undercurrents of suspicion, secrecy, and conflicting cultural values. I remember that these surfaced vividly in the debates relating to the siting of Swaziland's first House of Parliament. The building was to be Britain's parting gift, a symbol of Swaziland's new status. Francis Lloyd had appointed a committee, chaired by the Chief Government Secretary, Athel Long, to select the site and the plans. British officials considered that the buildings would be, and should be, at the present administrative capital, Mbabane—a modern town. Swazi members, including Prince Makhosini, informed the committee that the Swazi wanted Parliament to be in the ambiance of Lobamba on land allocated (in 1957) by the *Ngwenyama* for national purposes. The British did not treat this seriously and chose a site on the Mbabane hill, had plans drawn, and incurred architectural expenses. When the matter came before the full Legislative Council, several Swazi members refused to accept the committee's decision, resting their argument on sentiment and historical association. "To the amazement" of the Chief Secretary as chairman, one member of Legco went so far as to deny all previous knowledge of the issue. Exchanges were charged with bitterness and personal animosity. In the end Prince Makhosini produced his own version, which contradicted that of the Chief Secretary. "Obviously," one member said, "we have two factual statements, neither of which bears much relationship to the other." The Legco majority condemned the chairman of the committee and overruled his decision. Parliament of the independent kingdom of Swaziland would be sited at Lobamba.

Elections of members of Parliament were set for April 19 and 20, 1967. This time only four parties were registered: the INM, the NNLC, the SPP, and the Swaziland United Front (SUF), a weak alliance of different factions. The INM and the NNLC were able to put forward the full number of candidates, the other two, eight, and seven respectively. The USA had virtually disintegrated after the total rejection by the INM majority of a motion by the USA members in Legco to give South Africans living in Swaziland the right to vote beyond a deadline set by the British. Since all voters were now registered on a common roll, the INM no longer needed an organized diplomatic alliance with Whites. While there was little doubt of an INM victory, the NNLC hoped to win several seats. But the country was divided into eight three-member constituencies. The NNLC had requested a division into sixty one-member (one-man–one-vote) constituencies. The effective concentration of their supporters in urban centers was diminished by the broader boundaries, whereas the INM retained a national network. Moreover, the NNLC had been weakened by internal quarreling and public resignations.

Two weeks before the election, the king addressed representatives of business and industry at the office of the SNC and told them that he had heard there was fear that their future security in Swaziland was in jeopardy. He pointed out that race tensions existed and could not be ignored, since they were played upon by irresponsible politicians. "I would like everyone to ask himself," he continued, "am I an asset or am I a liability to Swaziland? If your answer is an 'asset,' there lies your security. Everyone who is good for the country is welcomed."

Eighty percent of registered voters came to the polls. The INM received 79.4 percent of the votes; among the winning candidates were two former defeated leaders of the SDP. In only one constituency, where Dr. Zwane was an NNLC candidate, was voting close: 11,266 for the INM and 10,242 for the NNLC. This constituency had the highest percentage of foreign-born Africans and also the lowest number of Swazi actually born in the district. The Swazi were mainly employed on two sugar-growing complexes, with no immediate ties to adjacent rural areas. The NNLC had won 20.2 percent of all votes, but the INM was nevertheless still able to fill every seat. Again the political leaders protested against the limited number of constituencies and the absence of proportional representation, and attempted to challenge the vote in certain areas and to press charges against some of the candidates. But their efforts were in vain. On the basis of a general election Swaziland became, in effect, a one-party state under a hereditary monarchy.

On April 24, 1967, the *Ngwenyama* signed an agreement with the British which changed the status of Swaziland from that of a colony to that of a protected state. And on the following day, before a crowd of some 20,000, Sobhuza was officially installed as King of Swaziland. The day was named *Somhlolo* Day—a new annual public holiday commemorating Sobhuza's namesake Sobhuza I, statesman and strategist, better known as *Somhlolo* (Worker of Wonders), who had seen in a vision the coming of Whites and had advised his people never to shed their blood. In his address, he summed up his position:

> It is the tradition of all African kings that their kings are leaders as well as kings. This is also true of Swaziland. Now, rightly or wrongly, some people have mistaken this dual capacity as a dictatorship. I would like to assure you here and now that in our kingdom the king both leads and is led by his people. I am my people's mouthpiece.

The flag of the British had been lowered and the flag of the new Kingdom of Swaziland was raised on the plain of Lobamba, from which, twenty-five years earlier, Sobhuza had sent Swazi troops to fight alongside the British, to remind them of past promises made in the reign of his grandfather.

Sobhuza wore the unassuming everyday dress of his age regiment but a few bright red feathers of the lourie in his hair showed his royal birth, and two long, strong feathers of the thunderbird showed his unique position among the princes. On the platform were dignitaries of both governments: the *ndvuna* (governor) of Lobamba, a couple of senior princes, and, on the British side, the queen's commissioner and his deputy, the chief justice, three appeal court judges, the attorney general, the master of the high court, and the commissioner of police.

In the final scene Sobhuza stood alone to take the salute. Thousands of chanting warriors loped past, their shields raised above their heads, their eyes averted in deference, and then some hundred Western-trained police marched by, saluting and looking directly at him. When the ceremony was over, the earlier protocol of departure was reversed, and instead of the representative of the British government taking precedence, the car of the *Ngwenyama* led the way, followed by the car with the *Ndlovukazi*, and then the British queen's commissioner.

LIMBO PERIOD OF "SELF-GOVERNMENT"

Sobhuza had still to appoint six additional members to the Assembly and six to the Senate. Since the INM now held every elected seat, these appointments were of less concern to the Swazi majority than to the Whites, who regarded this as a test of the king's good faith and an indication of their own future. They were reassured when he included four Whites among his appointments to the House of Assembly. To his senators, elected by the House, he added a Swazi woman welfare worker, three Swazi men—a lawyer, a minister, and a rural development officer— and two Whites, one of them Carl Todd. Sobhuza had thought about these appointments for some time but had kept his ideas so much to himself that the final list came as a pleasant surprise to those he selected and a great disappointment to others who had anticipated their own selection. The names did not tally with those published in the South African press, which had included some of the extreme members of the USA. From the parliamentarians Sobhuza now selected his cabinet, with Prince Makhosini as prime minister. All were Swazi except for Leo Lovell, a South African-trained lawyer, a liberal in his politics and former member of the South African Labor party. He had settled in Swaziland in 1961, and though he had not joined any of the local political parties he openly criticized racist trends in the country. On independence, Sobhuza appointed him minister of finance, commerce, and industry.

Sobhuza had expressed his desire to include Dr. Zwane as one of his appointees in a government which he hoped would draw together all sections of the people. But Dr. Zwane refused to accept an appointment as an individual; instead he suggested a coalition in which he would be recognized as leader of an opposition party. This suggestion was refused, and he continued to appeal to international organizations, protesting the "fraudulent constitution" and calling for a new election. At the same time, he expressed his loyalty to Sobhuza and regularly attended the *Ncwala*, albeit in Western clothes.

There were difficulties inherent in the conditions imposed during self-government, and it had come as a great shock to learn at the last meeting of Legco that every permanent secretary would be a British expatriate, with Swazi only in super-numerary posts. The British did not seem prepared to hurry the process of localiza-tion and the Swazi were not prepared to wait.

Sobhuza, as king, attended the official opening of Swaziland's first parliament on July 7, 1967 dressed for the occasion with Western formality. The ceremony was modeled on that of the British, a ceremony developed in the seventeenth century to signify the supremacy of the elected representatives of the people over the arbitrary actions of an individual king. The president of the Senate escorted the King to the door of the House and left him there with the Speaker, while the usher announced "Mister Speaker, King Sobhuza II of Swaziland seeks admission." Came the reply: "Let His Majesty, King Sobhuza II King of Swaziland be admitted."

In his Speech from the Throne Sobhuza expressed his appreciation for "the unique constitutional arrangement," adding that "My government is already looking forward to further constitutional advancement and is therefore proposing that Swaziland be granted independence in September 1968." This speech was followed by a request from the Swazi parliament, and on November 3 the British government gave its consent. British officials in the country expressed their dis-appointment, arguing that there were as yet too few Swazi capable of filling the positions necessary for running a modern government. The Swazi replied that the fault lay with the British for their reluctance, over the long period of coloniza-tion, to educate and train the necessary personnel.

New proposals for the final independence constitution were drawn up by the cabinet and presented by the prime minister on January 27, 1968, to the House of Assembly and then to the Senate. But, at the same time, he indicated that there were still some unresolved grievances relating particularly to minerals and land. It seems that Leo Lovell as minister of finance had played a leading role in formulating a compromise under which minerals would be vested in the king, in trust for the nation; but the king would be advised by a Mineral Committee consisting of the commissioner of mines, a government official, and four or six members, half of whom would be appointed by Sobhuza as *Ngwenyama* of the Swazi, in consultation with the SNC, and half by him as King of Swaziland acting on the advice of the cabinet. When the prime minister presented this motion, he dwelt on the difficulty experienced by the cabinet in reaching this compromise between two "irreconcilable views." The reaction was hostile and the discussion acrimonious. The first-speaker from the floor bluntly condemned "the nerve, the temerity, and audacity to grant power to the cabinet to exercise control over Swazi private property, which is under the trusteeship of the *Ngwenyama*." He therefore proposed as "an amendment" returning to the *Ngwenyama*-in-Libandla [SNC] the right to appoint all members of the Minerals Commission. When the vote was finally taken, this amendment was carried by twenty-one to nine. The following day the prime minister presented the same address to the Senate. The reaction was almost identical. This time the amendment was passed by eight votes to four. While no White in either house had voted for the amendment, the prime minister himself went against the compromise reached by his own cabinet and expressed himself in favor of the amendment. Sobhuza supported him on the ground that a person in authority must be advised by the council and the people who had given him his position.

The Secretary of State for Commonwealth Affairs convened another conference in London to finalize the independence constitution. The Swaziland delegation, led by the prime minister, included the minister of finance and four Swazi cabinet members. The view of the local British officials was presented by the queen's commissioner, the attorney general, and the secretary to the cabinet. Though there was already a framework of agreement, and most of the proposals were accepted with minor modifications and limited opposition, there was again a direct confrontation on the control of minerals and land. The British expressed regret that their unilateral proposals on minerals, embodied in the existing constitution, were unacceptable, and tried to persuade the Swazi representatives to revert at least to the compromise accepted by the cabinet and submitted by the Prime Minister to Parliament. But the prime minister insisted that now only the amendment granting control to the *Ngwenyama* and the committee chosen by him, independent of the cabinet, had the full support of Parliament. He also informed the conference that there was already in draft a new Swazi National Fund, to be managed by the committee appointed by the *Ngwenyama*, into which mineral royalties would be paid for the general welfare of the Swazi nation. The British government, "recognizing the strong feelings held in Swaziland on this subject," finally agreed that the independence constitution would place control over minerals in the hands of Sobhuza as *Ngwenyama*-in-council rather than of Sobhuza as head of a nonracial state obliged to act on the advice of a cabinet linked to an elected parliament.

Before returning to Swaziland Makhosini, acting on instructions from Sobhuza, also raised the land issue (a perpetual grievance), though it was not on the official agenda. Forty-three percent of the country was still in the hands of Whites. Much of it was undeveloped. Sobhuza's own people needed land for food. Swazi areas were congested, farm tenants were insecure, and the grievance of concessions was kept alive by the peasants' discontent. One of the great fears of Whites was that land they had bought would be expropriated after independence. Sobhuza recognized their fears, but pointed out that since the time of his grandmother the Swazi had been buying back their own land, often at inflated prices. Now his approach was different. He placed the onus on Britain and, citing as precedent the British purchase of the white-owned highlands in Kenya for African use, suggested that the United Kingdom do the same for the Swazi. The delegates claimed compensation for the alienation of land under the Partition Proclamation of 1907, and for a further 500,000 acres which had been sold by the British to finance its administration of the country. The British rejected this claim, but suggested that a practical way of tackling what they acknowledged as a serious problem might be for the Swaziland government to include suitable land-settlement schemes in the development plans they were now formulating. The Swaziland delegation stated that they claimed the restoration of the land as a right, and that it was an issue separate from any development aid program.

Before leaving London, Makhosini expressed himself rather frankly at a press conference, saying that it was as if the British government had planted a time bomb in Swaziland and were giving independence before the bomb exploded.

However, the granting of independence would not be delayed. Makhosini and a small delegation returned in July for further discussions. The approach of the Swazi was more diplomatic this time, and Britain agreed to consider more detailed proposals on land shortage and land use and to send a team of experts to examine the situation.

The constitutional battle was over. Sobhuza had proved his political skill and leadership in his dealings with three alien forces—white settlers, Western-oriented politicians, and a paternalist colonial power.

INDEPENDENCE CELEBRATIONS

Independence would be celebrated in a stadium near the Lobamba site chosen by the Swazi for the House of Parliament. Sobhuza named it Somhlolo Stadium. The list of guests was impressive. Official representatives came from forty-two countries, rich and poor, large and small, developed and developing, from all over the world—Europe, the Middle East, Asia, America—as well as Africa. The largest delegation was from Great Britain, followed by South Africa, Portugal, and the United States. Politically they ranged from extreme right to moderate left. Communist countries were excluded since at that time all flights into Swaziland came through South Africa. Individual VIPs included leading industrialists, churchmen, judges, farmers, lawyers, and scholars. Among Sobhuza's few personal guests on the public list, and the only other king, was King Moshoeshoe of Lesotho. Then there was another circle, less official and less conspicuous, of chiefs, kin, priests, and friends who lived across the border in South Africa. And finally, but by no means least important, thousands of Sobhuza's loyal subjects, who were essential witnesses and participants.

Unlike the traditional rituals which followed the rhythm of nature, Independence celebrations were planned by the written calender and, especially for the main day, by the minute hands of the clock. Events reflected the complex interaction of Western and Swazi traditions, but since the British were already experienced in independence celebrations, they provided the more formal blueprint, while the Swazi contributed the uniqueness of their culture. Public programmed events began on August 31 with the opening of the Swazi Independence Exhibition in the Manzini showgrounds and ended on September 8 with a national day of prayer. For those who so wished, there was the alternative of a polo match or a visit to the iron-ore mine that had commenced production in 1964 and by 1968 had outstripped all other Swazi mineral exports, including asbestos.

In a pre-independence meeting with the SNC, Sobhuza had re-emphasized two aspects of Independence. One was joy in the rebirth of the nation, the other the struggles that lay ahead to make independence meaningful. He instructed the age-regiments to wear full traditional battle dress—the costume and regalia of the main day of *Ncwala*. Following custom, all Swazi were ordered to "throw off the ropes of mourning." It was a day for strength and rejoicing, hence public display of personal bereavement was prohibited.

According to the British model, the post of queen's commissioner would come to an end at independence, the present incumbent would leave before the celebrations, and British government interests in Swaziland would be represented by the office of a high commissioner. A high-ranking official from London, the Secretary of State for Commonwealth Affairs, would hand over the documents of independence, and the British royal family would be represented in all social activities by the Duke of Kent, cousin of Queen Elizabeth and Prince Philip and son of Princess Marina of Greece. The program was already in print when news came that Princess Marina had died. The inner council wrote to the queen's commissioner that "it would be out of Swazi custom to receive a royal guest soon after a bereavement." It was left to the British to find a suitable substitute. At this short notice, the queen's commissioner was selected, and he was told to remain until after independence. For the rest the program would stand.

September 6, 1968, the day of independence, was an unforgettable experience. The stadium, marked by flags of the different countries, was alive with choirs singing, schoolchildren performing acrobatics and gymnastics, hospital nurses and government officials parading in full uniform, the police band playing loudly, Swazi maidens in traditional short beaded skirts dancing and chanting, thousands of Swazi warriors in *Ncwala* costume in the background, and, close by, aging but

Sobhuza II, Ngwenyama and King of Swaziland with Sir Francis Lloyd, the last representative of the Colonial Government prior to Independence. Both in full traditional regalia, 1968.

proud veterans of World War II in their old army uniforms. The air was crystal clear, and beyond the stadium rose the majestic Mdimba mountains, associated with memories of old battles and sacred burial caves of royalty.

People arrived in their brightest and finest: As in all Swazi national rituals, individual display was merged with group identity. The actors included the audience. Present in the crowd were prominent Westernized Swazi in traditional clothing. Rows of plumed warriors faced the grandstand. The queens and princesses in their traditionally distinctive dress were strikingly beautiful as they walked single file to their appointed seats, heralded by bards.

The arrival of notables, announced by loudspeaker, was a magnificent show of protocol and status. Every last detail, from the type of limousine they arrived in and the number of their escorts to the ceremonial seating in the royal stand reflected an official hierarchy of prestige and rank. Sobhuza's entry, in full *Ncwala* costume, and the playing of the new Swazi national anthem set the stage for the transfer of sovereignty.

At high noon, under a blazing sun, George Thomson, British Secretary for Commonwealth Affairs, handed "His Majesty, King Sobhuza II" the "Articles of Independence." The formal transfer and accompanying speeches acknowledging the new relationship between Swaziland and Great Britain were solemn but rather mundane. Then unexpectedly the stadium rang with the haunting singing of the traditional epic anthem, *Inqabakanqofula* (The Fortress of Nqofula). The king, accompanied by the prime minister, left the grandstand to join the regiments in their dance. The royal queens and princesses responded and danced back and forth in joyous homage. In the final movement, the warriors crouched behind their shields, leapt forward in unison, then raised their shields high in triumph. It was superb, euphoric, an African ballet royal, temporarily transforming a Western-designed political ceremony into a sacred ritual, rich in allusion and associations.

But how long can euphoria last? It is a truism that the future of a country depends on its leadership, and in a monarchy the position of the king is crucial. By 1968 at independence, Sobhuza held at least four different positions. First, he was head of the state of Swaziland as a territorial entity with a racially and culturally diversified population. Second, he was trustee of Swazi national land and controller of mineral revenue in an economy dependent on foreign investment. Third, he was the recognized founder of the political party in power. And, finally, he was *Ngwenyama,* priest-king of the Swazi in a country of competing religions. He had emerged as a major strategist in the arena of modern politics. The king, rather than the kingship, became hedged with divinity, a process the reverse of the routinization of charisma—a hereditary monarch appeared to have successfully embellished a declining office by the charisma of his personality. But what of the future? What would independence bring?

9 / Independence: dream or reality:
1968-1973

Independence is an elusive concept, an ideal for which people throughout the world have been prepared to fight, to die, and to kill. In Swaziland, the British described their role as "granting independence"; the Swazi spoke of "regaining freedom." Legally, independence is a formal transfer of sovereignty from an external power to internal leadership. Freedom has no legal formula. In Swaziland, nominal independence was achieved without bloodshed largely through Sobhuza's diplomatic leadership. Freedom was more difficult to win. In terms of action, the official recognition of independence was not a finale, but a major event projecting Swaziland and the Swazi into new political orbits and more diverse connections, both external and internal. Paradoxically, independence made the Swazi more dependent on the rest of the world.

THE NEW ELITE

Independence gave rise to a Swazi political elite that would be more numerous, conspicuous, and competitive than the outgoing British. It would involve members of the royal family, chiefs, and prominent officials of the traditional structure competing with the new elite of parliamentarians, top-ranking civil servants, and Western-oriented entrepreneurs. It was clear that the number of candidates would exceed the number of available coveted positions.

In the traditional hierarchical system, rank by clan and lineage gave access to major resources of wealth and privilege within the precapitalist context of a predominantly subsistence economy. In the early colonial period, the dominant cleavage was along the visible line of color expressed in a conflict for control of land and minerals. Literally and metaphorically the ground was prepared for the emergence of class differences in a racial context. Toward the end of the colonial period, during the meetings of the first constitutional committee, a general law prohibiting racial discrimination helped open new developments for the Swazi as a nation and a wider range of opportunities for Western-educated Africans. But legislation alone did not remove deeply entrenched inequalities, and class divisions developed within racial categories. Swaziland provides a classic example of the interaction of race, ethnicity, class, and nationalism—four overlapping but analytically distinct factors—reflected in the character of the ruling elite.

Until the period of rising nationalism, it had been assumed that the population was racially divided, but also that all the Africans were Swazi, speaking one language and recognizing Sobhuza as their leader. By the time of independence, it was clear that the true position was not so simple. The total population, estimated as 400,300, was classified into three racial categories: Africans, Europeans, and Eur-Africans or Coloreds (people of mixed race). Roughly 90 percent of the Africans, 20 percent of the Europeans, and 70 percent of the Eur-Africans were born in Swaziland. But within these groups, there were significant differences in national loyalty and language.

While the majority of Africans born in Swaziland were identified with clans classified into the three historic time groups—true Swazi, "those found ahead," and the latecomers—incorporated under Dlamini hegemony (see page 11), there were significant numbers of non-Swazi who had settled in the country since the beginning of the century without becoming clients to Swazi chiefs and without the consent of the Swazi rulers. Some had been brought in by the colonial government—as police, teachers, hospital staff; others by settlers as domestic servants and laborers. Others had come independently to seek work or find political asylum. The British colonial government had not worried particularly about their specific ethnic or national identity as long as they registered and paid the necessary tax; and though at different periods Sobhuza had raised the question of the allegiance of "foreign Africans," it was with the opening of new opportunities that citizenship as well as race became directly related to positions of power and access to economic resources.

In 1964 the British had introduced a public service commission, an essentially British institution, to deal with appointments, promotions, and the discipline of members of the civil service. It was designed to ensure that appointments be made by a body aloof from the political struggle and that would base selection on individual qualification and promotion on the British model of merit, experience, and seniority. From the Swazi viewpoint, this approach had resulted in the appointment of too many non-Swazi (mainly South African political refugees) to new positions and coveted scholarships, and in preferential treatment of expatriates (the new term applied to British civil servants). A report on localization and training in Swaziland was requested from J. O. Udoji, a highly respected judge from Nigeria appointed to the task by the cabinet. It revealed the extent to which in 1969 key positions were still held by expatriates and it also contained recommendations designed to develop a national civil service.

On the basis of his experience of other African countries, Udoji pointed out the need to ensure the appointment to the commission of people who were not only mature, responsible, of good reputation and education, but whose sympathies with the aims and aspirations of the government also would not be in doubt. Under the independence constitution, appointments were to be made by the king on the advice of a newly constituted judicial service commission, an impartial and independent body. A wide range of people, including parliamentarians and civil servants, were specifically excluded from appointment to the public service commission on the grounds of political involvement, but in a small country like

Swaziland, people of the required quality were "either in Parliament or in the civil service." Udoji also suggested that more important than constitutional reform and the introduction of appropriate localization machinery was the need for attitudinal reform on the part of some expatriates who did not seem to have had any experience in working in a "staff political atmosphere."

The expressed policy of government was "to localize as rapidly as possible without lowering standards." But localization was being differently interpreted. Sobhuza's ideal was to develop a single modern nation that would be characteristically African in culture and nonracist in demographic composition. He spoke of "black Swazi and white Swazi" and stated that "any person irrespective of color or creed who had genuinely become a citizen of this country and identified with us is a Swazi." He fully accepted as black Swazi those non-Swazi Africans who had made Swaziland their home and had contributed or were still contributing valued services to his people, especially in the field of education and other professional knowledge. He sent emissaries to educated Swazi living in South Africa and abroad and invited non-Swazi whom he trusted into his country. They were a relatively small but influential group of people, and the more conservative and ambitious established Swazi lumped them with a number of opportunists and entrepreneurs who claimed Swazi citizenship for their individual benefit. These people were described as *Emaswati entsambama* (Swazi-of-the-late-afternoon), a term that reflected a new period in Swazi national development.

Sobhuza himself also recognized as his true subjects Whites and Eur-Africans who had availed themselves of the opportunity of registering through chiefs or becoming Swazi citizens by naturalization based on qualification of residence and affirmation of loyalty stipulated in the independence constitution. In fact, very few Whites born in Swaziland had become Swazi citizens. The majority of Whites in public service were expatriates, and the unexpected and apparently arbitrary termination of contracts of some senior civil servants appeared to many Whites a racial threat. While Sobhuza advocated that the few Whites and Eur-Africans granted Swazi citizenship receive positions of responsibility, many Swazi saw Whites in government as competitors for a limited number of highly paid positions. White settlers—traders, farmers, missionaries, managers, professionals, who retained their previous citizenship—were treated as individuals whose future security depended on the role they played in helping Swazi development. Localization in the private sector was made part of government policy.

To many Swazi in and out of government, localization was not Africanization, nor was it a sharing with the Whites. It was the tangible reward of independence and the exclusive monopoly of the "true Swazi". Moreover, even among the Swazi, traditional criteria of differentiation continued. Clanship (family), national service, and loyalty were considered legitimate factors in political appointments, and group identity overruled individual qualifications. Individuals without aristocratic connections complained that they were automatically disqualified.

Increasing efforts to define a Swazi resulted in a narrowing of those in control. There was increasing competition between the educated commoners and the royals, who were only beginning to recognize the necessity of Western education to secure their position as leaders. Sobhuza had always stressed the need for his own children to be school-educated, but facilities were limited and the tradition of book learning was not established. The educated elites were drawn mainly from the children of converts to Christianity. By the time of independence, attitudes had changed and princes became more eager to receive education (without conversion to any particular church). Accepting the custom that mothers were mainly responsible for the raising of children, a number of royals sought as wives (though not necessarily as main wives) school-educated women, nurses, and teachers. Because of the continued influence of royalty, nonroyal educated elites were suitors for the king's daughters. Lowly birth was a handicap, and high birth gave one a head start on the narrow road of upward mobility.

Despite the establishment of additional training centers, crash courses, and new educational directions emphasizing science, technology, and other "practical" subjects, there were rumblings that localization was going ahead too rapidly for efficiency or for morale. There was a dreadful shortage of well-trained Swazi teachers. Volunteers from England and from America were welcomed, but many of them were also unqualified, and communication between them and the locals was not always satisfactory. Peace Corps volunteers who attempted to "go Swazi" by wearing beads and no shoes were appreciated by neither the elites nor the traditionalists.

The quality of Swazi life was being changed radically by the extension of large- and small-scale capitalist enterprises and investments associated with an influx of representatives from different countries (Britain, the United States, Germany, Denmark, Canada, Israel, Taiwan, the Republic of China, Portugal) and multinational and international organizations. "Experts" of varying efficiency and conversant mainly in their own language were often recruited from outside for jobs that generally carried salaries grossly disporportionate to indigenous scales and with living standards much higher than their skills would command in their own countries.

With increasing modernization the number of civil servants, the political bureaucracy, multiplied. The salaries of ministers and members of parliament were out of proportion to those of the rest of the civil service.

Class distinctions became more marked, with housing and cars conspicuous status symbols. When the post of queen's commissioner was replaced by a high commissioner, the British built an elaborate house for its new representative, the Swazi prime minister moved into the vacated residency while a new, somewhat smaller house was built nearby for the deputy prime minister. Ministers and deputies were allotted the better houses previously occupied by British civil servants in the urban areas. The growing staff of clerks, messengers, drivers, mechanics, and service people lived mainly in the peripheral townships which were less serviced and more congested.

YOU CAN'T EAT INDEPENDENCE

Swazi leaders realized that political authority without the backing of economic power was frustrating and meaningless. One old councilor commented, "You can't eat independence." Experts had been brought in mainly to help the Swazi gain the economic benefits of their new political status. The first postindependence development plan, published in 1969, aimed primarily at "improving the living conditions of the masses." It was framed within the restrictions of the national budget, without utopian expectations, and stated clearly that despite major developments in mining, industry, and commerce, Swaziland would remain for the foreseeable future a predominantly agricultural country in which the majority of the labor force would depend on the cultivation of the soil for its livelihood.

Expansion had taken place in limited sectors of the economy and in limited areas of the country without sufficient improvement in the living conditions of the majority. Per capita income in 1966–1967 was about $170 per annum. Though this was higher than in most countries south of the Sahara, there was a marked contrast in standards of living between the modern and traditional sectors, and a similar distinction between modern and traditional land use.

The dual structure, rooted in the Land Concession Proclamation of 1907, still distorted the national economy of the independent kingdom. Some 45 percent of the total area was mostly owned by non-Swazi under freehold title. Pressure on Swazi national land had increased, but agricultural technology had not kept pace. In the countryside and in the developed urban areas, the cost of land had rocketed beyond the means but not the legitimate aspirations of the rising black middle class. Some Swazi suggested outright confiscation of white farms; others advised that Swazi already on white farms refuse to move if evicted by landlords. Sobhuza rejected both these approaches; he and his council decided instead that every future land transaction involving non-Swazi be scrutinized by a special board appointed by the king and independent of the courts of law. It would decide whether the particular transaction would help the people and the country as a whole or serve only the interests of outsiders. It was with this aim in view that the Land Speculation Bill was introduced. The government specified that it aimed to achieve maximum Swazi participation without alienating foreign investors and genuine expatriate farmers who were seen to have a continuing role to play in the country's development.

The announcement of the bill created a temporary panic in the white community and led to another open disagreement between Prince Makhosini as prime minister and Leo Lovell as minister of finance. The bill was introduced by the minister of agriculture under a certificate of urgency while the finance minister and two Swazi members of cabinet known to be sympathetic to the private sector were in the United States negotiating a loan from the World Bank. By the time they returned, the bill had passed its first reading in both houses. Whereupon the minister of finance, though not a member of the Senate, went to a Senate meeting and protested against the undue haste, criticized the drafting, and suggested an amendment.

The following day, the prime minster came in person to the Senate, denounced the minister of finance for flouting the principle of collective responsibility of the cabinet, refuted his charge of undue haste, and concluded "To me, Mr. President, all his Majesty's Ministers are useful, but none of them is indispensable." The original bill was unanimously passed by both houses on December 16, 1971.

The king gave the bill his assent in February after the long break for *Ncwala*. It became law only in December 1972, by which time further legal opinions had been obtained, clauses were amended, warning to speculators had been given, and guarantees to genuine investors spelled out. The banks had recovered from their initial nervous reaction and were again prepared to grant loans and receive mortgages on landed property. The prime minister described the conflict as "a storm in a tea cup." He had not removed the minister of finance, nor had the minister resigned. Sobhuza's choice of the specific members, white and black, to the two boards (a lower board and a board of appeal) constituted under the Land Speculation Control Act, reassured many Whites of his determination not to expropriate or exclude non-Swazi genuinely interested in development and not in speculation for private profit.

The transfer of land to private individuals and corporations affected the Swazi middle class more than the peasant. Discussions with the British on additional land for the nation continued as a separate issue. The British finally agreed to grant a large sum of money to buy land for settlement schemes, but at the same time stipulated conditions of control and development the Swazi government considered derogated their national independence and dignity. The purchase was delayed but negotiations continued.

In the meantime Sobhuza had developed his own policy of economic and social development. On August 19, 1968 (in the very last period of self-government), he had registered by Royal Charter the national fund known as Tibiyo Taka Ngwane (the minerals of Ngwane). This was the fund mentioned on page 108 into which all mineral royalties were vested in Sobhuza with the rights of a traditional African king. Tibiyo was charged with the task of assisting the government in its efforts to further the interests of "the people of Swaziland," and specifically to promote harmonious relations between the different races, to advance the material welfare and education of the Swazi people, and at the same time "to support customs and traditional institutions in such a way as to prevent the disillusionment and instability which has followed the rapid breakdown of tradition in different parts of the world." One of Tibiyo's first projects was a modest land-purchase program and the allocation of a limited amount of money to fund scholarships for the higher education of royals. Over the years, Tibiyo developed subsidiary organizations and diversified its interests and investments, becoming the single most powerful economic organization in the country. It was controlled by the king independent of government, separate from the treasury, and not accountable to Parliament or to the public for its expenditures.

The expansion of Tibiyo reflected the entrepreneurial ability of the director (Sishayi Nxumalo) and the committee appointed by the king. No outsider knew or dared to inquire to what extent, if any, the property vested in the king in trust for the nation was distinguished from his own personal and private resources. But the king's own lifestyle continued to be simple and unostentatious.

To the outsider it appeared that there was both stability and progress. Participation of the Swazi as a group was increasing. The country was developing a firm, modern infrastructure, a network of good roads, and the extension of irrigation and electricity. New industries (particularly since 1964) were being efficiently and profitably run. But in every field, the division between the haves and have-nots reflected the continuation of early discrimination. Most of the Swazi were have-nots living off the land or selling their labor to Whites, so the rural districts were periodically drained of active manpower. The Swazi authorities were well aware of this.

The growth of a Swazi middle class, recruited from the better-paid upper echelons of government, was being encouraged by white businessmen. Swazi were able to obtain licenses for liquor, for the lucrative and desirable transport businesses, and as general dealers; many of them, however, had little capital or experience. Under Sobhuza's patronage a cooperative organization, the Commercial Emadoda, was established to protect the small Swazi trader from competition by non-Swazi in Swazi areas, but it had a difficult and checkered career. In 1970 the Swaziland government set up SEDCO, a small-enterprise development corporation to help the small businessman. Big business was in the hands of individual Whites and of large private and multinational corporations, such as the Commonwealth Development Corporation, Peak Timbers, Lonhro, Coca-Cola, Libby, Heinrich Breweries, and Swaki, with investments in forestry, minerals, canned foods and drinks, petroleum, agricultural tools, and fertilizers. It was in such ventures that Sobhuza wanted the Swazi nation to have a share through Tibiyo. He saw this as the means by which the Swazi would benefit from external and private investments and realize full independence. He explained to me that his reason for establishing in 1971 the National Industrial Development Corporation as an autonomous, statutory body was to promote and assist private investments in industry, commerce, agriculture, and mining and provide employment opportunities, with adequate pay, for the growing Swazi labor force. Public and private enter-

Rural National Development Projects, 1973.

prises would be encouraged, not forced, to train Swazi personnel in every field of development. For Sobhuza development did not mean simply more money, more Western goods, and more efficient technology. His was a broader humanist concept of using material goods for advancing personal dignity and national pride. "Development" was based on his dream of an economic empire that would benefit all segments of his people. It was an idealistic dream—naive, perhaps Quixotic, but not Machiavellian.

FOREIGN RELATIONS

Immediately after independence, Swaziland became a member of the British Commonwealth, the Organization of African Unity, and the United Nations and subsequently joined the World Bank and the International Monetary Fund. But Swaziland remained geographically encapsulated between the racist Republic of South Africa and the Portuguese territory of Mozambique, where the struggle for liberation was being fought. Without the direct protection of the British, Swaziland had become more vulnerable to political disturbances and actual violence from outside. The prime minister, enunciating the new Swazi foreign policy, made explicit that his government was "constrained by geographic and economic circumstances to follow a policy of enlightened self-interest, relying upon a maximum of wisdom and a minimum of heroics. . . . It would maintain a policy of non-intervention in the internal affairs of other states since it was in no position to enter the lists of international power politics in the spirit of a medieval crusade."

By this time, South Africa had abandoned the idea of trying to incorporate Swaziland. Instead, it directed its policies to winning the confidence of the Swazi government by indicating and emphasizing its recognition of traditional African cultures, while at the same time retaining its influence over Swaziland's developing economy. In 1969, Swaziland, with Botswana and Lesotho (which had gained their independence in 1966) jointly exerted pressure on South Africa to renegotiate the Customs Unions Agreement entered into in 1910. Swaziland was the main beneficiary, and for the first time since the colonial era was able to balance its current budget and enter into bilateral trade agreements with states outside the continent. Sobhuza's government, seeking to loosen its economic dependence on South Africa, established a remarkably wide range of trade relations with other nations in Africa (Zambia, Kenya, Uganda, Nigeria, Tanzania, Malawi) and elsewhere (the United Kingdom, the United States, the Republic of China, France, Sweden, The Netherlands, Norway, West Germany, Portugal, Canada, South Korea, Israel). But 90 percent of its imports were still from South Africa, and South Africans were using Swaziland as a base for establishing subsidiary companies to extend trade into African countries hostile to South Africa's *apartheid* system.

Swaziland's economic involvement with South Africa was demonstrated by its decision to have an integrated electric power system and its realization of the importance of a railway link to South Africa as well as to the harbor of Lourenço Marques—later Maputo—in Mozambique. In March 1972, the prime minister of Swaziland met the prime minister of South Africa in Capetown to discuss matters of mutual interest. Though Swaziland had established its own currency and postage stamps, credit and savings banks, it was still bound to the economy of South Africa and largely dependent on external aid from the United Kingdom.

The government of Swaziland was continuously trying to separate its political principles from economic necessity. But it always made the point that change should be by peaceful effort, negotiation, and discussion. Sobhuza once described his policy as "dedication to the right of self-determination and human dignity; we do not beg, we ask as human beings, speaking to other human beings"—but added typically, "we must be prepared to defend ourselves against violations of our rights."

In international affairs, Swaziland followed a policy of nonalignment but voted most frequently with the noncommunist group. It went contrary to the majority of African countries in maintaining friendship with Israel and Taiwan. Sobhuza's spokesmen at the United Nations expressed their support of these countries and, in the case of Taiwan, voted with the minority against the Albanian resolution that led to the admission of the People's Republic of China and the expulsion of Taiwan.

POSTINDEPENDENCE: TENSIONS AND CONTRADICTIONS

As in many countries, the removal of the colonial masters released individual ambitions submerged in the common struggle for independence and opened, particularly for government officials, temptations and opportunities for personal aggrandizement. The early harmonious cooperation in the government was disturbed by differences of opinion in the cabinet and in the inner council of the Swaziland National Council on a variety of issues related to development, appointments, salaries of staff, investments, licenses, and citizenship as well as land policy. In July 1971 there had been a major reshuffle of ministers and senior civil servants. Some of the more conscientious complained of a general apathy, a lack of courtesy, a general frustration, and an absence of control.

Despite overlapping membership, there were structural tensions between the traditional councils, described in Chapter 3, and the latest Westminster institution, parliament, described in Chapter 8. Their members met at different times and separate places. The inner council, the liqoqo, met privately and generally with the king at his residence. The Swazi National Council (the *libandla* laka Ngwane), which included in addition to all Swazi-born citizens non-Swazi adults who had been accepted through the traditional process of allegiance, met either at an office built by the colonial government or, when addressed by the king, in the *sibaya* at Lobamba. Members of parliament assembled in the House of Parliament, to which the king came only for the opening or closing session or for very particular occasions. At a public meeting in 1972 Sobhuza stated "Parliament is not the Nation." To him, parliament and the Swazi National Council were separate channels of control but neither could nor should function adequately without the support of the other. However, on another occasion, he said that the greater authority was vested in parliament and the secretary of the Swazi National Council was no longer entitled to sign himself secretary of the Swazi nation. Advisers closest to the king were not necessarily members of cabinet or parliament, but included senior princes, chiefs, and governors of royal villages whom he summoned when he pleased, and constituted the liqoqo described on page 36.

An increasing number of matters were dealt with by parliament and the administration without Sobhuza's knowledge. Decisions, not always acceptable to him or to councilors active in the SNC, were taken to the cabinet before he could intervene. The prime minister explained that this was often necessary because of the complexity and pressure of time in the modern world. The cabinet made decisions on public matters and then took them to the king for approval. It did not ask him first, and if he did not approve, further discussions and long delays would result.

During the colonial period it had been easier for Sobhuza to stand out and express the wishes of his people. He was their recognized mouthpiece, speaking for an oppressed section of the population. The institutions developed during the process of independence, and particularly the institution of parliament, changed his position. His information and contacts were more indirect, his obligations to different sectors more difficult to disentangle, and the process by which these obligations could be met more complicated because of the diversity of groups simultaneously putting forward contradictory claims.

Sobhuza and his people had welcomed independence, but from an early stage they found themselves confused by the Westminster constitution: "It gave with the right hand what it took away with the left." The legalistic document included a new schedule (No. 4) listing some hundred "entrenched provisions" and "specially entrenched provisions." Amendments required lengthy and elaborate procedures. When Sobhuza consulted legal experts, he received conflicting opinions and advice on such major issues as immigration, human rights, the power of parliament, and citizenship.

However, following the procedure laid down in the independence constitution of 1967, Parliament was dissolved in March 1972 and elections were set for May 1972. Sobhuza had told warriors, after their final service at the annual *Ncwala*, that they should vote; abstention would simply increase the chances of those opposed to his policies. His own opposition to the parliamentary system had not weakened. At a meeting shortly before the elections he likened political parties to "nations, each fighting a battle to be in power, each wanting to rule the other." At a farewell party he congratulated the outgoing parliamentarians—"the highly educated, the less educated, white and black"—for working together as if they were all members of one family, demonstrating that the absence of an official opposition did not stifle differences of opinion, since "every one of you knows that there has been a type of opposition which emanates from within the hearts of members. Such opposition was spontaneous, genuine, and constructive, born of facts rather than out of fear and jealousy; you did not oppose for the sake of opposing but because you had alternative ideas you strongly believed could better solve the problems put before you."

The question of citizenship was of crucial importance in registering voters. The population had become increasingly diversified and the traditional system of incorporation by acceptance of allegiance was now more complicated. Allegiance had become but one form of naturalization. Moreover, many non-Swazi had been brought in by Whites in competition with, not complementary to, the Swazi-born. Their loyalty was to their employers. Their customs, particularly their marriage customs, were different, and their kinship ties were weakened by distance. They were accused of increasing illegitimacy and crime. There was a wide range of derogatory terms describing them as aliens, transients, and thugs. Those who were prepared to *khonta* (declare allegiance) to chiefs, needed land to support them and their families but land was scarce, and some foreigners were not prepared to give Swazi chiefs the necessary respect and services.

At different times during the colonial period, Sobhuza, on behalf of his people, had seen the dangers of foreign labor, but the question became of major significance in the process of nationalization and localization and was thus associated with the controversial issue of the right to vote. The general procedure was familiar. The chief electoral officer was an experienced expatriate who had settled with his family in Swaziland and whose son was one of the few Whites given a position as a Swazi in government. There would be no changes in the boundaries and numbers of constituencies and the qualifications of voters had been stated simply to be any person who had attained the age of twenty-one and "was a Swazi citizen." But citizenship was a privilege, not a right; a commitment, not a label.

In addition to non-Swazi Africans in Swaziland who wished to become Swazi after independence, some 700,000 Africans in the Republic of South Africa were classified as Swazi. Throughout the colonial period Swazi chiefs living on the other side of the arbitrarily drawn border had requested, without success, to be reunited with their people under their own King Sobhuza. He responded favorably, but to accept them now, *en masse*, without land to support them, would threaten the political and economic stability of the entire nation. He therefore urged them to be patient while he, as representative of an independent state, negotiated with the government of South Africa. This would be a major commitment to the future. He would negotiate in his own way, guided by an image of a great precolonial Swazi empire. In the meantime he faced the problem of immediate demands for citizenship.

Those who were accepted into Swaziland, like those born outside, were put into the category of non-Swazi Africans and had to be accepted by chiefs in Swaziland, who would then apply on their behalf to the SNC and have their acceptance validated by papers. It was a long and cumbersome procedure. Non-Africans could apply for naturalization through the immigration office, which fell under the aegis of the deputy prime minister, whose decisions appeared arbitrary and were final. The essentially personal procedure of the traditional system of *khonta* took on the impersonality of modern bureaucratic complexities and the accompanying individual frustrations, except in a few cases in which the king himself interceded directly.

The policy was generally confused, and in 1970 Sobhuza had appointed a committee from the SNC to investigate the different categories of people in the country. According to its findings, 6000 adults in Swaziland did not have any of the necessary evidence of traditional citizenship or documents entitling them to residence. They included non-Swazi Africans most of whom had been brought into Swaziland as employees, and also Africans who identified themselves as Swazi but had been born outside Swaziland. The final number of voters registered by the closing of January 31, 1972, was lower than calculated in terms of the population.

The twenty-four elected seats were contested by five political parties, but this time only the Imbokodvo nominated the full quota of twenty-four candidates. The NNLC had split on personal rather than ideological grounds into two separate competing factions, one led by Dr. Zwane and the other by his former deputy; they put forward nineteen and fourteen candidates respectively, the Swazi United Front six, and the Swaziland Progressive Party five.

John Nquku, the veteran leader of the Progressives, did not stand—he could not document his status as a Swazi citizen. He did not appeal his exclusion but considered it contrary to the king's own outlook. Of the Imbokodvo candidates, seventeen had been in the previous parliament and seven were new nominees. Once again, Imbokodvo candidates were chosen by the traditional regional committees and after being accepted by the king were presented at a meeting in Lobamba. It was stated clearly that each candidate was appointed to represent the interests of the country as a whole, not simply his own constituency or his own local district, and therefore would not necessarily stand in the area from which he came or in which he was well known. The king had sent out his messengers to explain Imbokodvo policy, and was assured that the party would gain a total victory. Dr. Zwane's NNLC, the strongest opposition, stood on the same party platform as in 1964, while the Imbokodvo modified its conservative approach. It felt that it had achieved a good deal, and that its 1969 development plan had responded to the needs of different segments of the population.

An official opposition was seen as the equivalent of having in one's midst a subversive and persistent enemy committed not to national unity but to partisan policy. For some time the king and prime minister had hoped the position would change and had indicated that Dr. Zwane could be welcomed back "like a prodigal son." But Dr. Zwane persisted in his refusal to join as an individual: he wanted to be accepted in what he now called a federation of his party with that of the Imbokodvo, a condition the Imbokodvo found unacceptable.

The final result was indeed an overwhelming majority for the Imbokodvo, which obtained 78.3 percent of all votes. But 18.2 percent of opposition votes went to the NNLC, and in one constituency, which in the previous election had received strong support from the NNLC, Dr. Zwane and his two adjutants defeated the Imbokodvo candidates, one of whom was Prince Mfanasibili, a high-ranking prince and minister of local affairs. For the first time there would be an organized opposition party in the parliament.

A CASE OF DISPUTED CITIZENSHIP

The situation was complicated by the fact that one of three winning NNLC candidates was Thomas Bekindlela Ngwenya. His success in the election sparked a bitter and dramatic battle in which two issues, one related to the citizenship of a particular individual and the other to the broad interpretation of national sovereignty and rights to land, became inextricably confused.

At the time of nominations, Prince Mfanasibili (the defeated Imbokodvo candidate who had been on the committee appointed by the king to examine claims for citizenship) had complained to the electoral officer that Ngwenya, though Swazi, had been born on the South African side of the border and hence could not be recognized as a voter. But since Ngwenya had voted in earlier elections and was a progressive farmer at a scheme sponsored by the Colonial Development Corporation, the chief electoral officer to whom the matter was reported did not treat the objection seriously and no formal objection was lodged. Once elected, however, the position changed. Prince Mfanasibili took his complaint to the deputy prime minister—who, without informing the king, declared Ngwenya a prohibited immigrant under Immigration Act 32 of 1964. Ngwenya was described as a South African and deported across the border on May 25, 1972, the day before the opening of the new parliament. When the king questioned the deportation, the deputy prime minister (who found restrictions on his independent actions irksome) referred to the need to deal effectively with illegal immigrants and people who had no claim to citizenship under the existing constitution.

The defeat of the prince was treated as a different and separate matter; a number of royals came to Sobhuza requesting that he give his "son" (his dead brother's child) a position befitting his rank and his qualifications which they, although not the electorate, rated highly. Initially Sobhuza refused. The victory of NNLC candidates was the result of a party system he condemned, but it was embodied in the constitution he had signed. The argument that finally convinced him was that in Botswana and Tanzania there had been similar situations in which candidates who had lost elections had been given high offices by their respective presidents, the internationally respected Sir Seretse Khama and Julius Nyerere.

Parliament opened as scheduled on May 26, 1972. Members were duly sworn in, and the king announced his nominees to both houses and to the cabinet. Prince Makhosini was again appointed prime minister and the new cabinet had many familiar faces. The two who were conspicuously absent were Leo Lovell, the outspoken former minister of finance, and Mfundza Sukati, the equally forthright former deputy prime minister. But Prince Mfanasibili was appointed to a new ministry of commerce and cooperatives, departments that formerly were part of the portfolio of Sishayi Nxumalo, who was left with mines and tourism. Prince Gabheni, one of the king's own sons, was made minister for local administration. Ten elected members of parliament were Dlamini. Fears of white settlers were assuaged by the appointment in Lovell's place of R. P. Stephens, who had been a member of the EAC in the 1950s and 1960s and was elected to the Legco as a member of the USA.

Superficially, parliament was set to continue as before, but the presence of two NNLC members was a constant reminder of organized opposition and the atmosphere was tense. In his maiden speech, Dr. Zwane attacked the government policy of trying to obtain loans from Great Britain to buy land that rightfully belonged to

Sobhuza on the steps of parliament in 1972, a year before he repealed the "West-minster" Independence Constitution.

Swaziland anyway, and he objected to the creation of the new ministry, for which he said he could see no reason except to provide a job for the minister he had defeated.

Hanging over parliamentary discussions was the issue of Ngwenya, whose seat remained empty. The NNLC had decided to fight his case. Ngwenya had secretly come back to Swaziland and been rearrested by Swazi police on instructions from the deputy prime minister. He was charged with being in the country illegally, found guilty, and sentenced to twelve days' imprisonment. He applied to the high court in Mbabane to set aside the order pronouncing him a prohibited immigrant. His lawyer was Musa Shongwe, a young Swazi whose parents were Sobhuza's close and trusted friends and kin. Shongwe briefed a white advocate from Johannesburg who had acted for Dr. Zwane and the NNLC at the time of the strikes. He approached the situation as a political trial in which his client was being victimized because he had defeated a member of the Imbokodvo. The fact that two other members of the winning NNLC trio were both admitted and sitting in parliament did not affect his charge. The South African press constantly referred to Ngwenya as "the member who had defeated the candidate of the majority royalist party."

On July 12 Dr. Zwane tabled a motion of no confidence in the government and stated that he would "give a long litany on its sins of commission." But the majority of the members of the house were deliberately absent and a prince appointed as a minister in the new government interrupted Dr. Zwane to point out that "we seem to have no quorum." The speaker had to agree and had "no alternative but to adjourn the House until tomorrow." That tomorrow did not come.

On August 29, a week before the eighth anniversary of independence, Judge Pike, who was then chief justice of the Swaziland high court, declared in a fourteen-page judgment that Ngwenya was a Swazi citizen. There was deep consternation in many quarters. Though the case could still be brought before the Swaziland appeal court, the King-in-council realized that the judges would start off with the same assumptions and the same legal criteria. The independence celebrations were nevertheless spectacular and no outsider would have suspected that there were any internal anxieties.

At the annual conference of the NNLC, held on October 7 and 8, a motion of confidence in the leadership was passed and Ngwenya was elected one of the officers. A meeting of the House of Assembly had been called by the Speaker for October 11 on previous instructions from the prime minister. In terms of Judge Pike's decision, Ngwenya could take his place in parliament. Would he try to do so? If he did, how would the hotheads in the Imbokodvo react? The king instructed his people not to use violence. Ngwenya arrived and went with the other two NNLC members into the House. All the Imbokodvo members stayed in their rooms. The clerk rang the bell. They made no move. After a long wait, the Speaker "regretted that there was no quorum," and adjourned the meeting "to a date and time to be fixed by the chair."

Local newspapers reported the Imbokodvo action as a boycott. The king as well as the cabinet objected to the term. Whom, he asked, were they boycotting? Themselves? The orders of the king? No. It was simply a technique to avoid violence and signify disapproval.

Two weeks later the king came to parliament to celebrate United Nations Day, recognized as a new public holiday. Before a crowd of some 2000 he spoke of the many historic events enacted on that site and expressed his hopes for the fulfillment of the high ideals of the United Nations.

When parliament finally met again on November 13, a "legal solution" to the citizenship dispute was presented. An immigration amendment bill, tabled by the deputy prime minister under a certificate of urgency, provided for the establishment of a special tribunal of five to decide cases of doubtful citizenship. The members of the tribunal would be appointed by the prime minister and an appeal could be lodged with him. The verdict would then be final and would also supersede and render ineffective any previous judgments of the courts.

The justification given by the deputy prime minister for the extensive power of the tribunal was that cases of citizenship

often involved matters relating to traditional customs with which our courts are not familiar. . . . Moreover, we are anxious to protect our courts against the criticisms of the public in respect of decisions which although probably sound in law and in accordance with the evidence placed before the courts at the time, do not in fact accord with our own people's views and our own knowledge of the facts. Such criticisms can only lead to a disrespect for our courts and their decisions. And I need hardly emphasise how important it is that such a situation should be avoided.

Strong criticism of the bill was voiced by Dr. Zwane, who raised two major objections—first, that the power of deciding who came into the country and who went out is reserved "for the Prime Minister." He did not elaborate. Dr. Zwane as well as others wondered at the wisdom of this, since the traditional right of accepting or rejecting subjects was vested in the king. Was the prime minister usurping the authority of the king? Second, Dr. Zwane challenged the power of the House, in view of the rights entrenched in the constitution, to make laws that were not subject to the jurisdiction of the court. How much had been agreed to by the king? Did he know what he was being asked to sign?

The attorney general, David Cohen, responding to Dr. Zwane's challenge, specifically avoided comment on the political merits and demerits of the bill and limited himself to its legality. Very cautiously, he gave his considered opinion that the bill did not intend to change the constitution, and he compared the tribunal to any other quasi-judicial body, "such as the Liquor Licensing Board," the decision of which was not likely to be appealed in the high court, "though if it were to act in an arbitrary or unconstitutional and illegal manner, it would be subject to review." So he advised the government that the bill was not inconsistent with the constitution and did not attempt to change the constitution. The question of the entrenched clauses did not arise.

The bill, which passed all three readings in both houses within thirty hours, was taken by the prime minister to the king. He already knew the contents and, having previously received the official reassurance of the attorney general, he gave his assent. The bill immediately became law. The members of the tribunal had already been selected and their names were made public the following day, November 13, in the *Government Gazette Extraordinary*. The first meeting of the tribunal was held at the Lobamba office that afternoon, but it would take some time finding witnesses and sorting out the evidence.

The deputy prime minister's appeal against the decision of the high court (lodged on August 31) was still pending when, on November 16, he further claimed an order setting aside the decision on the ground that it was obtained by perjured evidence. In response Ngwenya's lawyers applied to the high court for an order against the deputy prime minister and chief immigration officer, on the grounds (among others) that the immigration amendment act was *ultra vires* (outside the law) and the special tribunal unconstitutional.

For reasons not made public, Chief Justice Pike, who had given the original decision against Ngwenya, had been removed from office and replaced by Judge Hill. On January 9, 1973, soon after the main public rites of the *Ncwala* were ended, Chief Justice Hill declared that the establishment of the tribunal was *intra vires* (within the law) and dismissed Ngwenya's case with costs. The government members were deeply relieved. The opinion of the attorney general appeared correct. The hearings before the tribunal continued. Several new witnesses had been found, and on January 29 Mr. Troughton, the chairman, delivered the tribunal's unanimous decision that "Ngwenya is not a citizen of Swaziland. Although his ancestors may have been resident in Swaziland, he himself was born in South Africa and therefore is not a person who belongs to Swaziland in terms of the present law." But the matter was not at an end. Ngwenya appealed the verdict of Judge Hill to the highest court in the country, the Swaziland court of appeal which had replaced the old British privy council.

Three prominent and nonpartisan judges from South Africa heard the case in the court of appeal. Their decision, expected on March 17, was awaited with some anxiety. A routine meeting of the nation had been called at Lobamba for the nineteenth. The ex-servicemen were told to arrive a few days in advance and several thousand people, anticipating a major constitutional announcement, came to the capital. But the judges had not made their decision, and the king, referring to "the matter which they were expecting to hear about," told them that his "advisers had not yet fully decided their line of guidance." He then posed to the nation the crucial question:

> Ask yourselves: Is Parliament fully independent as other Parliaments are? Is it fully independent as for instance, in other states such as England or France? Or is it a token independence?

On March 27 the judicial answer came. Judge Schreiner, facing a crowded and tense courtroom, declared the immigration amendment act "beyond the power of Parliament to enact, save in accordance with Section 134 of the Constitution. Hence the Act was void." What should be done?

REPEAL OF A WESTMINSTER CONSTITUTION

In its election manifesto drawn up in 1972 the INM had pledged itself to amend the Westminster constitution. On March 19, 1973, a week before the elections, the king had made it known that this was being closely studied with a view "to make it consonant with the spirit of a Sovereign Independent Swaziland." The Ngwenya case provided the final straw that destroyed the Westminster constitution. The officials (particularly the DPM) who initiated the case against Ngwenya were interested in the immediate local situation and were either not concerned with or unaware of the effect on Swazi across the border. This would be the burden of the future (see Chapter 11).

Parliament was due to meet early in April. The situation was volatile. On April 12, the prime minister presented first to the Senate, then to the House of Assembly, a resolution expressing "complete lack of confidence in the 1968 Constitution which had proved to be the direct cause of many difficult and sometimes insoluble problems," and called "upon His Majesty-in-Council to consider ways and means of resolving the crisis." The king was waiting at Embo, the state house, in the company of councilors, including the chief immigration officer and Rev. Bhengu, a renowned minister from South Africa who had come to visit and whom he asked to pray with him. He had accepted a decision made by others; he considered that there was no alternative.

The prime minister and cabinet went from parliament to bring the King to Lobamba, where some 7000 people were already assembled. For the first time a few hundred Swazi equipped with FN rifles appeared before the public. It was a modern army, albeit small in number, including a core of veterans from World

War II. The meeting took place not inside the *sibaya*, with its sacred enclosure and ritual associations, but on an open space adjoining the barracks of the regiment that had fought in World War II. There were chairs for the king and the main officials; the rest sat on the ground. The king and a few of his councilors wore simple traditional dress.

Prince Makhosini, as prime minister, standing in front of the microphone, announced briefly and bluntly that the two houses of parliament had found the constitution unworkable and that it had to be replaced. The prime minister was followed by a senior prince, representing the Swazi National Council. He addressed the king in the name of "the nation" which "would like to be completely sovereign and independent and not have the Father Christmas type of independence."

Then Sobhuza got up, and the crowd listened in silence as he read, slowly and very quietly, the irrevocable proclamation dated April 12, 1973. It stated that the existing constitution had failed to provide machinery for the maintenance of peace and order but was a cause of growing unrest, permitting the importation of foreign political practices incompatible with the Swazi way of life, "and designed to disrupt and destroy our own peaceful and constructive and essentially democratic method of political activity." Since the method prescribed by the existing constitution for effecting necessary amendments would bring about the disorder which any constitution is meant to inhibit, it was essential for the achieving of full freedom and independence to create their own constitution without outside pressures.

The proclamation continued: "*Now, therefore I, Sobhuza II, King of Swaziland, hereby declare that in collaboration with my Cabinet Ministers, and supported by the whole nation, I have assumed supreme power in the Kingdom of Swaziland.* All legislative, executive, and judicial power is vested in myself, and shall for the meantime be exercised in collaboration with a Council constituted by my Cabinet Ministers." It declared further that "to ensure the continued maintenance of peace, order and good government, my armed forces, in conjunction with the Royal Swaziland Police Force, have been posted to all strategic places, and have taken charge of all government places and all public services."

The constitution of the Kingdom of Swaziland, which commenced on September 6, 1968, was "hereby repealed." All other laws "shall continue to operate with full force and effect . . . with such modifications, adaptations, qualifications and exceptions as may be necessary to bring them into conformity with this and ensuing decrees."

Sobhuza then called on the attorney general "to read out the decrees designed to provide for the continuation of administration, essential services, and normal life in our country." There would be no immediate radical changes. All judges and other judicial officers, government officials, public servants, members of the police force, the prison service, and the armed forces were to continue in office; the prime minister, deputy prime minister, cabinet ministers, secretary to the cabinet, and attorney general would remain in office at the discretion of the king; and all members of the Senate and the House of Assembly would continue to receive the emoluments to which they were entitled.

But at the same time, restrictions similar to those operating in South Africa were imposed on individual freedom. Political parties were dissolved; political meetings, processions, and demonstrations disallowed without prior written consent of the commissioner of police; and the government was given the power to detain a person without trial for a period of sixty days, which could be renewed as often as deemed necessary in the public interest.

The meeting ended quietly. Voices were discreetly hushed. The press outside Swaziland reported "Swazi King Scraps the Constitution"; "King Seizes Supreme Power"; "Another African Dictatorship." Inside Swaziland many people openly expressed joy and pride in the king. Others expressed, less openly, their anxiety as the fear of detention without trial cast its shadow: How far had the repeal of the Westminster constitution solved the real problems, political and economic, of independence?

10/The limits of cultural
nationalism: 1973-1981

Sobhuza now bore the full burden of sovereignty. But in interpreting his role as a traditional African king he did not desire or attempt to convert a sacred kingship into a dictatorship, secular or sacred. Much of the machinery of government had been retained. The cabinet, officially renamed the Council of Ministers, continued to meet regularly and the liqoqo (at that stage still a loosely defined inner council of the Swazi National Council) was involved in constant discussion. The king was the fulcrum. New legislation, initiated by the appropriate minister and drafted by the attorney general, was submitted after cabinet approval to Sobhuza for him to accept, amend, or reject. Once accepted by him it was gazetted as a King's Order in Council.

Sobhuza guided Swaziland into the modern postcolonial era while trying to maintain its unique cultural identity. Changes required to make traditional institutions responsive to modern needs had to be based on the Swazi cultural heritage as a model. The success of this process of cultural nationalism depended on Sobhuza's skillful blending and balancing of a traditional Swazi institutional infractructure with Western symbols and of new Western-style organizations with traditional Swazi symbols. This synthesis brought tension and conflict as individuals sought to resist change or to take advantage of new power relationships for personal gain. To ensure the continued unity and prosperity of Swaziland, Sobhuza had to confront the limits to cultural nationalism.

MABUTFO, SOLDIERS, AND POLICE

In modern nation-states a broad distinction is drawn between soldiers and police. Soldiers and police are instruments of government, the former for national defense against external armed enemies, the latter for maintaining law and order and internal security. In the traditional Swazi system, the functions of soldiers and police were both performed by the *emabutfo* (age regiments), in which every male was automatically recruited (as described on p. 55).

The colonial power introduced the police as a separate arm of a civil administration distinct from the *mabutfo*. In the police force the officers were white, the other ranks black, and originally most of them were Zulu, traditional enemies of the Swazi. Subsequently Swazi were enlisted, but their position was ambivalent.

Though their loyalty was to the *Ngwenyama*, they were paid and protected by the British. The *emabutfo* were prohibited from carrying weapons, including traditional spears, except for approved national occasions; the police were armed and included a paramilitary unit. At the time of independence four out of thirty-four gazetted officers were Africans, of whom only two were Swazi and hence automatically members of the *emabutfo*.

Historically, the Swazi were known as a military nation. When, in World War II, the British appealed to Sobhuza to send a contingent to help the Allies, Sobhuza agreed on condition that the Swazi serve as soldiers, not simply as laborers, and that they be recruited and demobilized as a national unit. They left with traditional rituals and under men appointed by him. In his farewell speech, Sobhuza emphasized that by their actions they would remind the British of the promises they had made in the reign of his grandfather Mbandzeni that Swaziland would be independent. When they returned home a few were given positions in land resettlement projects, and in the civil service; there was no talk of keeping them on as soldiers.

The possibility of a modern Swazi army was raised after British troops had been brought into Swaziland to quell the 1963 labor strikes. Their status as soldiers was obviously higher than that of the police, but some of the princes who expressed the desire to receive military training were refused. A request by the prime minister that the barracks, specially constructed for the British troops who remained in Swaziland until 1966, be kept for the Swazi army that would be formed after independence was also refused on the grounds that an army was a political luxury a small country could not afford; after all, "Whom are you going to fight?" But the *emabutfo* continued, their structure seemingly unchanged though their functions had been curtailed.

After the strikes, conditions of the police had been improved and the gulf between them and the *emabutfo* became accentuated. In 1965, a police college was built, and education became a qualification for selection. For the *emabutfo*, age remained the basis of recruitment. Police salaries were regular and relatively high; *emabutfo* provided labor and performed services for the traditional authorities and received, irregularly, meat and beer as their reward.

In 1969 the force was renamed the Royal Swazi Police Force and the king became commander-in-chief. He spoke of it proudly, and the members were described as *Bafana Bembube* (Attendants of the Lion). In 1972, at the time of the Ngwenya case, the king prevented a violent confrontation between police and *emabutfo*. The contract of the last white commissioner of police was subsequently terminated and a Swazi appointed in his stead. The choice was Timothy Mtetwa, son of the traditional prime minister of the Swazi nation.

But it was from the *emabutfo* that the new army, demanded by national pride, would be created. On the last day of the first independence celebrations, Sobhuza announced the formation of the next age regiment, to which he gave the name *Gcina* (End [of an Era]), with a junior section, the *Tinkanyeti* (Stars [Lights of Night]). He then addressed the veterans of World War II, stressing that whereas Whites called them ex-soldiers, no Swazi ever lost his position in the *emabutfo*, and it would be their responsibility to hand on their knowledge to the young.

Sobhuza inspecting veterans of World War II accompanied by two senior police officers, 1970.

The *Gcina* was a group already in existence. The name had been given by Sobhuza to a camp started, in 1967, as a service by the Israeli government at the request of the incoming Swazi government. The camp officials trained in community activities and agriculture youths who were not in school or employed. After two years, they were expected to carry back the knowledge gained to their rural home areas. A request to include military training was firmly refused: initially the emphasis was on agriculture, not arms. But since the youths were strictly disciplined and trained to obey they were called on for national occasions, including the *Ncwala*; five years later (1973) the *Gcina* appeared as the nucleus of the new army, which Sobhuza designated the Royal Umbutfo Defense Force. The word *Umbutfo* applied to the corporate group of warriors in permanent residence at royal villages; the word *emabutfo* referred to the entire category. The distinction was subtle but significant. The Umbutfo were the permanent core of the defense force of royalty.

Following independence, a few carefully selected Swazi were sent to different countries, mainly in Africa, to find out about modern military organization and training. At the end of the *Ncwala* of 1972, before Sobhuza dismissed the *emabutfo*, he hinted that the time had come when young Swazi men should be well trained in modern methods and techniques to deal with trouble that may threaten the peace of the country, and in a stirring speech he exhorted them to live up to the spirit of heroic achievements of the past. England accepted the development of a Swazi army; South Africa supplied the equipment, paid for from Swazi national funds. One of the first decrees passed in 1973, after the king repealed the constitution, was to establish the amed forces financed from general revenue, and with the king as commander-in-chief.

Sobhuza made a deliberate effort to establish a harmonious balance between the *emabutfo*, the army, and the police in terms of payment and living conditions.

He also brought them together on public occasions. New holidays had been created for the new state. Important among them was the king's birthday, the exact date of which he had "discovered" only in 1965. At this celebration the police played a prominent part, whereas in the *Ncwala* the warriors dominated the scene. At the king's birthday celebrations in July 1973 the *emabutfo*, the police, and the new army, each with its own potential as a national force, appeared together on the playing field at Mankaiana to honor their king. The *emabutfo*, still in traditional costume, were the most numerous, and the police outnumbered the army.

Swazi leaders were aware of the frequency of military coups that followed in the wake of independence, not only in Africa. The most recent, and to some extent the most disturbing, was the deposition of Emperor Haile Selassie of Ethiopia in 1974, and, in the following year, the abolition of his ancient empire. Events closer to home made it increasingly difficult for Sobhuza to maintain Swaziland's neutrality. At the same time internal unity required recognition of a common enemy. In 1975 the Africans of Mozambique, more numerous and more diverse than those in Swaziland, freed themselves from Portuguese domination after a long and bloody struggle. Samora Machel, recognized by the Organization of African Unity as the leader of the winning party, Frelimo, proclaimed a policy of radical socialism.

In the same period, the racist national government in South Africa was entrenching its *apartheid* regime, and in 1976 more than 100 South African blacks, mainly students, sought refuge in Swaziland. The position of Swaziland was graphically described by a high-ranking Swazi minister as that of a "louse between two thumbs" or, more sympathetically, "a single grain between the upper and the lower grindstone." Sobhuza's emissaries, expressing the king's own point of view, criticized *apartheid* but at the same time made it clear that South Africa had sufficient economic as well as military power to cut off supplies of essential foods and to close employment to thousands of Swazi working in the gold mines. They acclaimed the success of Frelimo in Mozambique and expressed support for freedom fighters in Rhodesia (now Zimbabwe) at the same time they prohibited political refugees from taking part in any political activity or using Swaziland as a military training base. The South African police had close contacts inside Swaziland, and some of Sobhuza's own trusted people acted as informers.

The army was directly under the king. Its organization was separate from the rest of the administration. The camps in which the soldiers lived were out of bounds to the populace. The first Swazi commander of the army, publicly appointed by Sobhuza in 1975, was Prince Maphevu. Maphevu looked—and was—impressive. He was over six feet tall, with a fine carriage, and large gleaming eyes in a noble face. He had grown up in a traditional royal village, served with the Swazi Pioneer Corps in World War II, joined the Royal Umbutfo Force as a reserve, and showed outstanding qualities of leadership in addition to a sense of military discipline.

Sobhuza, who had previously informed the nation that Prince Makhosini was due for retirement, appointed Colonel Maphevu prime minister as well as commander of the army. The choice came to many as a surprise and to some as a disappointment. Maphevu was relatively unknown to the general public. Though he was Western-educated, he did not hold a white-collar office job. At the time of his appointment he was serving as a veterinary officer, seeking to raise the living standards of the peasantry. Moreover, apart from serving as a member of the committee on the mineral royalty fund and on the land speculation control board, he had held no national office. He had never been a member of Parliment. Those who had worked with him respected him for his integrity, seriousness, and disinterest in intrigue. By appointing Maphevu to the two highest positions in the new government Sobhuza attempted to secure for the monarchy double protection and a national stability. Maphevu was able to work closely with the Western-trained chief commissioner of police, the son of a former traditional prime minister, and also with the present traditional prime minister Bembhe, who was in charge of *emabutfo* and also a veteran of the second World War.

Traditionally every male subject was a soldier; under the new plan every soldier would be a citizen. Marching and drill were only part of the duty of a Swazi soldier. Soldiers, as citizens, would also cultivate the fields. Land bought with money from the mineral royalty fund was allocated for them to grow crops for their own needs and for the benefit of the nation. By building a modern army based on recruitment through the traditional age-group systems Sobhuza created a uniquely Swazi institution, but the effort to apply the concept of cultural nationalism to the armed forces was not without serious social costs. The agricultural aspect of the system worked well in the beginning, and two of the first camps produced sufficient food for a surplus to be sold at low prices to villages in the vicinity. But the army subsequently grew too rapidly to be self-supporting and became a drain on the limited national resources. By 1978 there were some 5000 regulars on the payroll and several thousand weekend volunteers. The number of trained officers was not sufficient to maintain adequate control and the army was accused of becoming a law unto itself. The number of police, however, remained relatively stable; recruitment was more selective, and stricter discipline was maintained.

The functions of army and police traditionally performed by *emabutfo* as a single national organization, had in the historical process of development become compartmentalized and competitive. Thus when soldiers became aggressive and domineering, and the police intervened and wished to take the culprits to the court, Maphevu claimed they should be reported to, and dealt with by, the army. The police were outnumbered by the army in a ratio of roughly one to four, and individual police were intimidated by gangs of soldiers.

But Swazi soldiers and police were still automatically *emabutfo* and participated as such in the annual ritual of kingship. There, a single national identity prevailed and members of regiments bonded by age which cut across boundaries of kinship, locality, and occupation, performed their roles in relation to the king. When the *Ncwala* was over, everyday problems again took precedence.

DEVELOPMENT OF AN UNWRITTEN CONSTITUTION

The new constitution Sobhuza had promised when he repealed the written Westminster constitution proved more difficult to formulate than he had anticipated. It was easy enough to state general guidelines and principles. It was much more difficult to make these specific. First he appointed a royal constitutional commission, under the chairmanship of the minister of justice, Polycarp Dlamini, to inquire into fundamental principles of Swazi history, as well as the modern principles of constitutional and international law, with which they needed to be harmonized. Sobhuza insisted that the inquiry be thorough; some thought too thorough. In addition to inviting and receiving suggestions, the commission held regional meetings throughout the country. Then, having sampled local opinion, selected members were sent to other countries in Africa—Malawi, Zambia, Kenya, Tanzania—as well as overseas—to Israel, England, Switzerland, and Denmark—to see different systems at work and to learn from them. The report, which was finally presented to the king in July 1975, was not made public.

On November 26, Sobhuza appointed, as a second stage, a constitutional advisory committee to make more definite suggestions for the actual constitution. In July 1976 their recommendations were handed to the king. He compared himself to a man carrying a clay pot of such value that he himself has to be carried lest he stumble and fall and the treasure break.

The issue became increasingly urgent. The five-year term of office of parliamentarians elected in 1972 and still being paid drew to a close. On March 24, 1977, Sobhuza announced that the kingdom would be governed through traditional institutions and that former members of parliament would be replaced by a new team chosen through *tinkundla*. He selected a committee of seven to work out the details of the "experiment." No written constitution was produced. His emissaries had informed him that this was the position in England and Israel, countries that were considered democratic.

The situation in the kingdom was becoming tense. In an article in *The Times* of London on September 6, 1978, under the ominous heading EXTENDED DETENSION CURBS DISSENT, the writer referred to specific cases of oppression and injustice, and mentioned the distribution of a pamphlet by an illegal organization calling itself Swalimo (Swaziland Liberation Movement) urging people to stay away from the celebrations marking ten years of independence "because our country is not yet free and independent." Swalimo claimed responsibility for "rescuing" Dr. Zwane from prison, where he had again been detained, and demanded the immediate release of all other political prisoners in Swaziland.

The Ngwane National Liberation Congress was a banned organization. The sixty-day detention act was no longer merely a threat. Teachers had gone on strike for higher pay. Their unions had been banned. Students, demonstrating their support for the teachers, were confronted by armed police who had been given permission to shoot if necessary. Two ministers were stoned. Clandestinely distributed leaflets threatened destruction of ministerial buildings and death to the prime minister and deputy prime minister. Officials blamed the violence and subversion on South African refugees, including students from the black township of Soweto. In April 1978 some 100 black refugees, mainly members of the Pan-African Congress, were arrested and put into detention camps.

The committee of seven finally completed its work, and on October 21, 1978, the king signed two orders-in-council, detailing a complicated electoral system to a bicameral parliament. The number of *tinkundla*, each with its own *indvuna* and committee of chiefs, was increased from twenty-two to forty, grouped in four regions, each with a regional administrator to coordinate local and central activities. Each of the forty *tinkundla* would send two representatives, selected by public acclamation (the Swazi method) to the capital. These eighty would form an electoral college. No member of the electoral college or the committee of seven could be elected. The eighty members would elect by secret ballot (Western method) forty people to serve in the House of Assembly. To this forty, the king would appoint ten additional members. The Senate was to consist of twenty members, ten elected by the House and ten nominated by the king. To eliminate, as far as possible, "campaigning" by individuals, election to the *tinkundla* would take place on the day of nomination, and in the case of the electoral college not more than five days after completion of the nomination.

Everyone claiming Swazi citizenship, urban as well as rural, Black as well as White, was attached to specific *inkundla*. At the head of the *tinkundla* bureaucracy was *indvuna yetinkundla* (a governor of *tinkundla*), appointed by the king. The system of local administration under district commissioners and sub-commissioners developed by the British was not immediately abolished, but there was an implicit threat to its position in the future. The committee of seven was retained to serve as an evaluatory and mediating council between the *tinkundla* and the more Western system of local and central government.

Much of the system introduced after the repeal of the constitution continued. Every bill passed by the parliament would become law after the king gave his consent and the bill was published in the *Gazette*. Executive authority was vested in the king, who appointed the prime minister from members of the House. All other ministers and deputy ministers were appointed by the king in consultation with the prime minister.

In outline it sounded an appealing example of a hybrid system in which modern cuttings were carefully grafted onto an ancient trunk. But its critics argued that it was a master plan in which twentieth-century liberal concepts of individual rights were subordinated to the interests of an autocratic aristocracy.

Elections duly took place on October 24 under strict security supervision. In effect, the traditional method gave the appearance of free choice but lacked its substance. Since the names of the candidates were announced on the day of election, there was no opportunity for free and open discussion of their merits. Four candidates of each *tinkundla* sat on chairs in a cleared space. Each voter walked through a gateway, lined up in front of the candidate of his choice, then went through the exit behind him and past the returning officers, who were there to count the number of votes cast for each candidate. Each person voted for only one candidate, and the two top candidates were sent to the electoral college. Only 55 percent of registered voters chose to vote. Some who refrained from voting explained privately that they were not prepared to risk making three enemies for one friend. It did not matter that Sobhuza had urged people to vote for qualities other than those of personal friendship.

Superficially, the new parliament had many new faces and reflected, to some extent, the king's effort to include educated and uneducated, young and old, in-experienced and experienced. Maphevu continued the double role of prime minister and head of defense. Six of the ten new ministers were Dlamini (two were sons of

Sobhuza), two were non-Dlamini Swazi but part of the in-law network, and two were white Swazi. At the same time, it must be remembered that the Dlamini outnumbered any other clan, that polygamy based on clan exogamy was an integral part of traditional culture, and that even within the circle of Dlamini royals dissent was known to exist though its extent was uncertain.

After the elections there was little public protest. Sobhuza sent two of his emissaries, one the head of foreign affairs and the other the Swazi ambassador to the United States, to fetch Dr. Ambrose Zwane from his exile in Tanzania, where he had obtained refuge after escaping from his third period of detention in prison. He came willingly, expressing disillusionment with the governments of Mozambique and Tanzania, and returned to his private medical practice.

THE PERILS OF OFFICE

The image of Swaziland was improving abroad. Representatives invited to international meetings throughout the world were welcomed in countries as far apart ideologically as South Africa and Cuba. Oliver Tambo, exiled leader of the banned African National Congress, publicly praised the work of Sobhuza at a meeting of nonaligned countries.

But the role of Maphevu as both prime minister and commander of the army had become increasingly difficult and dangerous. He was invited everywhere and was often out of the country. In his absence the army became more aggressive toward civilians. Maphevu had enemies, rivals. His life was in danger and he knew it. There had been threats against him and omens of misfortune. Then in 1977, on a mission to Switzerland, he was seriously injured in an automobile accident the details of which were never made public. When he returned home in April 1978, after months in a Swiss hospital, those who knew him well said they were shocked by the change in his personality and appearance. He was embittered, forbidding, and crippled. He had lost the use of his right arm: the bone had been shattered. Interpreting right and left in traditional Swazi cultural idiom, right symbolizes male, left female; in warfare a warrior holds his spear in his right hand, his shield in his left; the right is aggression, the left is defense. The emphasis is on complementarity not opposition. "Hands wash each other": both hands are needed. There were rumors that Maphevu's physical handicap would automatically end his public career. But Sobhuza decided otherwise. He kept Maphevu on as both commander-in-chief and prime minister. Maphevu saluted with his left hand.

Maphevu never really recovered and, in August 1979 Sobhuza sent him for treatment to Johannesburg, where the doctors diagnosed cancer. Swazi asked "What is cancer? It it a new witchcraft?" Maphevu died on October 24, 1979. His funeral was carried out at two levels: a public state ceremony in which his coffin contained not his body but his Western accoutrements and an ancient traditional burial, when his soldiers carried his body to the royal caves in the Mdimba mountains.

Sobhuza had to find a new prime minister. He watched the indirect maneuvers of many eager candidates, and listened to those who came to sing their praises. But he gave no indication of his own preference until, in November, in a meeting at the ritual capital, he called on Bembhe as traditional prime minister and head of *emabutfo*, to announce Prince Mabandla as Maphevu's successor.

The choice was again as much a surprise to the people as to the candidate. Mabandla's involvement in politics had been minimal until 1978, when he was nominated by the king to the House of Assembly. However, his qualifications were both traditional and Western. His father, Prince Mancibane, grandson of King Mswati, was a highly respected chief in the Peak district. Mabandla was well educated, with a diploma in agriculture, commerce, and administration, and had studied irrigation and extension work in Israel. He was deeply attached to the soil, and at the time of his appointment was manager of a national sugar project financed by Tibiyo. In outlook and training, he was closer to the police than to the army. He was not a soldier and Sobhuza did not put him in charge of defense.

Mabandla's position was difficult. He inherited a parliament that included hostile, disappointed, and influential members and a cabinet in whose appointment he had had no say. He was relatively young, in his early fifties, and did not follow the footsteps of the older princes. As a member of a Protestant church and a practicing monogamist—his wife was also well-educated—many of his closest contacts were with the professional elite, both in the private sector and in the civil service.

As a new man Mabandla wanted to work out his own political approach to existing problems. Following the repeal of the constitution the civil service had become politicized, and there was a decline in morality and an increase in corruption. Sobhuza spoke out publicly and bitterly. "Corruption," he said, "breeds coups." A few individuals were charged and occasional scandals brought into the open. In 1977 a report by the auditor general referred to specific cases of corruption in government, the intimidation of civil servants, the disregard for regulations, and a complaint by the minister of finance that financial control had almost broken down in many industries.

In March 1980, less than five months after taking office, Mabandla secured Sobhuza's approval for a commission of enquiry with a broad mandate to look into corruption in government and official state agencies during the past four years. It soon became clear that the investigation, headed by a judge of the appeal court of South Africa, would undermine some of those in the highest positions in the government. The minister of justice, one of the closest and most long-term advisers to the king, was found guilty of misappropriating several thousand *emalangeni*, and the previous deputy prime minister was under investigation. While the hearings were still in progress, the king, acting under pressure from business groups and politicians, signed an order-in-council that excluded from investigation the defense force and the management of two major funds. The commission refused to continue its work under these conditions, and resigned. No action was taken against anyone, and the entire report was shelved.

There was a powerful reaction against Mabandla from those who had felt themselves threatened by the investigation, and Sobhuza's support weakened. He summoned Mabandla's father to inform him that his son was undermining national morale. He then summoned Mabandla, who justified his actions on the grounds

that he needed to know what had been happening in different departments before
he could get on with his job. Sobhuza warned him that it was his duty to look to
the future, not stir up troubles of the past. Rumors were rife that Mabandla would
be replaced, but the king told him that he must stay on. Mabandla described himself as "a man in the middle: a deep pool on one side, a fire on the other, and wild
animals all around."

Not only were there deep divisions between the pro-Mabandla and anti-
Mabandla factions in parliament and the cabinet, but the hoped-for integration
between parliament and *tinkundla*, the Western institutions and the traditional,
had also not been achieved. A small commission appointed by the King in 1981
to investigate why the *tinkundla* were not functioning gave the most obvious
reasons: first, the four regional administrators, essential cogs in the new system
set forth in the 1978 order-in-council, had never been appointed; and second, an
independent budget for the *tinkundla*, though accepted in principle, had not been
established. By contrast, the appointment of all members of parliament had been
legally confirmed and their salaries, like those of civil servants, were already
provided for in the budget. Some people considered that the nonimplementation
of regulations necessary for the effective functioning of *tinkundla* was symptomatic
of general neglect and ineptitude; others, more politically astute, related it to the
fundamental structural conflict between parliament and *tinkundla*, symbolized in
the unique position of the *indvuna yetinkundla*, Mdeni Shabalala, in the total
political hierarchy. Not only was he appointed directly by the king as head of the
tinkundla, he claimed that his was a permanent appointment and that, like the
prime minister, he had direct access to the king. While he recognized that the
prime minister headed the entire civil service, he also claimed ministerial status,
with his duties encompassing all aspects of cultural and customary activities.

It is difficult to know to what extent, if any, the conflict between the parliamentary minister of home affairs and the head of the traditional *tinkundla* was
exacerbated by personality differences. But regardless of any personality conflict,
there was an inherent structural tension between their positions. The minister of
home affairs dealt with a wide range of issues, including the system of local administration built up during the colonial regime, acting through district commissioners and subcommissioners. Under the *tinkundla* system, however, these
posts would be redundant, and the commissioners would be absorbed as far as
possible into the *tinkundla* bureaucracy. But the district commissioners continued in their posts. Liaison between them and the *tinkundla* officials, through the
committee of seven, was limited and constrained. The *indvuna yetinkundla* claimed
that all activities under Home Affairs fell within his jurisdiction. The relationship
between *tinkundla* and local administration was roughly parallel to that between
the army and the police. Weaknesses in institutional links are readily expressed
in terms of personal hostility and antagonism and are all too often dismissed as
such. In the past, the Swazi traditional council system acted as a shadow government
parallel to, and often in opposition to, the colonial regime. Now it was the Western
institutions that provided a shadow government, with its own dynamic processes,
imposing limits on cultural nationalism at the constitutional level.

The only unifying factor was the king. It was widely recognized that it was he alone who kept the nation together, and in his own personal behavior was able effectively to handle situations according to his interpretation of the Swazi way of life. But here too there were constitutional obstacles to cohesion. Decisions were inevitably difficult. The term "The King-in-Council" was itself misleading, since the council he consulted was not always the same. *Tinkundla* and parliament, army and police each contained their own council of elites.

However, there remained the religious and educational institutions, and Sobhuza placed great emphasis on their potential contribution to the fostering of cultural nationalism.

RELIGION AND EDUCATION IN CULTURAL NATIONALISM

Sobhuza went beyond the more familiar techniques of political diplomacy— commissions, conferences, meetings, petitions, court appeals, elections—and the essentially Western media of communication and propaganda—newspapers, radio, television, rallies—to familiar Swazi institutions and the deeper resources of Swazi culture to build up patriotism and national pride. We have seen how traditional warriors were forged into modern soldiers and an elected parliamentary system was based on a model of dispersed royal villages. Old customs were revitalized, new ceremonies incorporating ancient themes were created, and throughout the years the *Ncwala* remained a symbolic ritual of kingship, its significance reflected in an increasing range of participants—including not only new regiments but also new priests.

Traditional sovereignty was both sacred and secular. Religion was power. The person of the king was sacrosanct. His mother was the guardian of ritual. Lobamba remained the *umpakatsi*—the sacred center, the *axis mundi*. But Christianity was on the increase, not as a single religious movement but as divergent and at times conflicting sects.

The majority of Swazi belonged to African Independent churches, some of which retained the liturgy, hymn books, and catechism of the particular European churches from which they had broken away. Others, who described themselves as Emazioni, emphasized divine healing and prophecy. All were under Sobhuza's patronage and, in cases of dispute over leadership, appealed to him for his intervention. Sobhuza himself was very susceptible to those who claimed divine inspiration; though the falsity of several prophets he had befriended was exposed, he never challenged the power of the Holy Spirit.

Good Friday had become the main annual Christian celebration, with priests from churches both within and across the borders of Swaziland coming with their congregations to Lobamba to pray for the health of the rulers and the well-being of the nation. Sobhuza always attended and, in giving his thanks, pleaded for unity, harmony, and peace. During the Easter celebration of 1971 a "prophet" recounted a vision in which Jesus had told him that the national church started in the 1940s (referred to on page 70) must be completed. The vision was taken to heart: the church of the nation, an unusual and impressive building close to the

Somhlolo stadium and to the parliament, was consecrated in 1978, ten years after independence.

Sobhuza was increasingly known as a Christian; he spoke of himself as *likholwa* (believer) and expressed his belief in Nkulunkulu (Great Great One), a missionary translation into siSwati of the English word for "God." The more orthodox churches, notably the Anglican and Catholic, responded to the king's affirmation of Christianity. They increased the number of African clergy in the church hierarchy and appointed a few to higher positions. Sobhuza set an example of tolerance by his willingness to listen and to join in prayers by Christians of all denominations as he continued to carry out traditional rituals and to send his priests on annual pilgrimages to ancestral burial grounds to pray and offer sacrifices. To Sobhuza there was no basic incompatibility between Christianity and the religion of his forefathers. To him both revealed a universal ethic, and he openly criticized division and quarrels among leaders of different sects who, using the same Bible, claimed that theirs was the one and only true religion.

Many of the queens came from families of different Christian denominations, and Sobhuza encouraged them to attend Sunday services at Lobamba and to hold evening prayers in their own quarters. These services were delightfully informal and held sitting on mats in a hut lit by a single candle (until the 1960s there was no electricity even at Lobamba). One or two of the queens chose a text and led the service, and there was singing of hymns and a feeling of warm sociability. Some people attended more regularly than others, but no one ever questioned why anyone was absent.

The question of the particular church to which the queens or queen mothers belonged as individuals was never a major issue, and, in effect, their membership accentuated the sanctity of dual sovereignty. Both Lomawa, Sobhuza's mother (who died in September 1938), and her full sister Nukwase (who died in September 1957) were of the *Esikoteni* branch of the Ndwandwe clan. They were historically associated with the first missionaries, Wesleyans, in the south. (see page 69) Nukwase's successor Zihlati was not a "mother" but a senior wife of the same clan, the Ndwandwe, but of a different branch, the *Elwandle*. This group had special responsibilities in the annual rituals of kingship and was not affiliated to any particular church. Once appointed and granted the sacred insignia of office, Zihlati was symbolically transformed from queen to queen mother and was addressed by Sobhuza as "Mother." Zihlati died in January 1975, and Sobhuza selected as her replacement Seneleleni, another Ndwandwe queen, also from the *Elwandle*. Seneleleni, who was a member of a fundamentalist church, was already old and in poor health. She died in June 1980, and though there was another Ndwandwe among his queens, after much deliberation Sobhuza chose Dzeliwe, who was a Shongwe not an Ndwandwe, to the onerous position of his "twin" in the dual monarchy.

Dzeliwe was a practicing Catholic who came from a well-known Christian family. One of her brothers had been a chaplain with the Swazi forces in World War II, and she had been a novice in a convent before being taken as a queen. She was able to read the Bible in Zulu (it was not yet translated into siSwati); though she understood some English she was not fluent in speaking or able to read it. At the time of her appointment she was in her mid-fifties, strong, energetic, intelligent, and childless. She retained her close relationship with the Catholic church, and Mandla Zwane, the first African Catholic bishop, was her confessor and good friend. He was a man of outstanding ability whose influence spread beyond the limits of his own congregation. He was acceptable to Sobhuza, a friend of Mabandla, and a defender of the rights of refugees. He was killed in a car accident on August 9, 1980.

Sobhuza had been friends with several Catholic priests whom he found understanding and tolerant of such Swazi customs as polygamy, beer drinking, divination, and reverence of ancestors, but he refused to identify himself with any particular denomination, explaining that the traditional ancestral religion was non-sectarian. He frequently reflected that "the Book" Sobhuza I had told his people to accept from the Whites was to bring peace, not conflict.

In his youth, Western education and Western religion were one. To read from the Bible was to be educated. Missionaries used the Bible primarily for conversion, though they also included genuine scholars and teachers interested in furthering wider knowledge through literacy. After independence Sobhuza appointed several leading clergy to political positions. One was made secretary of the Swazi National Council, two became ministers of education; others were less directly influential in national affairs, but most Swazi in the upper ranks of the civil service and many parliamentarians, including the successive prime ministers, were regular churchgoers. The appointment of educated officials meant in most cases the appointment of Christians.

With the passing of time, Sobhuza argued that education should not be secularized but it should also not be confused with Christianity. If education developed apart from religion, it would undermine the unity of the sacred kingdom. The worst allegation against communism was that it was against religion. Sobhuza's efforts were directed at bringing together people of diverse religions and of different standards of education.

In the several development plans drawn up by the government after independence, education was given a high priority but not conceived as a basic search for knowledge as much as for training to meet the practical needs of the country. The number of children attending primary schools increased rapidly. New technical and training schools were opened.

Most of the schools were still run by the missions, and mission-school education was based on the principle of promoting the Swazi way of life and the Christian way of life, which was an advance from the earlier approach, in which only the "Christian way of life" was the final goal. All schools had been desegregated since 1964 as a result of the recommendation of the first constitutional commission and, particularly after independence, the education department became more Swazi-oriented. It had extended the Swazi section of the curriculum, and siSwati, the language of the people, was being taught in all schools. There was an attempt to get interesting siSwati textbooks, and a genuine effort was made to inculcate into the students a pride in Swazi history and a knowledge of Swazi customs. The government had also financed a museum and had built a fine storing place for the archives, all in the Lobamba vicinity.

The University of Swaziland started with a campus initially focused on agriculture. Later it was extended to the social sciences, which included history, anthropology, sociology, and political science. For specialized training in engineering, medicine, and geology it was necessary to go outside the country, so a limited number of scholarships were provided. But, as in most developing countries, the scholarships were given in terms of practical rather than theoretical knowledge.

Within Swaziland, emphasis was placed on research related to Swazi interests. Canada, The Netherlands, West Germany, England, and the United States, among others, contributed funds. The staff was drawn from different countries. Though more than 98 percent of the students were African, they came from many different states—particularly Lesotho, Botswana, Zimbabwe, and Zambia and as far afield as Zaire. The University was nevertheless to some extent a little apart from the rest of Swaziland. It was more Western and yet more isolated. The students were more privileged than their peers and perceived themselves as future leaders. At times the relationships between government and university was strained; government felt that the faculty was inculcating subversive or radical ideas; the faculty and students reacted to government restraints. The conflict between the more Westernized and the most traditional Swazi, hinted at in earlier chapters, was becoming more marked.

Sobhuza was one of the few traditional Swazi who continued to incorporate selected Western customs and values into his own lifestyle. Others found it more difficult. The more Western-oriented were criticized by the semi-educated as well as the more traditional as un-Swazi; those who were ardent traditionalists, even if educated, were criticized by the Western-educated as backward or reactionary. Sobhuza appealed to teachers as leaders in modern knowledge and to priests as leaders in ancient wisdom, but he never denigrated ordinary people: "I have learnt much from those others called fools." To him development was neither segregation from nor integration into Western culture. He described his approach simply as "Swazi"—a vague term for a humane and tolerant philosophy of cultural nationalism.

KING SOBHUZA'S DIAMOND JUBILEE—
A DRAMA OF CULTURAL NATIONALISM

In 1980 Sobhuza was acclaimed the longest-living reigning monarch in the world. He agreed to a suggestion by the British high commissioner that the country celebrate in 1981 his "Diamond Jubilee," to commemorate his eighty-second birthday (he was born July 22, 1899); sixty years since his public installation as *Ngwenyama*, traditional sovereign of the Swazi (December 21, 1921); and thirteen years of peaceful postcolonial independence under his leadership as king and head of state (September 6, 1968). Celebration of these historic events was telescoped into the period of one week, from September 1 to 6 (September being a propitious moon in the Swazi calendar). The Swazi translation for Jubilee was *sibhimbi*, officially defined as "a prayer, a thanksgiving, a rejoicing, it is all these things and more."

Sobhuza, the hero, the central character, wrote his own script and directed as well as authorized the entire performance. The actual production (the programming of events, the care of VIPs, and all the minutiae of organization) were the responsibility of his representatives, both in different departments of government and in the SNC. Prince Gabheni, then minister of home affairs, whose portfolio included cultural activities, sports, and housing, played a leading role. Less conspicuous to the foreign public were more traditional councilors, with Mdeni Shabalala, *ndvuna yetinkundla*, at the forefront. Structural tensions stemming from the double system of authority were kept offstage through Sobhuza's skill as director.

The invitation list had been carefully constructed. Selection was both ideological and pragmatic. No one refused. In all, twenty-five countries, with political philosophies ranging from conservative to radical socialist, sent official representatives. Prominent were the presidents of four front-line African states—Zimbabwe, Zambia, Botswana, and Mozambique. President Julius Nyerere of Tanzania, who sent his good wishes and regrets for not being able to attend in person, was represented by a former vice-president, then minister of defense and a member of the central committee. African royalty was represented by the King of Zululand, who was accompanied by his wife, a daughter of Sobhuza, and by the Queen of Lesotho. Queen Elizabeth II of Britain was represented by her sister, Princess Margaret. The few surviving monarchies of Europe, The Netherlands, Sweden, Norway, and Spain, sent high-ranking officials. The largest delegation came from the United States, led by the secretary of the United States Air Force. The second largest came from Britain, and the third from the Republic of China (Taiwan). There were also envoys from the United Nations and the Organization of African Unity.

The absence of any official representative of South Africa was conspicuous. At the same time it was widely known that there was continuous communication between the two governments and that negotiations were going ahead on a controversial issue of land which Sobhuza claimed belonged historically to Swaziland.

The major events of the Jubilee took place within the orbit of the two centers of traditional power—Lobamba, the ritual capital and residence of the queen mother, and Lozitha, the first village established by the king after his installation as *Ngwenyama*. In Lobamba were three buildings completed for Swaziland's first independence celebrations: Embo (Sobhuza's first state house, named after the mythical place of Swazi origin), parliament, and the Somblolo national stadium. The Lozitha complex included an increasing range and number of office buildings, of which the most impressive was for Tibiyo (the mineral royalty fund). Adjoining the old traditional village of Lozitha, which had increased in size over the years, was Lozitha palace, a rather grand two-story residence costing some eleven million *emalangeni*. Each site carried its own message, one predominantly Western, the other essentially Swazi. Together they reflected the complexity of contemporary Swaziland, with Swazi culture at the center, indicating Sobhuza's first principle for modernization: Take the best of the West and join it to the best of our own.

The official program listed as the only event of the first day the arrival of heads of state, their welcome by the prime minister, and their departure to the guest houses. At the airport security was tight; officials, soldiers, and police were much in evidence. Onlookers were kept at a safe distance; the VIP lounge was well guarded. Each arrival was regulated by protocol with consideration given both to relations with the country and to the position of the delegate in his or her own government. A few dignitaries and envoys already in the country were also invited to watch the final act of the traditional annual ceremony, the *Umhlanga* (Reed Dance) at Lobamba. Action thus took place more or less simultaneously at two contrasting sites, the airport at Manzini and the ritual capital of the nation. Crowds, interested and voluble, served as a backdrop for both events.

The performers in the *Umhlanga* were unmarried girls who had been summoned to the capital from all parts of the country, and the ceremony itself had different levels of meaning. In practical terms, the girls performed a national service for the *Ndlovukazi*, as mother of the nation and of the king. They had walked many miles to gather bundles of the long flexible reeds required for the fences surrounding the royal quarters. At a more symbolic level, the reeds, the costumes, and the dance songs conveyed their own message in terms of Swazi concepts of fertility, chastity, and the power of womanhood.

The king and his mother had to be present while the girls threw down their bundles before performing the reed dances in front of an eager audience, including this time the foreign guests. The girls danced and sang with unabated energy until sunset. In contrast with the airport, security at Lobamba was minimal and the atmosphere casual and relaxed.

The main event scheduled for the following day was the private audience given by the king to representatives of each country. Hedged by protocol, the sessions could have been an assembly line of meaningless formality, but Sobhuza's warmth and genuine interest made each audience a personal and memorable experience. Some of the guests were friends of long standing, and with them he caught up on the past. From those he was meeting for the first time he inquired about the countries from which they came, the conditions of life, and the customs of the people. He asked the Egyptians about embalming and the symbolism of the Sphinx. From the Dutch representative he wanted to know if his people still had to fight against the sea, and he inquired about dykes and irrigation. With the South Koreans, who had presented him with a scroll, he discussed calligraphy. He asked the representatives from Zaire about their continuing French connection. That afternoon he saw representatives from eighteen different countries; the rest he would see on the morrow. Except for England, which he had visited on two occasions, he had been to none of the countries. His questions were stimulating: he wanted to know, to learn more, to understand better.

Sobhuza did not consider these private sessions at the Jubilee suitable for discussing controversial political issues. He would make his political statement later and publicly. But several of the incidents brought home to him the threat to established power. A Spanish representative informed him that King Juan Carlos could not come in person, since he had received a serious injury escaping through a window in the latest attempted coup. The Egyptian envoy, who had come in from Maputo, explained that it was difficult for President Sadat to leave the country at a critical time (Sadat was assassinated thirty-two days later). The day before Queen Mamahoto had left Lesotho for Swaziland a bomb had been exploded outside the main airport. The attempt on the life of President Ronald Reagan was still front-page news.

Many of the guests gave the king personal presents, most of them beautiful and valuable. Each was carefully recorded. They included a crystal vase from the queen of Sweden, a bison carved in jade from the government of Canada, a handsome television set and recorder from The Netherlands, an exquisite ivory carving from Taiwan, and a Steuben crystal eagle on an ebony stand (as well as a photograph of the president) from the United States. Some had already given substantial gifts, including a fleet of Mercedes provided by the government of West Germany for the use of those attending the ceremony.

By the third day all the chief guests had arrived for "The Loyal Address" to be given at noon, at a joint session of both houses of parliament. This scene was covered by television, press, and radio. Heads of state, ministers, parliamentarians,

Sobhuza on the steps of parliament in 1981 after receiving the "loyal address" on his Diamond Jubilee. On his right are a high ranking police official and an army officer. On his left are the Speaker of the House, and the then-prime minister, Prince Mabandla, 1973.

and senators were shown to their allotted places on opposite sides of two tables that ran the length of the chamber. The upstairs galleries were crowded with privileged onlookers. Uniformed police stood guard. When everyone was seated, Sobhuza made his entry. He was in traditional battle dress—a leopard skin on top of a print loin cloth. Everyone stood up. Someone from the gallery recited his traditional praises He took his seat on the dais, with Princess Margaret on the right, Queen Mamahotho on his left; to the right of Princess Margaret was President Banaana of Zimbabwe; to the left of Queen Mamahatho, Ndlovukazi Dzeliwe.

The two main speakers, Queen Momahatho, followed by Princess Margaret, paid tribute to Sobhuza in their respective cultural idioms. Thus Queen Mamahotho quoted a Lesotho and Swazi axiom "A King is King because of his people" and congratulated Sobhuza, not only for his long and wise rule "learning from the great ancestors of Africa," but for winning the confidence and love of his neighbors. Princess Margaret pointed out that this was "an important Commonwealth occasion" and referred to Sobhuza as the longest-serving king and valued member "in the family of the Commonwealth." The session was then formally closed. As in theater, the main character may say nothing and yet dominate the scene. So Sobhuza, listening with intense concentration, had been the most powerful, albeit silent, presence.

A garden party at Lozitha palace was scheduled for the afternoon. But this was no ordinary garden party. It was described officially "as a *Sibhimbi* to celebrate the birth and initiation of Lozitha Palace, performed in a way both the living and the dead will appreciate." Once again the main action took place in two distinct but interacting and complementary settings. The queens, all in traditional dress, moved together into an area of the palace gardens adjoining the old village to perform ancient dance songs. In another section of the garden, with access more restricted and guarded, there was a huge canopy with several rows of chairs. Here the heads of state and other dignitaries were taken on their arrival.

On each chair were two documents: a special supplement on Swaziland in *The Times* of London, September 1, 1982, and a mimeographed brochure titled *Lozitha Palace (sigodlo)*. The former featured factual information, dealing primarily with developments and resources in Swaziland. The latter expressed the Swazi ethos in relation to a modern architectural structure, a structure described as "practical and functional, but which, to have any meaningful value, had to embody the essence of our nationhood. And that essence, the umbilical cord that links us with the spirit of our forefathers, is culture. Culture, to define it, is that which instinctively rules and governs our every action and is distinct from science and technology."

The VIPs seated under the canopy could hear but not see the *sibhimbi* dancers. Opposite them was a military band, and when Sobhuza came from the *sibhimbi* to join the dignitaries, the band struck up the Swazi national anthem.

An eloquent speech by Prince Mabandla as prime minister was published the following day in the inaugural issue of *The Swazi Observer*, the first postindependence newspaper, financed by Tibiyo. It was a speech of gratitude, appreciation, and loyalty, in which the prince told how, when the king took control, some foreign observers openly expressed the fear that he would rule "with unbridled tyranny and despotism." But as they could see, this prediction had proved false.

After the speech came a royal feast. For the dignitaries under the canopy it included delicate sandwiches, hors d'oeuvres, canapés, chicken, and champagne. For the others the emphasis was on grilled meat and beer, Swazi favorites.

That night a state ball, held at the Royal Swazi Hotel, was hosted by the prime minister. It was known that Sobhuza would not be present. The affair had been organized to please the people who enjoy "that sort of thing." It was also described as "a page from British etiquette." For those not invited to the ball there was a dazzling display of fireworks at the Somhlolo stadium, the scene of activities for the following day, September 4, when Sobhuza would speak to the "peoples of the world."

That day was comparable to the spectacular celebration of independence in 1968. It began with wonderful displays of physical skills and beautiful dancing and singing; the schoolchildren excelled themselves, the bands included in their repertoire Beethoven's "Ode to Joy" and "Hold Him Down You Swazi Warriors"; the king and his prime minister, both in traditional *Ncwala* costume, joined their respective age regiments for the great traditional anthem, and all the royal women played their part. The police, the defense force, and the prison service performed, each in distinctive uniform; security was conspicuous.

Sobhuza had thought about his Jubilee speech for some time and had originally recorded it in siSwati, but, because of the wide audience he wanted to reach, he had it translated into English and read the revised English version. His starting point was what he saw as "a confusion in the entire world" which he attributed to the "lack of mutual trust without which quality, whether it be on an international or an interpersonal level, nothing can succeed." To establish trust, people must talk to each other. "Language differentiates people from wild animals. . . . Talk with your enemies. He who regards himself as my enemy cannot succeed because I will spare no effort in getting closer to him until there is a conference. Do not approach him as an enemy, but in the spirit of helping another human being, your brother." The alternative, he warned, was "confrontation, arms manufacturing, and stockpiling of military weapons."

Focusing next on the problem of "strife, confusion, and unrest in Africa," he identified its root cause "as culture conflict, or, more specifically, the alienation through education of Africans from their own culture." He referred to Professor Bronislaw Malinowski, whom he had met at a conference on education in South Africa in the 1930s, and pointed out that the problem was not inherent in education, but rather in the confusion of Christianity with education; the missionaries had treated them as "indissolubly tied together." Mission-educated Africans then adopted European customs of food, clothing, and marriage, rejecting their own as inferior and undesirable. "In that way," Sobhuza said, "we have lost much of our own old culture. We do not know what is bound to what. Now we are trying to find ourselves." He contrasted this development with that of Asian countries which had effectively kept their own customs—religion, food,

Some of Sobhuza's wives watching the parade at the Diamond Jubilee, 1981.

and clothing. But, he added, "we shall not copy the East and we shall not copy the West. We must produce what is best for us." He then thanked the Swazi people for their unity, cultural pride, and cooperation which together had made possible the celebration of the Jubilee, and at the same time gave advice and warning: "The Roman Empire fell because of luxury and complacency."

The crowd applauded enthusiastically, but it was clear that their enthusiasm was for the speaker rather than the speech. It was not the speech of a politician; it did not boast of past achievements and made no promises for a glorious future. Those who had hoped to hear a stirring appeal to nationalism were left unmoved, and those who had expected Sobhuza to speak directly on Swaziland's position in current politics were disappointed. After a few more events, the production ended with a grand parade and an impressive exit.

The following day the king and queen mother stayed in their respective homes and saw official guests privately. Among them were fifteen Swazi chiefs from the Republic of South Africa who had come with many followers to express allegiance to Sobhuza and to request that they be brought into the kingdom. Organized tours of economic developments in Swaziland (the sugar estates, the impressive forestation schemes, the pineapple plantations) were arranged for official visitors.

The last public act of Jubilee week (Sunday, September 6, the date of independence) was programmed as a thanksgiving service at Somhlolo stadium. The king, the queen mother, queens and other royals, all in Swazi clothing, attended the service. Though the audience was smaller than on the preceding day it numbered several thousands. A wide range of ministers prayed and preached and the Bible Society presented the king and queen mother with copies of the Bible, translated into siSwati.

The Jubilee was over. But what was its message? Or really, the messages? What did the Jubilee say?

INTERPRETATION

Like any well-constructed drama, the Jubilee unfolded in tightly directed scenes, each with its own symbolic actions, drawn together in such a way that they expressed Sobhuza's personal philosophy of cultural synthesis and national integration. For Sobhuza, it was more than a jubilation and a tribute, it was an opportunity to express, in his last public message to the world, his hopes, fears, and philosophy.

For the Jubilee there was no clear script but a flexible text that incorporated elements from other performances, more especially previous celebrations of independence. The main characters were the same but they played additional roles, selecting, adapting, or improvising, both intuitively and deliberately, items they considered the best and most suitable for the occasion. It was a process of routinization through repetition and of innovation through new contacts. The organizers were not interested in reproducing Swazi history as something static, but in expressing its continuity. What was best in Swazi culture was a selection from a dynamic past. And, in the same way, what was Western was a mixture of many cultures.

The use of the metaphor of theater is deliberate, but it must be emphasized that the Jubilee was in fact not theater. The performance was not a play. Theater produces reality through illusion. The Jubilee produced illusion through reality. The characters were both themselves and idealized projections of themselves.

The Jubilee was a complex communication made in different languages or symbols—social space, dress, animal imagery. Throughout the Jubilee all the available "languages" of cultural nationalism were evident, conveying both general and specific, explicit and implicit messages. What was clear was a sense of appropriateness, a deliberate interweaving of cultural symbols in particular events, though the final construction did not necessarily receive the same interpretation. For example, throughout the Jubilee Sobhuza wore different styles of Swazi clothing; on the main day he wore the most elaborate style, symbolizing the significance of the occasion. To some this appeared a display of Swazi nationalism, to others an anti-Western statement, but taken in the context of his speech, in which he emphasized the appropriateness of maintaining one's own customs, it was a demonstration of his position: in a celebration of Swazi kingship, his dress was symbol of the continuity between past and present. Changes from Western to Swazi clothing reflected his interpretation of particular situations; in the past he had worn a Western suit at the opening and closing of parliament, but because of his perception of his role at the "Loyal Address" in parliament during the Jubilee, he appeared in Swazi dress.

To Swazi traditionalists, Lobamba remained *umphakatsi* (the "within," the sacred center, the *axis mundi*, the dominant ambiance). To Western visitors, Lobamba was an old-fashioned village—a collection of huts grouped around a cattle byre. To the Swazi, the costumes had specific ritual associations; Westerners described them as picturesque or primitive. For Sobhuza and other leading Swazi the Jubilee was a sacred totality, operating within a national framework. The garden party, for example, with the dancing of the *sibhimbi* at one end and the band playing near the canopy at the other, were complementary and interacting, rather than opposed, messages, and both were incorporated into the "*sibhimbi* of the palace."

While the Jubilee communicated many messages, perhaps its most important were political statements—a warning against dangers ahead; the vulnerability of a small country; and the need for trust built on discussion as a basis for peace and stability. For this, allies were necessary, as reflected in the invitation list.

Internally, the Jubilee put forward a statement of unity, an affirmation of the monarchy at a time when, unlike the situation in the past, the future of the kingship was itself in jeopardy. The Jubilee revealed the support of Sobhuza, and gave him the opportunity of an international platform from which to express his policy of building on established customs rather than blindly aping other cultures. It was a declaration of his faith, and a plea for peace and harmony within, as well as without, the borders of Swaziland. For those at odds with the monarchy as a system of government, the recognition of Sobhuza given by presidents of African states advocating radical socialism was particularly important.

Sobhuza had always argued that political stability required a sound economic base, and the question of economic cost was an important element in his calculations. It was his hope that, despite the heavy expenses, the publicity given the event and the enthusiastic responses of invited guests would yield future financial returns through new investments and tourism, already one of Swaziland's more important industries.

It was largely the ideal of political stability and economic promise, of harmony and progress, that was communicated through the media—through newspaper articles, photographs, film, and television, as well as by symbols and signs of traditional rituals; and it is this ideal portrayal that will be perpetuated as part of Swazi cultural history. Existing conflicts and tensions were contrary to this central message. The Jubilee was a statement of what ought to be—of ideal relationships that are seldom enacted in everyday reality but which were the goals of a Swazi king seeking national stability and peaceful international relations.

11 / The monarch and
the monarchy: 1981-1983

Sobhuza was old and frail. At the time of the Jubilee it was widely known that he was suffering from leukemia, an incurable illness. The period of remission was indefinite but limited, and he was trying desperately to complete difficult and controversial political negotiations with South Africa affecting the borders of the kingdom itself.

He had taken no queen as a main wife and he knew that his successor would only be chosen after his death. There were constitutional safeguards, but conflict was traditional in succession to the monarchy. So Sobhuza tried to provide for a peaceful interregnum. But all his wisdom and efforts could not control the future. Discord was already present: conflict is the germ of history.

ROYAL AMBITION OR SACRED MISSION?

During the colonial period Sobhuza had struggled to regain for his people land within the small area designated as Swaziland. The enemy was the British, the goal independence. Sobhuza's success was acknowledged; it was a major political achievement. But after independence the campaign was extended, and though the techniques of peaceful diplomacy were the same, the enemy was different, the stakes higher, and the dangers greater.

Swazi rulers had always challenged the validity of the borders drawn by representatives of British, Boers, and Portuguese in the last half of the nineteeth century. Until independence there seemed little possibility of success. Indeed, the reverse seemed the more likely. The Republic (initially the Union) of South Africa had made many efforts to incorporate Swaziland, the last being as late as 1965. But as a result of independence the situation in both countries had changed. Sobhuza, as head of an independent state, took up the issue of land with the government of South Africa not on the basis of incorporation, but as the renegotiation of boundaries in the light of historical and documentary evidence.

Sobhuza's approach and policy were consistent, but the reaction of the government of South Africa appeared to have changed. Instead of speaking of incorporating Swaziland, it now expressed a willingness for Swaziland to incorporate specific areas of land in the Republic to further "ethnic unification"! As the

National Party in power in South Africa refined its ruthless policy of dividing its African population permanently into eight major ethnic groups segregated into so-called Bantustans (subsequently translated as "homelands"), Swaziland, with Sobhuza as its head, assumed a new significance. South Africa was interested in having Swaziland join the so-called Constellation, a confederation of Southern African homeland states. The members would all have an equal voice in formulating regional policy, while retaining autonomy in their own territories. It was part of Prime Minister Botha's latest strategy to appear to extend a measure of political power to the Blacks while in fact maintaining white supremacy in his economically dominant domain. To bring in Swaziland, an internationally recognized independent state, would give substantial strength which the confederation lacked, and it was hoped that it might encourage Lesotho and even Botswana to join. According to the census of 1975 more than 750,000 Swazi were living in South Africa. The total population of the Kingdom of Swaziland was roughly 500,000.

In 1976 South Africa created for the Swazi within its borders a "homeland" called KaNgwane, with its own territorial authority and national legislative assembly (KNLA). KaNgwane, totaling 787,500 acres, fell in the Eastern Transvaal, adjoining Swaziland's northwestern border. It had a Swazi population of some 300,000. The population was ethnically homogeneous but split into two rival factions: One was represented by Chief Mkolishi Dlamini, a Swazi royal acceptable to Sobhuza and the original chief minister of the KaNgwane legislative assembly. Mkolishi's faction regarded Swazi ethnicity as the overriding bond and through its chiefs had persistently petitioned to come under the authority of Sobhuza. To be citizens of the independent Swazi kingdom would be the fulfillment of many years of endeavor, and they had confidence that their future would be better than their present.

The rival faction was headed by Enoch J, Mabuza, a non-Dlamini, a former school inspector, subsequently elected chief minister of KNLA. Mabuza represented a small but established bourgeoisie—generally better educated, relatively wealthy and enterprising—teachers, civil servants, and traders. At the same time that Mabuza affirmed loyalty to Sobhuza and identified with Swazi culture he was afraid of the economic and political consequences of coming into a country which could not find employment for its own population and where Swazi from South Africa were in danger of being treated, if not as foreigners, at least as second-class citizens.

People had not forgotten the case of Ngwenya, the Swazi who had been declared a prohibited immigrant because he was born on the South African side of the border and banished from Swaziland after he had won a seat in the 1973 election. Mabuza was not prepared to accept the status of an "independent" homeland on the conditions offered by South Africa—conditions that restricted political advancement, closed the possibility of Africans ever becoming full citizens of South Africa, and would make them increasingly vulnerable to South Africa's control over cheap labor.

Not only were KaNgwane and its people and resources involved in the calculations of the South African government, South Africa was also ready to negotiate the transfer to Swaziland of another area, Ngwavuma, an artificially defined political strip on South Africa's border with Mozambique, that would give the Swazi limited access to the sea. The population of Ngwavuma was estimated at 100,000 and was ethnically diversified. The two major groups were Swazi and Zulu. In 1976 the South African government had demarcated Ngwavuma as part of *KwaZulu* (the homeland of the Zulu). The Zulu were some six million strong, the largest single ethnic group in South Africa. Their leader, Chief Gatsha Buthelezi, had persistently refused to accept independence of the KwaZulu homeland on the terms offered by South Africa for reasons similar to those of Mabuza, albeit more forcefully expressed.

The South African government worked with different leaders of various homelands in terms of its own interests, political, and economic. The complex behind-the-scenes negotiations in the present case deserve a monograph of their own; the public documents are full of contradictory statements, manipulation of figures, denials, allegations, intrigue, and the exploitation of Swazi ethnicity in the broader context of white South African racism.

Sobhuza figured in the background, acting through selected messengers, especially Sishayi Nxumalo (director of Tibiyo) and R. V. Dlamini (minister of foreign affairs). Most Swazi officials were neither consulted nor kept informed. All dealings were with accredited representatives of the South African government on the grounds that international boundaries could only be negotiated by heads of independent states, not leaders of dependent homelands. The first public announcement of Sobhuza's stand on the land issue appeared in the South African press; it evoked consternation and a barrage of unfavorable criticism.

Sobhuza responded by calling a meeting on March 19, 1982, at Lozitha palace to clarify the position of his government. It was attended by approximately thirty resident and nonresident chiefs of diplomatic missions or their representatives (including British, Taiwanese, Israeli, American, Egyptian, French, West German, Tanzanian, Swedish, and South Korean) as well as all of Swaziland's ambassadors and high commissioners called home from abroad, and by members of parliament, permanent secretaries, and the Swazi National Council. In his opening remarks, Sobhuza emphasized that the confusion arose from media reports that Swaziland was negotiating with South Africa for the incorporation of territories inhabited by ethnic Swazi whereas the Swaziland government position was that borders and boundaries had never been legally established and that both nations had long recognized that fact. He again referred to the importance of speaking to opponents and convincing them of the justice of one's cause.

An official statement was then read by the minister of foreign affairs describing the history of Swaziland's claims to the two areas. Negotiations for the return of Swazi territory had started long before South Africa formulated its policy of Bantustans. Following the establishment of the Union of South Africa in 1910, Swaziland had negotiated through the British. In 1966, when KaNgwane was pronounced a Bantustan, Sobhuza requested the British to ask the South Africans to hold the matter in abeyance. Direct discussions were resumed soon after independence. The claim for the return of KaNgwane had not changed.

Ngwavuma had a different history. The Swazi had previously protested that the British annexation of Ngwavuma after they (the British) had defeated the Zulu infringed British treaty obligations and promises to the Swazi. It was only incorporated into KwaZulu in 1976 by the unilateral decision of the South African government. The Swazi government had objected to this decision, which resulted in about 15,000 Swazi who were not prepared to pay allegiance to the Zulu fleeing into Swaziland, where they were being maintained by the high commission for refugees as well as by the Swaziland government.

Three months after the palace meeting in June 1982, proclamations in the South African government gazette officially abolished the KaNgwane legislative assembly and excised the Ngwavuma district from the administration of the KwaZulu legislative assembly. Pretoria demanded that Swaziland accept all South African-born Swazi as a precondition to the land transfer and made it clear that South African-born Swazi would forfeit all claims to future South African citizenship. It was officially estimated that Swaziland's population of roughly 600,000 would be increased by between 750,000 and 850,000.

Reactions against South Africa's actions were immediate. Buthelezi, speaking on behalf of the people of Ngwavuma, and Mabuza, representing the KaNgwane legislative assembly, appealed separately to the courts of law in their respective provinces of Natal and the Transvaal against the unilateral decisions by proclamation of the South African government.

On June 30, 1982, the High Court of Durban (in Natal) nullified the transfer of Ngwavuma and returned control to the KwaZulu authorities. The South African government took the case on appeal to the full bench of the Supreme Court of Natal. Judgment was to be given on September 30.

Mabuza's case for KaNgwane was heard first in the Supreme Court of the Transvaal which, after lengthy argument, decided to refer the case to the appeal court in Bloemfontein, the highest court in the Republic. Judgment was to be delivered on November 25. According to legal opinion, there could be no further appeal and no redress in international law. But if judgment went against the South African government it could simply pass legislation depriving Swazi in South Africa of any claim to South African nationality.

Meanwhile, Sobhuza persisted in his efforts at redefining the boundaries. He had interpreted the offer of land by the South African government as an effort "to right the wrongs of the past." His approach implied that his claim would go beyond the demarcated homelands, which happened to lie within the area claimed by Swazi as theirs by historic right, and would include flourishing towns, developed largely by Swazi labor which fell within the traditional Swazi boundaries. His efforts were directed to document, as well as to justify, the legitimacy of his claims and have them accepted by other African countries. He was aware that this would be difficult: it was an international issue that would have international repercussions. In 1964, the Organization of African Unity had issued a major resolution on border disputes under which all member states pledged themselves "to respect the frontiers existing on their achievement of national independence." But the Swazi situation was unique. The territory being offered Sobhuza was not being seized by force. The stand he was taking was not new, and his attitude toward *apartheid* had not changed. His people inside Swaziland expressed tremendous pride and pleasure in the result of his negotiations. Sobhuza had won a great moral as well as political victory. Criticism was muted; doubts of the ultimate benefits (economic or political) were dismissed. Those who voiced objections were accused of disloyalty.

Sobhuza was therefore surprised and embarrassed by the interest and intensity of opposition from outside Swaziland and distressed by the judgment of the South African courts. He had been led to believe that his efforts had the full support of the vast majority of Swazi in South Africa as well as at home; he thought his approach might serve as a model for other Africans confronting border problems, that it would have the approval of all his friends and would be legally recognized. He was amazed to find that extreme right-wing Nationalists and more liberal Progressives, for diametrically opposite reasons, supported the claims of Buthelezi and Mabuza: the Nationalists for the very practical reason that it was giving away good land to an African country, the Progressives for moral as well as practical reasons. Thus the latter argued that additional land could not support the additional population; that it was beyond the capacity of the present government to provide for Swazi already in the kingdom; and that there was the danger that South Africa would treat migrant workers in the area as foreigners in terms of work opportunities, limited as they were. While it was true that Ngwavuma would give Swaziland access to the sea, this was meaningless without a harbor, and the country that financed the harbor would exert its own influence. Moreover, they argued further that the new population already contained an opposition: the proposed transfer of land would exacerbate tensions between Swazi and Zulu and play on old rivalries, while the very fact that negotiations were carried out with the sanction and help of South Africa would be seen as a threat to the security of Mozambique.

The Republic of South Africa, of course, would benefit economically and politically. It could control the employment of Swazi in the homeland while it reduced the number of its own unemployed by their forced exodus. Swaziland would become more, not less, dependent on South Africa, and its international standing as an independent state would lend respectability to the South African policy. Then too, the transfer of Ngwavuma to Swaziland would provide South Africa a buffer between it and Mozambique and at the same time indicate its power over Buthelezi for refusing to accept homeland "independence."

But Sobhuza was committed to what he described as a sacred mission. He believed he could negotiate so as to ensure that the welfare of his people would not be affected by the influx of population, and that the newcomers would benefit by being citizens of an African kingdom, not residents in a country where they were nationals but not citizens.

At the end of July he sent three groups of his top-level men to different countries in Africa to explain the situation and the justice of their cause. On their return, he called them to Lozitha palace to report. It was Friday, August 19. He seemed well, was alert, and questioned them closely. On Saturday, August 21, the South African broadcasting station announced that Sobhuza, King of Swaziland, was dead.

DEATH AND BURIAL

Sobhuza's death was sudden and the circumstances strange. No one was allowed to probe the details or follow up the rumors. The doctor, a white Swazi who had treated him for leukemia and was also minister of health, was with him at the end. Officially, King Sobhuza II died of heart failure. Close kin— brothers and sisters and the oldest children—contacted as soon as possible after the arrival of the doctor, were too late to bid him farewell. The preliminary announcement from South Africa was obviously an embarrassment to the Swaziland government, compelling those responsible for the funeral arrangements to act more speedily than tradition would otherwise have required.

The Swazi had been alerted, but not informed, by the fact that on Sunday, August 22, a major soccer match at Somhlolo stadium was canceled, and the regular Sunday radio service began with the hymn "Abide with Me." The following day the traditional governor of Lobamba broadcast in siSwati, "The Lion of the Nation is resting." The news spread like a veldt fire, leaving behind desolation and fear.

At the same time, it was known that sovereignty would remain with the surviving queen mother in a new capacity as queen regent, assisted by a senior prince and the inner council (liqoqo), until the new king was old enough to be fully installed with his own mother.

Swazi say "A King is King twice"—he is king of his own family and king of the nation. Decisions about funeral procedure were not made by a single group. Kin were distinct from cabinet, though a few members of the kin group were also members of the cabinet. The kin were concerned primarily with the selection of the heir, which was solely their responsibility, and with the more personal details of the mortuary ritual. It was clear that it would be difficult to reach rapid decisions on the basis of consensus. Their discussions were secret. The cabinet, on the other hand, representing the state of Swaziland, was obliged to act in the public arena, though its deliberations were confidential. Sobhuza was also an international figure. Foreign governments wanted to know when the funeral would be held so they could send their representatives to pay tribute and to condole. It was also expected that the names of the future king and queen mother would be announced.

Decisions were difficult; there were disagreements at many levels. Since no one involved in the burial of Sobhuza's own father was still alive, there was uncertainty over traditional treatment and procedures. Knowledge of the death rituals for a king had been limited to selected members of two clans. The left-hand blood brother traditionally played a major supervisory role. In the case of Sobhuza, the blood brother had died many years earlier and his heir was an ordained priest, trained at a theological college in the United States. However, he had been appointed by Sobhuza to investigate and record traditional customs, a task for which his ecclesiastical training had hardly prepared him. But his advice was sought, and he was involved in many of the decisions.

A major disagreement about the treatment of the corpse reflected the different perspectives of the traditional and the Westernized. Historically, the elaborate mortuary rites included a traditional embalming, a process of drying, or squeezing out, the "juices," in the course of which the spirit or soul manifested itself physically. The more Westernized, however, represented by the prime minister, accepted the suggestion of the minister of health (the doctor who had attended Sobhuza) that the ancient procedure be replaced by modern, scientific embalming. The minister of health first ascertained that this was compatible not only with the wishes of the prime minister and other members of cabinet but also acceptable to certain influential people of Lobamba, including the traditional governor and the heir of the left-hand ritual blood brother. He then phoned morticians in Johannesburg, who arrived speedily and did their work promptly and efficiently by injecting formalin.

The body had been moved by the family from Embo to Lobamba and placed in the hut associated with his marriage to his first ritual queen. By injecting formalin as a preservative, the corpse was kept supple and lifelike. But since it was not being preserved under controlled conditions, the doctor was obliged to administer further local injections when there were any visible signs of deterioration. The traditional embalmers, who had come to offer their services, were sent home. Many elders had not been consulted and reacted with anger and consternation, predicting dire consequences and cosmic disorder when they realized the effects of the modern process of embalmment. They asked that the process be reversed, but this was not scientifically possible, and the prime minister went ahead with the arrangements.

The state funeral took place on September 3. The site was a vast field with historic associations in the Lobamba area. Somhlolo stadium had been rejected because of taboos associated with death which would have prohibited its use by future kings. The central feature of the new arena was a high square mausoleum of glass, with a platform inside and an opening in the south. Rows of chairs under temporary shelters were provided for the mourners. But the majority sat or stood in the open for more than four hours.

The day was gray and gloomy. Huge crowds converged from all directions. Public transport had been commandeered, and all traffic moved silently at funeral pace. In the arena some 25,000 people, which included no children, sat quietly staring into space. In every society, the exhibition of universal human emotions, including sorrow, is regulated by custom and rationalized by beliefs. Among the Swazi natural expressions of grief—tears and sobs—should be controlled until the body is buried, when the spirit or soul joins the ancestors— "those below."

The difference in costume reflected both the mourning and the ongoing vitality of Swazi society. The *emabutfo* came by thousands wearing traditional battle dress and carrying shields and sticks but they were without their plumed headgear, leopard skins, and ceremonial decorations. The royal women were wrapped in drab-colored blankets and their heads were covered. No queens of Sobhuza were present—they were at Lobamba, secluded in their huts, their hair disheveled in the first stage of mourning. But the three sections of the modern armed forces (soldiers, police, and prison guards), each with its own band, appeared in vividly colored Western uniforms that contrasted sharply with the predominantly somber dress of other mourners.

The presence of Ndlovukazi, Dzeliwe, in full regalia, was required by tradition. She sat in the center of the front row, among the foreign diplomats, her face strained and haggard, but in control of herself. The head of the army and of the police then affirmed the loyalty of the armed forces by placing in the ground in front of her the flag of Swaziland.

There were rumors that the coffin might contain only the accoutrements, but not the body of the king. Suddenly there was a sound like thunder, the first of twenty-one cannon salvos quite different from the sound of the twenty-one gun salutes fired at celebrations in the king's lifetime. Then the hearse appeared; it was a gun carriage bearing a glass-fronted casket. Quite uncannily a gentle drizzle fell for a few seconds; people swear that rain had fallen when the coffin was taken out of the hut at Lobamba and followed the cortège.

Members of the defense force raised the casket above their heads and walked with it for all to see. The crowd gasped, and there was a burst of uncontrollable wailing and sobbing. They beheld Sobhuza in his dark-blue army uniform, with full decorations, sitting facing east, looking lifelike and benign, as relaxed as if in his limousine. The bands played the last post as the pallbearers placed the casket on the platform in the mausoleum and slowly walked away.

The king was not left on his own. Crouched in a corner, unrecognizable beneath an *Ncwala* cape, one of Sobhuza's close friends and councilors remained in attendance. The warriors chanted powerful traditional war songs recounting the deeds of Swazi kings.

Then came the tributes. Conducting this part of the ceremony was A. K. Hlope, a man close to the king who, as a member of the parliamentary cabinet and also of the liqoqo, reflected the integration of two cultural traditions. Funeral orations were given by a few carefully selected persons, who had known Sobhuza well. The main speaker was the prime minister; most of the others were ministers of different religious denominations. King Moshoeshoe II of Lesotho spoke on behalf of the heads of state. I followed the Prime Minister, speaking in my role as official biographer of the king and as an old friend.

After the speeches, wreaths were placed around the base of the mausoleum. The first was laid by Prince Sozisa, as senior prince and head of the liqoqo. Then came heads of state and other high officials. Nearly all the countries that had been welcomed at the Jubilee sent representatives of comparable or higher rank to the state funeral. The presidents of Mozambique and Botswana attended in person; Prince Michael, Duke of Kent, represented the United Kingdom. But in addition to mourners from countries one would have expected there were other prominent and more controversial figures: Oliver Tambo, president-in-exile of the African National Congress, banned in the Republic of South Africa; at the other extreme, the vice-president and the minister of foreign affairs of that same country.

The extremes of political ideology were thus more striking at the funeral than at the Jubilee, and while this was an indication of Sobhuza's personal charisma, it raised the question whether the new leaders of Swaziland would be able to maintain the peace and stability and the principled neutrality for which Sobhuza had worked throughout his long life.

When the ceremony was over, mourners went to condole with the Ndlovukazi who was waiting with Prince Sozisa at the House of Parliament. But at the arena regiments remained on guard, and late that night the casket was carried back to Lobamba. There the Western uniform was removed from the body, which was then ritually wrapped in the traditional black oxhide shroud.

The last rites were still to be performed. The king had chosen as his burial site a high mountain in the south of Swaziland, an area associated with the founders of the Swazi nation overlooking the Zulu border. The body was carried there during the night by *emabutfo* under the leadership of the governor of Lobamba. The cave tomb had already been prepared. Cattle were sacrificed to the ancestors who were asked to receive the king. The warriors returned to Lobamba on September 5 and reported to the queen regent. Until then, grief had been restrained. Now there was uninhibited weeping.

The death of Sobhuza marked the end of a period in Swazi history. But, in Swazi idiom, "A person goes [dies]; work remains." September 6, the day after the regiments returned from Sobhuza's grave, was the fourteenth anniversary of the postcolonial independent Kingdom of Swaziland. The public had not yet been told the name of the heir to the kingship, while the problems of independence confronted by Sobhuza had not been resolved, and new difficulties were arising.

DISPUTED SUCCESSION

Disputes over succession are characteristic of institutionalized leadership. They occur in a wide range of societies but appear to be chronic in centralized political systems in which there is no single unambiguous principle of succession and a plurality of legitimate candidates. In Swaziland the period between the death of one king and the acceptance by the people of his successor was characterized by dissension and disorder. A praise song to King Mswati ends with the dramatic declaration, "No king is installed without violence."

Polygamy, built into the traditional kingship, was a source both of strength and of disruption. Sobhuza, who had taken some sixty-five queens from thirty-two different clans, was survived by some thirty queens and 110 children of whom over forty were sons.

To legalize the traditional institutions of transition, Sobhuza had signed a decree dated June 21, 1982. This provided that the functions and responsibilities of the king would be performed by the Ndlovukazi as queen regent. A senior prince, described not as regent but as "the Authorized Person," would act on her behalf if, for any reason, she were unable to perform the functions of her office. A new Liqoqo would be appointed on the basis of individual merit. Liqoqo was spelled with a capital "L" and defined not simply as an advisory council but as "the Supreme Council of State whose function is to advise the King on all matters of State." Sobhuza died before the names were made public. On Sobhuza's death Mabandla, acting in terms of the decree, named Dzeliwe Ndlovukazi and regent. In this capacity, she put her signature to a list of fifteen names, submitted to her by senior princes and purported to have been left by Sobhuza but for which there was no evidence in his handwriting. Most of the names were familiar and expected, but the list included a few that raised doubts about its authenticity. The Liqoqo was not, however, a monolithic body. It reflected a range of opinion and included educated and uneducated, old and relatively young; at one end was Prince Mabandla's father, at the other Prince Gabheni. Dzeliwe also accepted as "the Authorized Person" Prince Sozisa, whose father had been prince regent during part of Sobhuza's minority.

The general principles of succession described on pages 23–24 were well known, and their application reduced the number of possible candidates to five. Disagreement and the development of factions were inevitable. Decisions were made by the *Lusendvo*, a council of kinsmen composed of senior princes (the late king's classificatory fathers and brothers), a senior princess (his "sister"), and the queen mother (his mother, real or surrogate). No "son" of the deceased king could participate directly. In the case of Sobhuza, the queen mother (his paternal grandmother) had played a decisive role in the selection.

Following customary procedure, no prince put himself forward. Outsiders irrespective of rank had no direct say, but maternal connections extending far beyond the immediate kin of a particular queen constituted the core of support for her son and at the same time reflected existing divisions within the inner circle of the Dlamini. This was the dynamics of succession: the resolution was not necessarily a finale. Discussions of the council are always private and details of what happened in the case of Sobhuza's heir must, for the present, remain confidential.

By the time Sobhuza was buried the choice of the future rulers had been made but not yet publicized, and dissent continued. Ntombi Twala, one of Sobhuza's younger queens, and her son Makhosetive were the chosen. The choice was unexpected. Mothers of three other candidates were historically higher in pedigree. But though the Twala clan was not historically one of those described as "Bearers of kings," it had strong traditional ties to kingship. The Twala clan was a branch of the Motsa, a clan which for generations had provided each Dlamini king with the second of his two ritual wives. The son of the first Motsa queen held a privileged position among the princes during his father's lifetime and was entitled to a special inheritance on his death. Both Sobhuza's first Motsa queen and her son were dead. Though Ntombi's father was not a chief, he was a respected headman in an area well known and frequented by Sobhuza. Overriding the fact that Ntombi's pedigree was not as high as that of other claimants were certain political considerations. Ntombi had only one child, and there would be no question of maternal favoritism or sibling rivalry. Moreover, he was a minor and he and his mother could be trained in the elaborate ritual associated with the dual sovereignty. Ntombi also had her personality in her favor. She had come into the *sigodlo* (queen's quarters) as a young handmaiden to Sobhuza's most Westernized and most publicized queen, at whose request Ntombi had subsequently been taken as a co-wife. Ntombi was intelligent, her character was beyond reproach; she was well known, liked, and respected. Her son was a bright and attractive child frequently seen in Sobhuza's company. Sobhuza had given him the name Makhosetive (King of Many Nations), since he was born in 1968 when leaders of different countries came to celebrate independence.

Ntombi had been separated from other queens and established in a modern residence known as *Phondvo* (Horns) or *Kanyamazane* (Wild Animals). The first name referred to the form of the adjacent ridge associated with the migration of Sobhuza I, the second to a private game reserve developed by a German count who had bought the land and built the house that had then been bought back with Swazi national funds.

Traditional mourning rituals varying in duration and intensity with the relationship of mourners to the deceased king had been imposed on the entire nation. Every male was commanded to shave his head completely, no weapons could be carried by the regiments, special clothing was specified, and for three moons, until the end of the public mourning, plowing was prohibited. Swazi obeyed more or less willingly. Some of the more modern, including many civil servants, considered the injunctions archaic. They thought they looked curious with their shaved heads and were at first embarrassed to appear in public, but it soon became a sign of social conformity and respect. Those few who persistently refused were fined by the courts—among them were members of the Jehovah's Witnesses movement who refused on religious grounds; their punishment was considered by outsiders a significant departure from the former practice of religious tolerance.

The prohibition on plowing applied to Whites as well as Blacks and had widespread economic effects. Rain, associated with the ancestors and the power of the king and his mother, was normally expected toward the end of August. In 1982 the first rains fell in October; they were short and heavy, but nothing could be planted and farmers were frustrated. The public mourning was officially ended on October 13 but the drought continued. Rain fell in November, but the crops were poor. Cattle died, food was scarce, the economy declined. Many interpreted the drought as a sign of the displeasure of the royal ancestors with the way the country was being ruled. It did not change this interpretation to know that Swaziland was not the only country suffering drought—the whole southern region, including South Africa, was affected and in deep recession.

To those who were not directly involved in Swazi politics, the surface was calm, albeit depressing. But beneath the surface, a bitter power struggle, less ideological than personal, erupted in a series of dramatic episodes shattering the tranquility of the country. It involved members of the inner circle of the Dlamini and officials in both the Liqoqo and parliamentary structure.

For the majority of Swazi, inside and outside the kingdom, the monarchy was not in question; it represented a cultural heritage and the main focus of national identity. The divisive issue was no longer limited to the choice of the heir but included the political direction of the nation. The battleground was extended beyond the boundaries of Swaziland into South Africa: with the death of Sobhuza Swaziland no longer spoke through the voice of one great man.

THE ANARCHIC INTERREGNUM

The death of Sobhuza had interrupted the land negotiations with South Africa. Soon after his death, on September 25, the Supreme Court of Natal found the excision of Ngwavuma unlawful and the Supreme Court of Bloemfontein had given judgment in favor of Mabuza and the KaNgwane legislative assembly. Temporally, Ngwavuma was again part of KwaZulu and KaNgwane's legislative assembly was reinstated. The Swaziland government was divided between members eager to push ahead in spite of opposition and a minority who were not prepared to accept the terms offered by South Africa.

Without Sobhuza's presence it became impossible to reconcile the two viewpoints—the one, represented officially by the minister of foreign affairs (R. V. Dlamini), expressing a conciliatory pro-South African view; the other, represented by the prime minister (Mabandla) who, while recognizing the historic validity of Swazi claims, opposed the conditions set by the South African government and foresaw danger to the economy and to the political stability of the kingdom itself.

Hostility to the ANC fed into the political crosscurrents. Mabandla's opponents never forgot that soon after his appointment he had been active in obtaining the release of ANC political detainees. After Sobhuza's death the South African police, with the permission of the minister of foreign affairs, were allowed to cross the border in pursuit of "terrorists." The Sobhuza policy of sympathy for the ANC had moved toward support of South Africa's policy of suppression. Raids by South African commandos against alleged ANC bases in Lesotho, in which innocent people were killed, brought fears that Swaziland, thought to be a launching site for ANC terrorist activities, would be the next target. The Ngwavuma case also brought pressure on the Swazi government to respond to the ANC crisis. Ninety ANC members in Swaziland, some of whom had lived there for twenty years, were put into a refugee camp. The Swaziland government described it as "protective custody [not detention], to ensure their safety."

The absence of Sobhuza was acutely obvious in December and January, the moons of the *Ncwala*. There was no ritual to bring together the police, army, and warriors to strengthen the king, symbol of the nation, against foes from within and enemies from across the borders. In January 1983 the political tensions surrounding Mabandla surfaced in press reports of a thwarted coup attempt. The papers stated that the police blocked the entry of arms into Mbabane by cordoning off the city.

Mabandla, confronted with antagonism from powerful individuals within the Liqoqo and from the cabinet, had decided to strengthen his own position by re-shuffling the cabinet and by reaffirming the strength of parliament. With the approval of Dzeliwe, he announced that the minister of justice, Polycarp Dlamini, would be "promoted" to the position of ambassador to the United States, a prestigious and well-paid post but far removed from the center of real political influence. His supporters protested against his removal so strongly that Dzeliwe acquiesced. Polycarp Dlamini stayed on, and hostility to Mabandla intensified.

At the opening of the fifth session of parliament a "speech from the throne" in the name of Dzeliwe was read by the minister of education, Canon Sipetse. In this speech the Liqoqo was given precedence over parliament. However, this speech was not identical with the original written by Mabandla, which placed power in the hands of an elected parliament. The original had been secretly intercepted by the minister of education, who had shown it to Prince Mfanasibili; it had then been rewritten. However, the original had already been officially sent to the Swaziland broadcasting station and was broadcast that evening.

In the dispute that resulted from the two conflicting speeches one of the members of parliament, Prince Bekhimpi, at that time a deputy minister in the office of the deputy prime minister, walked out in protest against remarks critical of the monarchy. Repercussions of the contradictory statements were felt throughout the country. The police and the army were on alert. The police were loyal to Mabandla; his opponents, led by Prince Mfanasibili, relied more on their contacts with the army. In February the violence of civil war, a danger Sobhuza had averted in the past, seemed inevitable.

Rumors spread that the police were being mobilized by Mabandla. Then two extraordinary incidents hit the news. On February 11 a huge leopard, an animal identified with both royalty and war but not seen in Swaziland for many years, appeared outside Mabandla's official residence in Mbabane. It was shot by one of his guards. A couple of days later an *impundze* (a small wild antelope) appeared and met the same fate. This was interpreted as another threatening omen. In March the public learned that on Mabandla's orders two members of the Liqoqo, Prince Mfanasibili and Chief Mfanawenkosi Maseko, were charged with making seditious statements against the police. Both were detained. Bail was refused to prevent the possibility of their interfering with witnesses while the case was being prepared. Some three weeks before the hearing, set for March 24, both men were unexpectedly released on an order signed by the attorney general, obeying instructions from the minister of justice.

On their release they came to Lobamba, where they were welcomed back with great joy by friends and allies. Mfanasibili openly threatened to destroy Mabandla and his supporters in the Liqoqo asked Dzeliwe to dismiss Mabandla. When she refused, they made it clear that they would remove him by force. She agreed reluctantly to sign the order for his dismissal, dated Sunday, March 20. The preceding day Mabandla had informed the press that his position was secure. When he was shown the order signed by Dzeliwe he immediately left his office, drove to his home, picked up his family, and crossed the nearest border, into South Africa. He was granted temporary asylum by the South African government and subsequently moved not to KaNgwane but to Bophutswana, an "independent" homeland for the Tswana in South Africa.

Initially a statement was issued in the name of the Liqoqo refuting outside press reports that it intended to charge the former prime minister with treason. It informed the nation, however, that Mabandla had prepared and disseminated a speech purporting to be the speech from the throne that usurped the powers of the monarchy, ran counter to proclamations by the king, and was designed to "take *Ncwala* from Lobamba [the ritual capital] and dance it at Mbabane [the government capital]."

Subsequently, in August 1983, a pamphlet headed "Mabandla's Litany of Betrayals" was issued in the name of the secretariat of the Liqoqo. It accused Mabandla of a wide range of crimes—subversion, abuse of power, taking control of the army from the monarch, interfering with the independence of the judiciary by politicizing the bench, corruption—and concluded that Mabandla was "a fugitive from the law and not a political refugee."

There were and probably will always be those who thought Mabandla guilty and those who thought him innocent of trying to subvert the power of the monarchy. Between these two extremes there appeared to be many who simply accepted the suppression of opposition and hoped that it would not disturb their own daily lives.

The position of prime minister was vacant. Prominent candidates included Polycarp Dlamini, minister of justice), Sipetse Dlamini (minister of education), R. V. Dlamini (minister of foreign affairs), Prince Mfanasibili (chairman of the civil service board), Sishayi Nxumalo (director of Tibiyo), and Prince Dumisa, the "rebel prince" who had been active in the NNLC. Following the model set by Sobhuza to avoid the inevitable bitterness had one of these controversial candidates been chosen, the final selection, acceptable to both Dzeliwe and the Liqoqo, was someone who had been less directly involved in the personal power struggle and was not a member of the Liqoqo.

On March 24, 1983, Sozisa announced that Mabandla had been replaced by Prince Bhekimpi of Nkaba Royal Residence. Bhekimpi was a minor public figure. He was the youngest veteran of World War II and had continued to identify himself with the army. He had also served on many political committees as an elected member of the first legislative council and of subsequent parliaments; but he had never been Sobhuza's first choice for national office. At the time of Sobhuza's death he was deputy minister in the office of the deputy prime minister. He was the member who had walked out of parliament in February 1983 in protest against what he considered an insult to the monarchy. Like previous prime ministers, Bhekimpi had not sought the office, but contrary to precedent his appointment had not been sanctioned by a meeting of the nation at the ritual capital. His position was indeed difficult, personally as well as politically. While he was a strong supporter of Sobhuza's approach to acquire land, one of his wives was a daughter of Gatsha Buthelezi, leader of the Zulu opposition to the Swazi claim to Ngwavuma.

The position of Dzeliwe had become increasingly critical; far from being the docile figurehead senior princes had expected, she proved to be a woman of character with a will of her own. She accepted Bhekimpi as prime minister but refused to sign a document, brought by Sozisa, that would have placed her under the control of the Liqoqo. She said she could not read English and would first need to have the document translated into siSwati; for this task she summoned a well-educated and Westernized senior civil servant whom the king had frequently chosen to interpret speeches from siSwazi into English. Having realized the contents, Dzeliwe was not prepared to submit to threats or persuasion. Instead, on August 2, in the presence of senior members of the royal family, she dismissed the entire Liqoqo. She did not mention replacements.

A week later the Liqoqo announced in an *Extraordinary Government Gazette*

Dzeliwe Shongwe, last Ndlovukazi appointed by Sobhuza. With her are her little attendant, her personal policewomen and visitors in the yard of her residence at the ritual capital of Lobamba, September 1981.

that they had deposed Dzeliwe and that Ntombi, mother of Prince Makhosetive, was to be *Ndlovukazi* and regent. In the lingo of the streets, "the employees had sacked the employer." Until virtually the last hour of August 10, Swaziland did not know whether or not this was true. Prince Gabheni, a strong supporter of Dzeliwe, had responded as minister of home affairs to an inquiry from the South African press that everything was normal and that Dzeliwe still held the reins of power. At the same time, the minister of foreign affairs informed ambassadors and the local press that Dzeliwe was no longer regent. Dzeliwe and her supporters, who included several princes including two on the Liqoqo, did not accept her dismissal.

In an urgent application to the high court Dzeliwe challenged the right of the Authorized Person, the Liqoqo, and the prime minister to remove her from office. Her lawyer was Douglas Lukhele, a name well known and widely respected. He had returned to private practice after having been "promoted" from the position of attorney general—a key political position requiring legal expertise and responsibility for the drafting of legislation—to the position of judge, a position higher in status but more remote from politics. He based his case on the argument that the Liqoqo was an advisory body without the legal authority to depose the queen regent and that in any case the Liqoqo had been officially dissolved. The defense claimed that there were sufficient powers to remove Dzeliwe and replace her with a new queen regent. An affidavit drawn up by Douglas Lukhele was submitted to the court on August 17 by the chief of the Lukhele clan, Dr. Dambuza Lukhele (a registrar in the University of Swaziland) appealing against the legality of the deposal of Dzeliwe and claiming to represent the views of the majority of the chiefs in the country.

The hearing was set for August 24; the nation awaited the result. Then the unexpected happened. Dzeliwe's opponents had moved silently to avoid an open hearing and there appeared in the next *Extraordinary Government Gazette* a decree signed by Prince Sozisa as the Authorized Person stating that the high court had no jurisdiction over the appointment or dismissal of a regent, since this was a matter of Swazi law and custom. The chief justice sitting with two other high court judges were in a dilemma. The minister of justice supported the Liqoqo. After deliberating for three days, the chief justice announced that the judges would not proceed with the case. The following day, August 25, *The Times of Swaziland* reported that the police detained both the lawyer who had been acting on behalf of Dzeliwe and the senior civil servant who had translated the document that Dzeliwe had refused to sign once she understood its contents; later, the chief who had submitted the affidavit was also imprisoned.

Dzeliwe was helpless and virtually alone. Organized protests against her deposition were quelled by police. Forty students were arrested. Dzeliwe's strongest supporter on the Liqoqo was Prince Gabheni. On August 26, *The Swazi Observer*, the local paper started at the climax of the Diamond Jubilee and financed largely by Tibiyo to express the interests of the monarchy, carried as front page news PRINCE GABHENI DETAINED. The next day Gabheni stated publicly that he had neither been detained nor put under house arrest. There is evidence that the order for his arrest had been drawn up but then canceled. The announcement in *The Swazi Observer* had shocked not only the Swazi but also local and foreign investors and diplomats. Prince Gabheni, the son most frequently appointed by Sobhuza in his later years to act as his personal representative and spokesman, was both highly respected and prominent. Two other sons of Sobhuza, less in the public eye, had been arrested on August 24, 1983.

After Dzeliwe's case had been removed from the jurisdiction of the high court, she was taken from Lobamba to Zombodze. She refused to return to Masundwini, the relatively modern residence, first referred to on page 6 where she had been one of Sobhuza's queens. Instead she elected to stay at Zombodze, a former ritual capital identified with the renowned Ndolovukazi Gwamile, and which continued to reflect the sanctity of sovereignty. Nor did she readily relinquish the symbolic crown of magic seeds topped with a red feather of the rain bird. When a few powerful men, including Sozisa and Mfanisibili, came to ask her for it, she challenged them to take it. Afraid of incurring the wrath of the ancestors by using force, they left it with her for the time being.

Initially Ntombi had been unwilling to assume Dzeliwe's position on the grounds that she was in mourning, and the period of seclusion would not be over for another two years. But after Dzeliwe had been banished from Lobamba, Ntombi could not withstand the pressure put on her and accepted her fate. She was ritually cleansed and officially announced both queen mother and regent on September 5, 1983. Dzeliwe gave up her royal insignia.

Ntombi remained at Phondvo until a more traditional village known as *Lusasa* was built. This would develop into the full ritual capital when Makhosetive was fully installed as *Ngwenyama*, entitled after taking his first ritual queens to dance his first *Ncwala* and establish a separate official homestead.

Bhekimpi had announced that the young king would soon be shown to his subjects. He had been taken in secret to be educated in a private school in England. The details of his departure, the choice of school, and the security surrounding the boy were matters of dispute and intrigue within the royal family. The main concern of the masses was to see "The Child of the Nation" in person.

Prince Makhosetive arrived in Swaziland on September 9 during his school holidays. Newspapers showed a tall, slender, handsome youth in a Western suit being greeted at the airport by the prime minister and a few members of the royal family and Liqoqo. Security was strong; the public was not invited. On the twelfth he made a brief appearance at Lobamba before a crowd called originally to receive instructions on the elections. For this occasion he wore traditional clothing and carried an ornamental battle axe. The audience, which included chiefs and spectators, was smaller than anticipated, but he was enthusiastically greeted with the royal salute *Bayethe*. He made a good impression. He sat between the prime minister and the Authorized Person, looking, according to reports and photographs, composed, pensive, and serious. Ntombi was not present and the meeting was held outside the *sibaya*. After he had been shown to the nation, Makhosetive was escorted to his limousine and driven back to his own quarters at Phondvo. He returned to school in England three weeks later; the interregnum was not yet over, but his trip was politically timely. His appearance was widely interpreted as an attempt by the Liqoqo to give legitimacy to the appointment of Bhekimpi and his supporters. Shortly afterward Ntombi signed that statement

Prince Makhosetive (with check mark over his head), Sobhuza's successor on the verandah of Mpondvo, the modern temporary residence of the new Ndlovukazi, his mother Ntombi. On his left are two of his older brothers, the senior princess (Nengwase, "sister" of Sobhuza) and younger sibling. On his right are the new Prime Minister, Prince Bhekimpi, guards and non-Dlamini councilors, 1983.

Dzeliwe had rejected, implicitly recognizing the supremacy of the Liqoqo over the queen regent.

ELECTION BY COERCION

The prime minister announced that elections would be held on October 28, in conformity with the Establishment of Parliament Order of 1978, which required elections every five years. The more ambitious members of the Liqoqo would be able to entrench their power on the basis of an electoral system that could legitimately be used to exclude political opponents from parliament. On September 13, 1983, Ntombi, as *Ndlovukazi* and regent, reaffirmed the appointment of members of the Liqoqo; Gabheni's name was not on the list. A week later the formation of a seven-member standing committee within the Liqoqo was gazetted under the signature of the Authorized Person. This small group would exercise the power of day-to-day decision making, but it did not present a united front or recognize a single leader. It included the two men who had been imprisoned by Mabandla and, as a co-opted member, the influential Princess Nengwase, "sister" of Sobhuza, kinswoman and friend of Prince Dumisa and Sishayi Nxumalo.

A new law, replacing the Sedition Act of 1938 introduced in the colonial period, was gazetted in the middle of October. Titled "The Sedition and Subversive Activities Amendment Act of 1983," it provided for a special tribunal appointed by the prime minister, and drastically increased the maximum period of punishment from three years to twenty years or, in the case of fine, from two hundred to twenty thousand *emalangeni*. The bill was detailed, complex, and deliberately frightening.

Fear, hostility, and distrust, attitudes that Sobhuza had considered causes of strife and conflict, reflected existing strife and conflict. Opposition was treated as sedition, demonstrators were warned of dire consequences, and civil servants were warned to stay out of politics. Protest was driven underground and subversion became a reality. In a statement to the public Bhekimpi alleged that the government had averted a coup involving Dzeliwe's defense lawyer, the civil servant, and princes who had unsuccessfully sought armed assistance from other countries. Among those arrested for distributing seditious pamphlets urging the public not to vote was a wife of Prince Gabheni.

On October 18, ten days before the elections, Sozisa addressed a meeting at Lobamba and threatened that all "disloyal" chiefs would be removed from office. "I cannot work with my enemies," he declaimed, adding that they "should be bashed to death as was done in the past." Nothing could have been in more direct contrast to Sobhuza's appeal: "Speak to your enemies."

The outside world was watching and reporting. Support in the elections was required to validate recent events. It was clear that there would be and could be no show of open opposition from either chiefs or subjects. An appearance of unity was necessary. Consensus by coercion was still consensus. In one extreme case a lesser chief had warned his people to "vote or get out of my area." Not to vote was described as illegal. Anyone found distributing or even reading a pamphlet denouncing the regime and telling people to stay away from the polls was liable to be charged with sedition. A few pamphlets still managed to get distributed, and the message spread. Elections duly took place on October 28, and the previous system of voting under the experimental constitution was effectively replicated.

The *tinkundla* network had been strengthened. In September 1982, almost at the same time that the names of the original Liqoqo were published, four regional administrators, two of whom were district commissioners, had been appointed and funds made available for their services. Organization of the elections was entrusted to a committee headed by *indvuna yetinkundla*. The chief electoral officer for the previous election (an efficient and intrepid auditor general) was replaced. Security was tight, police controlled the crowds, cars were stopped by roadblocks and searched, passengers were questioned; there were complaints of harassment but there was no bloodshed.

A new government in a one-party state was voted into power. Leading local officials asserted that there had been a magnificent response, though it was known that many people had stayed away in protest. Officially, 83 percent had voted. On November 14, the names of the forty members elected to the House of Assembly by the eighty member *tinkundla*-based electoral college were announced. Bhekimpi topped the list with eighty votes and would continue as prime minister. He had defeated several ambitious competitors.

The composition of the cabinet was changed, reflecting the power of the coalitions that ousted Mabandla and then Dzeliwe. The portfolio of home affairs (Gabheni's former post) and the position of deputy prime minister were eliminated. Three new portfolios were established, the most significant being a ministry of defense which brought under government control both the army, which was formerly directly controlled by the king, and the police, which had formerly been within the office of the prime minister. In addition to the cabinet ministers, and enjoying equal status, was an ombudsman empowered to investigate any public officer, including other government ministers but excluding the king, the queen regent, the Authorized Person, and members of the Liqoqo. No mention was made of the prime minister, implying that he too could be investigated, while the immunity of the Liqoqo signified the extent to which it could dominate parliament.

PERSPECTIVE

Our revised study has shown the complex process by which the tolerance and political pluralism that characterized Sobhuza's reign has been replaced by an autocratic polity. The traditional liqoqo has been transformed from a loosely structured advisory body into the official power center of the national government. By forceful maneuvering a few of its members, in collaboration with a few cabinet ministers and the Authorized Person, succeeded in removing the prime minister and the queen regent appointed by Sobhuza and in installing a new prime minister and a new queen regent whom they hoped would better suit their interests. Parliament as well as the queen mother and the cabinet were given a role secondary to the Liqoqo in decision making and power sharing. Economic and political ties with South Africa were strengthened. An analysis of the future of the new government in terms of personal alignments, interests, and policies must be reserved for a separate study.

It would have been easier to have concluded this study with the funeral of Sobhuza II, since his life covered an era of Swazi history. But this conclusion would have oversimplified the processual approach. Sobhuza built on pre-existing structures, and these were not automatically destroyed by his death. The anarchic interregnum was not a revolution with a new system overthrowing the old but a struggle for power among royals couched in the name of maintaining tradition. Though power has shifted away from the monarchy, there is still a queen mother, and the name of Sobhuza's successor—her son—has been announced. Though the Authorized Person is being criticized by many and may be replaced, with the installation of the new king the post itself will automatically fall away. Tensions between and within the Liqoqo, the cabinet, and the parliament have intensified; they are not new but were kept in check by Sobhuza. The present Swazi system is characterized by what can be described as coalitions of expediency rather than by permanent factions based on ideological principles.

The techniques of incorporating foreigners developed in the early period of nation building have not been forgotten but have been reinterpreted. Sobhuza attempted to create a nonracial state in which citizenship could be extended to include racial as well as cultural and ethnic differences. The closest preindependence analogies to the situation in Swaziland were not Lesotho or Botswana but Zimbabwe and Mozambique. Sobhuza incorporated Whites without violence into the polity and economy of the postindependence period.

Swaziland's stability was based largely on the rights to communal usage of national land and on Sobhuza's concept of national economic development. But this stability and the power of the monarchy are being threatened by increasing population pressure, urban unemployment, economic dependence on South Africa, personal internal power struggles and corruption. Whether the "lost lands" will be regained by the Swazi will depend, as in the past, less on historical claims than on the interests of Pretoria.

When (or if) the new king is fully installed the *Ncwala* will be performed once again. This will serve as a touchstone to the meaningfulness of future kingship to the Swazi nation. Ritual requires participants, not spectators. Should the *Ncwala* become merely a spectacle, Swazi kingship will have lost the traditional divinity that sanctions political control. But individual and collective identification as Swazi with a proud cultural heritage may remain, irrespective of the power of the monarchy.

Throughout the world, traditionally sanctified sovereigns have been removed or replaced by secular rulers. Sovereigns, sacred or secular, survive mainly in small states, with one dominant ethnic group. Though this case study deals specifically with the kingdom of Swaziland, it raises issues of more general interest. It illustrates the complex process of nation-building, the limitations on hereditary leadership, and the manipulatoin of resources—economic, political and ritual—in the struggle for power. It is also a study of the flexibility of tradition, the difference between praxis and ideology, and their intricate relationship in the processes of social change.

Appendix/Tribute to the late king his majesty, Sobhuza II at the state funeral: Friday, September 3rd, 1982

We have come here from countries throughout the world to mourn together the loss of Sobhuza II, Sovereign of Swaziland. This time last year, he was with us to celebrate his Diamond Jubilee. It was a wonderful and happy occasion marking his 82nd birthday (he was born July 22nd, 1899), 60 years since his installation as Ngwenyama, Lion of Swaziland, on 21st December 1921; and 13 years of independence from colonial rule regained on the 6th of September 1968. Today, we weep not for him but for ourselves.

We have lost a king among men. Here at home he was so deeply loved that he had become a legend in his lifetime. Stories were told of his wisdom, his kindness, his generosity, his tenderness towards children, his compassion, his efforts to protect the weak, his respect for the dignity of every person, his humility, his humanity, his insight to the joys and sorrows of the world.

People from all walks of life came to him with their problems and to them he gave sympathy and courage. But the burden of kingship he bore alone. He described himself as a traditional African king who ruled as well as reigned. But he never forgot that a king is king by his people; he was their mouthpiece.

His hereditary position of power was heavy with responsibilities. It was a sacred burden. A king must not weep, a king must not complain. It was in this spirit that he led his people and the country to independence, achieving peace and unity. Although he did not appear in person in international political arenas, his voice of reason was heard abroad, carried by his messengers, and representatives from countries near and far came to seek his help and obtain his advice. He was a statesman, not a politician. His wisdom through experience was respected. He never acted impetuously. He listened to what others said. He did not impose his own opinion and weighed each decision with the utmost care in his search for a solution that would be best for his people and the country. His vision extended beyond the boundaries of the present, but he never promised heaven on earth. He knew that hunger, poverty, and ignorance were the enemies of all mankind. But he also knew that development was not technology, that the welfare of the human spirit, the human element, was the most important and essential consideration in accepting anything that was new or rejecting anything that was old.

Sobhuza, Ngwenyama, the last of the great traditional kings of southern Africa, used tradition as a guide to the future not as a fetter to the past. May his approach be continued. The world would be a better place were there more rulers with his wisdom, his judgment, his commitment to peace with justice.

Today, we bid his body farewell, but his *lidloti,* his spirit, survives. Responsibility for the future is on us. May his spirit be our inspiration.

BAYETHE!

GLOSSARY AND ABBREVIATIONS

apartheid—South Africa's policy of racial separation and domination

Bantustans—Segregated Reservations for different ethnic groups in South Africa

Bayethe—a greeting reserved for royalty

bukhwele—the jealousy between co-wives

buntfu—humanity

Gcina—The End (name of a regiment)

hlehla—military dance

Imbokodvo—Grinding-Stone

impunzi—a buck

iNdlovukazi—She-elephant, traditional title of the Queen mother

indlunkulu—great hut

indvuna (pl., tindvuna)—governor, senior official

indvuna yetinkundla—the governor of regional committees

iNgwenyama—The Lion, traditional title of a Swazi king

inhlanti—subordinate co-wife

inkanyeti (pl., tinkanyeti)—star

iNkosi—Chief, general title of respect

inkundla (pl., tinkundla)—regional committee

insangu—drug similar to marijuana

insila (pl., tinsila)—ritually created blood-brother

inyanga (pl., tinyanga)—ritual specialist

khonta—offer allegiance

libandla (pl., emabandla)—a council

libutfo (pl., emabutfo)—age regiment

lichiba—hut of mourning for a headman

lidloti (pl., emadloti)—an ancestral spirit

lijaha (pl., emajaha)—warrior

likholwa (pl., emakholwa)—member of any Christian church

liqoqo—national inner advisory council

Liqoqo—Supreme Council

lobola—bridewealth, the transfer of cattle from the family of the groom to the family of the bride

lusendvo—family council

Mvelimqanti—The First to Appear, The Creator

Ncwala—Ritual of Kingship

Ngemandla—With Power

Nkulunkulu—Great Great One; term introduced by missionaries for God

phondvo—horn/pinnacle

qoma—girl taken by force to become a wife

sangoma (pl., tangoma)—a diviner

sibaya—cattle pen, also used as a traditional forum
sibhimbi—celebration of an event in the individual life cycle
sibonga (pl., tibonga)—clan praise name
siceme—platoon
sigcili (pl., tigcili)—slave
sigodlo—seraglio, quarters of the queens
sikhulu (pl., tikhulu)—a chief
sinanatelo (pl., tinanatelo)—extended clan praise name
sitfunjwa (pl., titfunjwa)—captive of war
tibiyo—minerals
Tibiyo Taka Ngwane—National Mineral Corporation
tikhonti—subjects by traditional naturalisation
umbutfo—royal regiment
umcwasho—ceremony for unmarried girls emphasizing morality
umhlanga—reed
umnumzana—headman
umphakatsi—royal village; ritual capital
umtsakatsi (pl., batsakatsi)—sorcerer, witch

Abbreviations

ANC—African National Congress

EAC—European Advisory Council

INM—Imbokodvo National Movement

Legco—Legislative Council

NNLC—Ngwane National Liberatory Congress

OAU—Organization of African Unity

SDP—Swaziland Democratic Party

SNC—Swazi National Council

SPP—Swaziland Progressive Party

SUF—Swaziland United Front

USA—United Swaziland Association

Recommended Readings

BARNES, JOHN A., 1954, *Politics in a Changing Society*. London: Oxford University Press for the Rhodes-Livingston Institute.

> An account of the Ngoni, a branch of the Swazi that moved to Northern Rhodesia.

BEATTIE, JOHN, 1960, *Bunyoro, An African Kingdom*. New York: Holt, Rinehart and Winston.

> An excellent case study of a people in East Africa with a political system somewhat similar to that of the Swazi.

BEEMER, HILDA, 1937, "The Development of the Military Organization in Swaziland," *Africa*, Vol. X, No. 1, pp. 55–74; No. 2, pp. 176–205.

> A detailed account of Swazi age groups.

*BOOTH, ALAN R., 1983, *Swaziland: Tradition and Change in a Southern African Kingdom*. Boulder, Colorado: Westview Press.

> A first-rate historical study which draws largely on dependency theory and class analysis.

*BONNER, PHILIP, 1983, *Kings, Commoners and Concessionaires: The Evolution and Dissolution of the Nineteenth-Century Swazi State*. Cambridge, Eng.: Cambridge University Press.

> An excellent study of the political economy of the Swazi state in the nineteenth century. Very relevant to the present situation.

CRONIN, A.M.D., 1941, "The Swazi," *The Bantu Tribes of South Africa*, Vol. VIII, Sec. 4. Cambridge University Press.

> A fine photographic record with an introductory article by Hilda Beemer.

FAIR, T.J.D.; G. MURDOCH; and H.M. JONES, 1969, *Development in Swaziland*. Johannesburg, University of Witwatersrand Press.

> An economic policy without the political dimension.

*GROTPETER, JOHN J., 1975, *Historical Dictionary of Swaziland*. New Jersey: Scarecrow Press.

> A useful dictionary of Swazi personalities with a comprehensive bibliography.

HALPERN, JACK, 1965, *South Africa's Hostages: Basutoland, Bechuamaland, and Swaziland*. Baltimore: Penguin.

> A stimulating and controversial comparative study of the last period of colonial history.

HOLLEMAN, J. F. (ed.), 1962, *Experiment in Swaziland*, Vols. 1, 2. Durban, South Africa: University of Natal, Institute for Social Research.

An interdisciplinary research experiment producing useful demographic, economic, and sociological data.

*HUGHES, A.J.R., "Some Swazi Views on Land Tenure, 1962," *Africa*, Vol. XXXII, No. 3, pp. 253–279.

*KUPER, HILDA, 1947, *An African Aristocracy: Rank Among the Swazis*. London: Oxford University Press. Reprinted 1980 by Holmes and Meier.

A standard reference on African culture and political systems.

*———, 1947, *The Uniform of Color*. Johannesburg: University of Witwatersrand Press. Reprinted 1969 by Greenwood Publishing Co., New York.

A study of race relations in Swaziland under colonialism.

*———, 1978, *Sobhuza: Ngwenyama and King of Swaziland*. New York: Holmes and Meier. Africana Press. First published in 1978 by Duckworth, London.

The authorized biography of Sobhuza from birth until 1978.

LEMARCHAND, RENE (ed.), 1977, *African Kingdoms in Perspective*. Frank Cass, Great Britain.

Eight case studies with theoretical introduction and conclusion by editor.

MARWICK, B.A., 1940, *The Swazi*. Cambridge: Cambridge University Press.

A useful ethnographic monograph.

*MATSEBULA, J. S. M., 1972, *A History of Swaziland*. Johannesburg: Longmans, South Africa.

Straightforward factual account, with good documentation on the land issue.

MOORE, SALLY FALK, 1978, *Law as Process: An Anthropological Approach*. London: Routledge & Kegan Paul.

Contains an illuminating discussion of "process" together with a suggestion for an analytic framework.

POTHOLM, CHRISTIAN P., 1972, *Swaziland: The Dynamics of Political Modernization*. Berkeley: University of California Press.

Vivid account of political developments between World War II and independence, 1968.

READ, MARGARET, 1959, *Children of Their Fathers*. London: Oxford University Press for the International African Institute.

A study of the Ngoni of Nyasaland, who retained many similarities with the Swazi despite separation in space and time.

* Asterisks indicate especially significant works.

Index